THE MYSTICAL SPACE
OF CARMEL

The Fiery Arrow Collection

Editors: Hein Blommestijn and Jos Huls of the Titus Brandsma Institute

Advisory Board:

Elizabeth Dreyer, Silver Spring, U.S.A.
Christopher O'Donnell, Dublin Ireland
Helen Rolfson, Collegeville, U.S.A.
V. F. Vineeth, Bangalore, India
John Welch, Washington, U.S.A.

The *Fiery Arrow* series aims at the publication of books which connect their readers with the legacy of great teachers of spirituality from the distant and more recent past. Readers are offered a language and conceptual framework which can lead them to a deepened understanding of the spiritual life. The treasures of the spiritual tradition form a veritable "school of love," which is accessible to all who in contemplation desire to be touched by the fire of divine love. In 1230 A.D. Nicholas of France, former prior general of the Carmelites, wrote a letter bearing the title *Fiery Arrow* to his fellow brothers to urge them to call to mind again the fire of the beginning in which, in silence and solitude, they were consumed by the inescapable claim of the One. Based on the Carmelite tradition, this series seeks to share this spiritual legacy – which presents itself in a multiplicity of cultures and   traditions   –   with all those who in a great variety of ways are in search of interior life and the fire of love. The series, which is grounded in scientific research, is aimed at a broad public interested in spirituality.

The Titus Brandsma Institute is an academic center of research in spirituality founded in 1967 by the Catholic University of Nijmegen and the Carmelite Order. Titus Brandsma, who from 1923 on was a professor of philosophy and the history of mysticism, especially that of the Low Countries, died in 1942 as a martyr in the Nazi death camp of Dachau and was beatified in 1985. The Institute continues his research in spirituality and mysticism with a staff of assistants and in collaboration with other researchers. In addition to this and other series, the Institute publishes the international periodical *Studies in Spirituality* and the series *Studies in Spirituality Supplement* (Peeters, Louvain).

Scheduled to be published in this series are:

1. Kees Waaijman
   The Mystical Space of Carmel
   An Interpretation of the Carmelite Rule

2. Henk van Os and Kees Waaijman
   Titus Brandsma, Image of Holiness

3. Frances Teresa
   *Poli*shing the Mirror
   Pathways to spiritual and mystical maturity in the life of Clare of Assisi

4. Hein Blommestijn, Jos Huls and Kees Waaijman
   School of Love
   Introduction into saint John of the Cross

5. Hein Blommestijn, Jos Huls, and Kees Waaijman
   Sounding the Depths of Nothingness
   Mysticism in Times of War and Crisis: Titus Brandsma, Edith Stein, Paul

The Mystical Space of Carmel

A COMMENTARY ON THE CARMELITE RULE

by
KEES WAAIJMAN

Translated by JOHN VRIEND

PEETERS
1999

ISBN 90-429-0773-8
D. 1999/0602/62

Table of Contents

1. Introduction

Mount Carmel, a mountain range which rises majestically from the Mediterranean Sea and the plain of Jezreel, is located in the extreme north of Israel. From time immemorial Mount Carmel has been viewed as a holy place.[1] Originally it was inhabited by fertility gods. These Baals had to give way to a group of prophets around Elijah who in the ninth century B.C. established the worship of Yahweh, the God of Israel, there (1 Kgs. 18).[2] Early Christianity viewed Elijah as the father of monasticism, and from that time hermits who sought God's presence in solitude lived on Mount Carmel.[3] With the expansion of Islam in the seventh century (C.E.), Mount Carmel became a sacred place to Muslims. Elijah appeared there as "the verdant, life-giving one".[4] In the wake of the Crusades (1095-1291) many a devout pilgrim or crusader found his way to Mount Carmel, one of the sacred places in Palestine recaptured from Islam. Pilgrims, "following the example of the holy hermit and prophet Elijah lived a life of solitude on Mount Carmel".[5] In our time the Bahais, an offshoot of Islam, have chosen Mount Carmel as the site for their central sanctuary, where they keep the relics of their founder. In Bahai eyes a new prophetic era has dawned here.[6] Thus, in the course of many centuries Mount Carmel gave shelter to a variety of religious traditions: earthy

[1] M. Mulder, *Karmel*, in: *Theologisches Wörterbuch zum Alten Testament*, Stuttgart-Berlin-Köln-Mainz, IV (1984), 340-351.

[2] K. Waaijman, *De profeet Elia*, Nijmegen 1985, 7-32.

[3] O. Steggink, *Elia, de profeet van de Karmel*, Almelo 1985.

[4] A. Augustinovíc, *'El-Kadr'and the Prophet Elijah*, Jerusalem 1972, 13-45.

[5] Report of Jacques de Vitry, bishop of Acre (1214-1228), in his *Historia Hierosolimitana*, in: *Gesta Dei per Francos* (ed. J. Bongars), Hanoviae 1611, I:1075. English: *The History of Jerusalem*, tr. Aubrey Stewart, London 1896.

[6] Bahá' u'lláh, *A declaration of the Bahá'i International Community*, The Hague 1992.

folk-religion and heaven-moving prophets, desertlike monasticism and thriving Islamic piety, solitary pilgrims and visionary Bahais. The Carmelite order is one of these religious traditions. It started with a group of hermits who around 1200 inhabited the Carmel mountain range "where in little comb-like cells, those bees of the Lord laid up sweet spiritual honey".[7] These hermits were fascinated by the solitude of Mount Carmel. They wished to lead a life like that of Elijah, the solitary one *par excellence* and the prototype of all hermits. By physically experiencing his solitude on Mount Carmel they hoped to realize contact with the same God before whose face he stood.

Their hunger for solitude is easily understood in light of their spiritual background. For at that time Western Europe from which they came, experienced a renewal of eremitic life inspired by a movement of Christ's poor.[8] People resolutely turned away from the world (*conversio*) in order to dedicate themselves totally to God in a life of penitence (*vivere in sancta poenitentia*). Pilgrimages are a striking symbol of this piety: people left behind established patterns of life in order to venture into the unknown. Pilgrimages to the Holy Land especially were regarded as the apex of a penitential life.[9] Some followed the implications of their religious choice to the limit: they chose the solitude of a mountain range or disappeared in the dense forests of Europe. The hermits of Mount Carmel were part of this movement. They withdrew to Mount Carmel because this mountain "offered quiet and rest in its solitude, protection in its caves, enchantment in its meadows, good clean air by its height, living water from its spring".[10] They

---

[7] Jacques de Vitry, *The History of Jerusalem*, London 1896, 27.

[8] *L'eremitismo in occidente nei secoli XI e XII*, Milan 1970; see also Carlo Cicconetti, *The Rule of Carmel: An Abridgement*, tr. Gabriel Pausback, ed. Paul Hoban, Darien (Ill.) 1984, 27-55 (hereafter: Cicconetti, *Rule*). The original edition: Carlo Cicconetti, *La Regola del Carmelo*, Roma 1973.

[9] Cf. Cicconetti, *Rule*, 39-43.

[10] *Decem libri de institutione et peculiaribus gestis religiosorum carmelitarum* (hereafter: *Decem libri*), 3.1. We quote from the textual edition of Paul Chandler (in preparation).

sought the Living One before whose Face Elijah stood. For these hermits Mount Carmel was a mystical space which drew them away from established patterns and into God. Accordingly, the oldest self-definition of the Carmelites – the so-called *Rubrica prima*[11] – views the Carmel mountain range as a place for people "who truly love the solitude of this mountain *with a view to contemplating* heavenly things".[12]

That the first Carmelites were imbued with the mystical space of Mount Carmel became evident when from around 1238 (C.E.) the advancing Saracens forced them to leave Palestine. This forced departure not only meant a physical assault and psychic uprooting for these men, but above all a spiritual challenge: "How can you remain a Carmelite apart from Mount Carmel?" Their answer was: "In whatever place you live, draw away from the finite and enter into the infinite space which is God. Turn every place into a Carmel". Accordingly, the *Book of the First Monks,* the most important early Carmelite document after the Rule, states that Carmelites living away from Mount Carmel *rightly* "insist on being called Carmelites" for the reason that in the spirit of Elijah they liberate themselves from the world in silence and solitariness in order to belong totally to God. All those who enter this mystical space of Carmel are true *Carmel*-ites, "those who live on Mount Carmel *as well as those who live elsewhere*".[13] A few centuries later the blind mystic John of Saint-Samson (1571-1636) was to voice the same thought:

> We must assume that the places where we live are so many Mount Carmels. And we must consecrate them to the extent possible to us with a very lively, very fervent, and very active desire for holiness, in accordance with the true spirit of our First Fathers and Founders. For their strict solitariness would not have been holy if they had not

[11] In the *Rubrica Prima,* the first rubric of the oldest *Constitutions* known to us (1281) the General Chapter lays down the official answer the junior members of the Carmelite order must give when someone asks them where the Carmelites come from. See A. Staring, *Medieval Carmelite Heritage,* Rome 1989, 33-43.

[12] Ibid., 40.

[13] *Decem libri,* 3.5.

totally abandoned themselves to the influences of God's Spirit. But because they did not erect any barrier against these influences they became very holy. And they made an enormous effort actively, and with all their powers, to flow back into God, completely faithful to the abundance of his grace and his Spirit.[14]

In the history of religion we see a parallel in Jewish mysticism. When the physical temple at Jerusalem still existed, "the place" could refer to the physical temple. But after the temple was destroyed in 70 (C.E.), devout Jews disconnected "the place" from the physical sanctuary. From that time on every place could become a sanctuary.

> The rabbi of Kobryn taught: God says to man, as he said to Moses: "Put off thy shoes from thy feet" – put off the habitual which encloses your foot, and you will know that the place on which you are now standing is holy ground. For there is no rung of human life on which we cannot find the holiness of God everywhere and at all times.[15]

We humans stand on holy ground. We are surrounded by the holiness of God. Habituation builds a shell around the Secret. Consequently we do not discern that holiness. But when we strip this habituation from us we become naked and again realize our true environment: God truly as our Place.

> They asked Rabbi Pinhas: "Why is God called 'makom', that is, place? He certainly is *the place of the world*, but then he ought to be called that, and not just 'place'." He replied: "Man should go into God, so that God may surround him and become his *place*".[16]

The parallel is clear: because the Carmelites were driven away from the physical Mount Carmel they were forced to read every place as a spiritual Carmel. Every day this Carmel has to be discovered anew. In this process the Rule of Carmel can serve as a resource.

---

[14] Jean de Saint-Samson, *Observations sur la Regle des Carmes,* in *Les Oeuvres spirituelles et mystiques* (ed. Donatien de Saint-Nicolas), Rennes 1658-1659, 848.

[15] Martin Buber, *Werke 3*, München-Heidelberg 1963, 560.

[16] Ibid., 242.

The Rule of Carmel was written by Albert of Avogadro, patriarch of Jerusalem.[17] Albert was born around 1150 (C.E.) at Castrum Gualterii, in the diocese of Parma. He joined the Canons Regular of the Holy Cross, who lived in accordance with the Rule of Augustine, and was chosen prior in 1180. He was bishop of Bobbio (1184) and for twenty years ruled the diocese of Vercelli (1185-1205). In 1205 he was elected Patriarch of Jerusalem by the canons of the Holy Sepulchre. Since Jerusalem was occupied by the Saracens he fixed his residence in Acre. Repeatedly he carried out delicate assignments for Pope Innocent III. He badly needed all his diplomatic talents to guide into constructive channels the differences of opinion among the Christians living in the Holy Land, an area that had shrunk to a narrow strip of coastal land from Jaffa to Acre. On September 14, 1214, almost 65 years old, he was stabbed to death during a procession. Albert was preeminently equipped to write the Carmelite Rule.[18] He was thoroughly informed about the then-current movements of religious renewal and well-versed in juridical matters. Between 1206 and 1214 he presented his Rule to the hermits on Mount Carmel.

Carmelites have reason to be happy with Albert's Rule. For although the Rule of Carmel is the most diminutive among its peers,[19] in its succinctness it has the expressiveness of a poem. In it several layers of meaning engage one another. We shall briefly review the most important.

1. From a *literary* point of view the Carmelite Rule is a letter. The twelfth century was the Golden Age of the art of letter writing.[20]

---

[17] On this topic see Cicconetti, *Rule,* 70-84; J. Smet, *The Carmelites: A History of the Brothers of Our Lady of Mount Carmel,* vol. I, *ca. 1200 until the Council of Trent,* rev. ed., Darien (III), 1988, 3 (hereafter: Smet, *Carmelites*), 1:6-7; V. Mosca, *Alberto Partriarca di Gerusalemme,* Rome 1992.

[18] For a brief and lucid overview of the context in which the Rule came into being, see Cicconetti, *Rule,* 23-49.

[19] See *Regole monastiche d'occidente,* Magnano 1989.

[20] For an overview see G. Constable, *Letters and Letter-Collections,* Turnhout 1976; C. Lanham, *Salutatio Formulas in Latin Letters to 1200:*

6 INTRODUCTION

There was a strong demand for good letter writers at the ecclesiastical and court chancelleries which were emerging at the time. To meet this demand special training was available for those who sought to learn "the art of letter writing" (*ars dictandi* or *ars dictaminis*). To help them learn this art, teachers as well as students had access to detailed handbooks containing numerous model letters.

The literary form of a letter offers many possibilities. To begin with, there is no end of variation in possible senders and addressees: high/low, private/public, living/dead, heaven/earth, far away/nearby, etc. Equally unlimited is the content: personal/business, juridical/poetic, fictitious/real, etc. This flexibility, however, does not imply formlessness. Persons who wrote a letter in accordance with the rules of the art adhered to the following standard form:

> Opening words (*salutatio* or *prologus*)
> Starting point (*exordium*)
> Exposition (*narratio*)
> Request (*petitio*)
> Conclusion (*conclusio*)

The Rule of Carmel, written at the beginning of the thirteenth century, corresponds to this standard form: following the opening greeting (*salutatio*), Albert unfolds his starting point, the core of the religious life (*exordium*), after which he gives an exposition of the Carmelite form of life (*narratio*). In this Carmelite form of life he aspires to see the core of the religious life realized (*petitio*). Finally Albert takes his leave (*conclusio*). Our explanation of the Rule follows this sequence.

2. From a *historical* point of view, the Rule of Carmel is interwoven with developments in the religious life of the eleventh, twelfth, and thirteenth century.

Syntax, Style and Theory, München 1975; both contain extensive bibliographies. For the spiritual literature see J. Leclercq, *Le genre épistolaire au moyen âge*, in *Revue du Moyen Age Latin*, 1946, II, 63-70; M. Kors, *Epistolaire aspecten van de geestelijke brief (ca. 1350-1550)*, in *Boeken voor de eeuwigheid*, Amsterdam 1993, 52-69.

In the eleventh century a large-scale religious movement arose and flourished whose aim was to follow Jesus in his poverty and in the preaching of the gospel. Its adherents called themselves "the poor of Christ". Many of them sought to practice the imitation of Christ by making pilgrimages and joining the crusades which took place between 1095 and 1291. The purpose of these crusades was to recapture the holy places in Palestine from the Saracens. For many a pilgrim or crusader the crusades paved the way to Mount Carmel. Here they yearned to complete their pilgrimage as hermits. These hermits were no part of any ecclesiastically recognized order. But neither were they any longer ordinary laymen like believers in a parish. They formed a middle way (*via media*) or an intermediate class (*status medius*) between the laity and official monasticism. They belonged to what is currently called *Semireligiosentum*,[21] a collective term for all persons and groups who wish to pursue a religious life without belonging to a monastic order. Often they were close to the laity, offering them a form of more intense Christian living and community without much in the way of juridical ceremonies.

In the twelfth century the élan of these semi-religious led to the inner reform of monasticism: canons and monks. This reform consisted in a return to the original charism embodied in the Rules of Augustine and Benedict. Key words were simplicity, poverty, and humility. The order of regular canons was renewed by the Premonstratensians and the Victorines. Among them the liturgy and the apostolate were stressed. The monastic order was reformed by the Cistercians. To them liturgy and manual labor were primary. In both renewals the life of the community held an important place.

In the thirteenth century a new phase in the development of the monastic system followed: the rise of the fraternal orders. They distinguished themselves from the older orders by a pronounced democratic form of life and by a radical renunciation of property.

[21] K. Elm, *Die Bruderschaft vom gemeinsamen Leben. Eine geistliche Lebensform zwischen Kloster und Welt, Mittelalter und Neuzeit*, in *Ons Geestelijk Erf* 69 (1985) 470-496.

For that reason they were called mendicants. The most important mendicant orders which originated in the beginning of the thirteenth century and gained ecclesiastical recognition were the Franciscans (Friars Minor) and Dominicans (Friars Preachers).

The rise of the Carmelite Order occurred in the context of these developments. In the earliest period of the order we can distinguish three phases:[22]

−1. The first is that of the *hermits*. It started when a few pilgrims opted for the solitude of Mount Carmel and regarded brother B. as their leader. (That is all we know of B; the letter B. has never yielded up its secret.[23]) The hermits lived in or by the Wadi ᶜAin-es-Siah, three kilometers from the northernmost point of Mount Carmel and one kilometer from the coast. The wadi has a surface of five hundred by fifteen hundred meters, offers a view of the sea, and lies a couple of hundred meters from two springs, the one to the north, the other to the south. The spring that is situated to the south was known among the crusaders as the Spring of Elijah, or simply the Spring.[24] The hermits lived in separate cells, reflected on Scripture, and applied themselves to prayer.

−2. The second phase is that of hermits-living-in-*community* on Mount Carmel. These hermits conceived a "plan" (*propositum*) to form a community. Albert developed it into a cenobitic "formula of life" (*formula vitae*). This formula of life combines eremitic elements (staying in the cell; reading Scripture day and night; combat with demonic powers; working in silence, etc.) with elements which structure the religious life of the community (having a prior; community of goods; regular joint celebration of the Eucharist, etc.).

[22] For a succinct description of the historical context of the Rule, along with bibliography, see C. Cicconetti, *The History of the Rule*, in *Albert's Way*, ed. M.Mulhall, Rome and Barrington, Ill. 1989, 23-49.

[23] A later tradition (ca. 1400) filled in the letter B. with Brocard of whom we also know nothing.

[24] E. Friedman, *The Latin Hermits of Mount Carmel*, Rome 1979, 52-55; 157-169.

−3. The third phase is that of *mendicancy* in Europe. The Carmelites did not stay on Mount Carmel long: Islam drove them away.[25] This exodus from Israel began in 1238. Hermitages were built on Cyprus and in Sicily, in southern England and southern France. Back in their country of origin the Carmelites encountered a changed situation.[26] Not only was there an increase in urbanization but the new religious movements had further developed their distinctive features as well. The mendicant brothers were enormously popular and the popes supported them, even keeping them outside the jurisdiction of the bishops. The Carmelites, who had sprung from the same renewal movement, felt attracted to the mendicant brothers. They succeeded in gaining the necessary preliminary conditions for this form of life: permission to celebrate the Eucharist in public, hearing confessions, having churches and cemeteries of their own, the recognition of the right to beg, etc. Gradually, driven in this direction especially by practical realities, the Carmelites opted for the way of living practiced by the fraternal orders.

The history of the rise of the Carmelite Order has left its traces in the Rule. The Rule of Carmel embodies three religious concepts: the eremitic way of life, the cenobitic form of life, and life as a mendicant brother. The combination of these three concepts is not the product of careful thought but of life lived within a single century: from hermit to cenobite, from cenobite to mendicant. The tensions between these three types of religious life have internally led to conflicts, down to this day. But they have also forced the Carmelites to go below the surface, to a deeper level, to look for the mystical space of contemplation, a level from the perspective of which all forms and concepts are relative.

---

[25] Cicconetti, *Rule*, 34-64.
[26] For a description of this episode, see Smet, *Carmelites*, 1:10-19; Cicconetti, *Rule*, 130-207.

3. From a *juridical* point of view,[27] the Rule of Carmel reflects the dialogue between the Carmelite community and the church leadership. This dialogue began the moment on which B. and the other hermits submitted the above-mentioned *plan* to Albert, patriarch of Jerusalem. It is probable that they presented the plan in the course of a conversation with him. Albert adopted their plan and confirmed Carmel as a religious community.[28] This does not yet mean that by this act the Carmelites became an order like others before them. If that had been Albert's or the brothers intention they could have adopted one of the existing Rules, but they refrained from doing so. Both parties opted for a new contemporary concept. By this fact the Carmelites were affirmed by the church in their semi-religious way of life. By endorsing their own rule of conduct the bishop of Jerusalem gave to the hermits of Mount Carmel confirmation of their actual life model: a way of their own between the ecclesiastically recognized monastic orders and the laity in general.[29]

However, having this form of life by no means made the position of the Carmelites stable and firm. The recognition was only episcopal and applied only locally. Accordingly, when in 1215 the Fourth Lateran Council sought to contain the explosion of new religious groupings, Carmelites felt their existence and growth potential were threatened.[30] Consequently they tried to gain papal approval for Albert's "formula of life". From Honorius III they received initial ratification in 1226, which was confirmed in 1229 in three letters from Gregory IX.

When the Carmelites were driven from Mount Carmel they were uprooted and became unsure about themselves. During this process of displacement and searching for an identity of their

[27] The juridical aspect of the Rule is central in Cicconetti, *Rule.*

[28] Cicconetti, *Rule*, 72-76 refers to the *Rubrica Prima* of 1281 where Albert's work is described as "in unum collegium adunare". See also V. Mosca, *Alberto Patriarca di Gerusalemme,* 103-136.

[29] Cf. Cicconetti, *Rule*, 57-65 and 76-84, where he offers several interesting examples.

[30] For a detailed account of this period, cf. *ibid.,* 85-129.

own, the general chapter of 1247 took place. The chapter sent two fellow brothers to Rome with the request that doubtful points in the Rule be clarified and corrected and that some duties be changed.[31] Pope Innocent IV put to work two Dominicans, who finished their assignment after only one month. The pope endorsed their work and sent the definitive text of the Rule to the prior general, adding a cover letter in which he instructed the receiver to correct all other copies of "your" Rule in accord with this definitive text. From this point on three things are clear. 1. Because the three vows (obedience, poverty, and chastity) occur at the beginning of the formula of life, Carmelites were from then on official religious.[32] 2. By a number of minor modifications (having houses in the cities, eating together in the refectory, praying the hours, going around begging as a form of apostolic life) the advisors bent the Rule in the direction of a mendicant Rule.[33] Innocent IV left no room for doubt that Albert's formula of life is a *Regula*. With this, a process that lasted a half century came to an end.

> At long last Hermits of Mount Carmel ... could celebrate the fact that they had their own rule approved and confirmed ... a true rule obligating to the three vows of religion! A rule approved by the apostolic see ... With this rule the Hermits constituted an Order.[34]

The clarifications introduced by Innocent IV had their effect. Internally the mendicant character of the order expanded, a fact which prompted resistance, especially among the proponents of the eremitic tradition who were horrified at having houses in the cities and going around begging. But opposition grew also from the outside, particularly from the side of bishops and priests who felt threatened in their pastoral territory. The biggest crisis, however, was still to come. The Second Council of Lyons in 1274 prohibited all new orders – except the Franciscans and the

---

[31] For the full text and a lengthy discussion of these points, see *ibid.*, 144-167.
[32] Ibid., 153-158.
[33] Ibid., 158-167.
[34] Ibid., 206.

Dominicans – from accepting new candidates for membership. In the long run this could have spelled the disappearance of the order. But everything turned out well. In 1298 the Carmelite Order definitively received the status of a mendicant order.[35] From this status John XXII drew the final implication: in 1317 he granted the order exemption from episcopal jurisdiction. In 1326 he extended to the Carmel Order the same rights as the Franciscans and Dominicans possessed. Around 1300 it numbered approximately 150 houses divided over 12 provinces.

Juridically the Rule can be viewed as the record of the lively exchanges which took place between the church leadership and Carmel. Starting with Albert's first letter, up until 1300, almost a hundred papal letters were to follow![36] The final exchange, as it concerns the Rule, took place in 1432. Pope Eugene IV granted two mitigations. The first concerned staying in the cell: from then on members could walk about freely in the church, in the cloister walkway and in the immediate vicinity of the monastery. The second concerned abstention from eating meat: this was restricted to three days a week. "The mitigation of 1432 can be regarded as the last phase in the process the Carmelites underwent to become mendicant".[37]

4. From an *intertextual* point of view, there are echoes in the Rule of several traditions. First of all biblical traditions: some passages in the Rule are a concatenation of Scripture quotations.[38] Next, specific religious traditions: ancient monastic rules, especially those of Augustine, classic spiritual authors like Cassian (ca. 365-435), and standard juridical expressions.[39] In the Rule we hear echoes of the religious past from which it came.

---

[35] For this period, see *Rule*, 208-251; Smet, *Carmelites*, 1:14-28.

[36] Mosca, *Alberto Patriarca di Gerusalemme*, 110.

[37] Smet, *Carmelites*, 1:72-73.

[38] The more than 30 Bible quotations are concentrated in the second half of the Rule where the life model gains mystical depth and is interiorized.

[39] These religious traditions, though they consistently resonate in the background, seldom appear in the text as quotations.

But there is still another intertextual resonance: the Rule still reverberates in the Carmelite traditions it brought into being![40] For example, the Rule resonates in the *Rubrica Prima*[41] to the degree that there the fundamental tension between the eremitic and cenobitic way of life is articulated.[42] There are echoes of the Rule in *The Book of the First Monks* to the degree that there the basic tension between the practical objective (asceticism) and final goal (mysticism) is portrayed in the figure of Elijah, the prototype of the Carmelites.[43] In Carmelite mysticism the Rule resonates to the degree that there the *plus*-dimension comes out which surpasses all the boundaries of the regulable.[44] In the *Familia Carmelitana* – all the orders, congregations and religious institutes which follow the Carmelite Rule[45] – the Rule is reflected to the degree that in this family the many forms of Carmelite life are lived out: by hermits somewhere in the lonely wilderness of Southern Colorado or the hills of Villefrance; by mendicants in the slums of a metropolis or a regional hospital; by cenobites who, praying and working, aspire to depict the original Jerusalem community in their apostolate or formation work. Thus the Rule is intertextually interwoven with traditions which preceded and shaped it and with traditions which followed and were created by it.

5. From a *spiritual* point of view a spiritual way becomes visible in the Carmelite Rule. The Rule is a spiritual structure in which the parts of the whole are so related to each other that together they form a way which leads to God, or rather, which gives God

[40] Technically this is the history of the Rule's reception, broadly understood.
[41] See footnote 11.
[42] K. Waaijman-H. Blommestijn, *The Dynamic Structure of the Rubrica Prima,* Rome 1994 (paper).
[43] *Decem libri,* 1.
[44] The mystical *supererogatio* with which the Rule ends.
[45] At this moment approximately 52.000 men and women have made a vow to keep the Carmelite Rule (source: John Malley, general of the Order of the Carmelites at the Provincial Chapter held May 13, 1993, at Boxmeer).

a chance to find us. This way begins with the elementary realities of daily life which are interiorized in such a way as to open up to God's impact and influence which knows no end. *The Book of the First Monks* puts it as follows:

> You will learn how we make straight the way of the Lord to our heart, make straight the paths by which God comes to us, in order that, when he comes and knocks, we immediately open the door to him who says: "Listen! I am standing at the door, knocking; if you hear my voice and open the door, I will come in to you and eat with you, and you with me".[46]

The Rule is designed to teach us to interiorize the elementary realities of life in such a way that they become the mystical space in which God can give God. The Carmelite Rule viewed as a spiritual way is central in our interpretation.

We regard this interpretation as an interim report on a search begun in 1975. In that year a renewed acquaintance with the Rule occurred in the Dutch province of the Carmelite Order. On the basis of some preliminary studies[47] the Rule was further explored in three directions: a deeper penetration of the historical context; a semantic inquiry into the spiritual terminology; a study of the biblical backgrounds.[48] In 1981, in the Italian Carmelite province, a comparable process of reflection started, focused on the structure of the Rule text.[49] During the first North American Congress on the Carmelite Rule, held in Niagara Falls, Sept. 21-26, 1986, these and other initiatives came together interactively.[50] This congress was inspiring because from it Rule-research received fresh impulses. Especially fascinating was

---

[46] *Decem libri* 1.1.

[47] See esp. Cicconetti, *La Regola del Carmelo*, Rome 1973, and H. Clarke-B. Edwards, *The Rule of Saint Albert*, Aylesford-Kensington 1973.

[48] See O. Steggink, J. Tigcheler, K. Waaijman, *Karmelregel*, Almelo 1978; translated as *Carmelite Rule*, by T.Vrakking and J.Smet, Almelo 1979.

[49] For a report see B. Secondin, *What is the Heart of the Rule?*, in: *Albert's Way*, 93-132.

[50] See reports in *Albert's Way*.

the presence of the *Familia Carmelitana*. It constitutes a living witness to the many-sidedness of the Rule. Inspired by the Congress, we further pursued our inquiry into the mystical-spiritual structure of the Rule via reflection,[51] celebration,[52] and study.[53] The commentary on the Rule which is now in your hands is a provisional terminus of this search.

I cordially thank Rudolf van Dijk who critically examined the manuscript from an historical perspective, and Paul Chandler who also read and commented on the whole work.

With this interpretation we hope to be of service not only to the brothers and sisters who have bound themselves to the Carmelite Rule for life but to all who aspire to see their "place" blossom in the mystical space of Mount Carmel.

Kees Waaijman
Nijmegen 1999

[51] Cf. R. van Dijk, *Karmelregel. Een leefregel voor bewuste christenen*, Nijmegen 1992.

[52] K. Waaijman, *Komen laat ik jullie in het land van de Karmel. Vieringen vanuit de Karmelregel*, Nijmegen 1989.

[53] H. Blommestijn-K. Waaijman, *The Carmelite Rule as a Model of Mystical Transformation*, in P.Chandler (ed.), *Approaches to the Rule of Saint Albert* Rome 1992, 108-134; K. Waaijman, *Silence*, in *Carmelus* 40 (1993) 11-42.

2. The Text of the Carmelite Rule

Before we can start commenting on the Rule, we have to decide which text we are going to read. Is it Albert's text, written between 1206 and 1214, or the text of Innocent IV, which was approved in 1247? In light of today's methods of editing texts this dilemma is no longer valid. Modern editors distance themselves from the notion that the so-called "authentic" or "original" text is self-evidently normative. They tend to view the text as a *history* of writing and reading, of re-writing and re-reading. What they are after is "the life of the text in the field of tension constituted by the author, the redactor, the copyist and printer, as well as public reception".[1] This historical dimension in the establishment of a critical edition can keep us from one-sidedly using the original Rule as *the* criterion for Carmelite life of today. Our commentary focuses on *both* texts, that of Albert (1206-14) and that of Innocent IV (1247), two foci of an ellipse which encompasses the entire period of the Carmelite Order's origination. Albert's text (1206-14) captures the moment in which the Carmelite hermits began to lead a more communal life. The text of Innocent IV (1247) captures the moment when the Carmelites adopted the model of the modern fraternal or mendicant orders.

2.1 Albert's text (1206-14)

Inasmuch as the first generation of Carmelites was not interested in documents,[2] Albert's letter was lost. But perhaps the *text* of

---

[1] K. Ruh, *Überlieferungsgeschichte mittelalterlicher Texten als methodischer Ansatz zu einer erweiterten Konzeption von Literaturgeschichte*, in *Überlieferungsgeschichtliche Prosaforschung*, Tübingen 1985, 262.

[2] Smet, *Carmelites*, 1:15.

Albert's Rule has in fact been preserved, and that in a collection of Carmelite writings which the Catalan provincial Philip Ribot (d. 1391) gathered up under the title *Ten books about the institution and noteworthy achievements of the Carmelites*.[3] In the eighth book Ribot brought together everything that relates to the Rule. The book opens with the so-called Epistle of Cyril[4] which states the reason why Albert wrote his Rule: "doubt and disagreement had arisen among the Carmelites" on ten points,[5] doubts and disagreements which Albert proceeded to remove. Next Ribot offers a literal transcript of Albert's Rule.[6] Then he does his best to show 'that Albert introduced little or nothing that had not been recorded earlier already by John XLIV in his *Book of the First Monks*. The only thing Albert did in his Rule was to define more precisely what John had described in general terms.[7] Following this Ribot demonstrates, item by item, the continuity between the old Rule of John XLIV and the new Rule of Albert.

Still more interesting to us is Sibert de Beka's *Treatise* which immediately follows the *Epistle of Cyril*.[8] In this *Treatise* Sibert discusses the endorsement of successive popes.[9] Finally he considers at length the changes made by Innocent IV in 1247.[10] This *Treatise* is especially interesting inasmuch as all the changes of Innocent IV relative to Albert's Rule are discussed in it.

Scholars do not generally consider Ribot very reliable. They should, however, be less distrustful with reference to his *Rule*-text. There are three reasons for this: First: where it concerns official documents, though Ribot orders them in his own historical perspective, he does not change the texts.[11] Second: he makes no attempt literarily to harmonize *The Book of the First Monks* and

---

[3] *Decem libri.*
[4] *Decem libri*, 8.1-3.
[5] Ibid., 8.2.
[6] Ibid., 8.3.
[7] Ibid., 8.4.
[8] Ibid., 8.5-6.
[9] Ibid., 8.5.
[10] Ibid., 8.6.
[11] Cf. Paul Chandler, *The Book of the First Monks. A Workbook*, Rome 1992, 4.

Albert's *Rule*. He only indicates where Albert's *Rule* can be found in the Rule of John XLIV. Third: in the case of all the changes Innocent IV introduced Ribot refers to grounds which at no point sound fictitious: the juridical necessity of the three vows; the uncooperative attitude of the bishops when it came to finding new places in which to live; the inconvenience of eating separately in one's cell; the uncertainty concerning the relation between the liturgy of the hours and saying the psalms; doubt about the way in which the community may acquire goods; the unreliability of an outsider as procurator; the necessity of a mitigated policy with respect to fasting and abstinence; the impracticability of an overly long night silence. These references are so divergent and so practice-oriented that they cannot possibly be viewed as a construction of a single author. They sound more like a report.

2.2 The text of Innocent IV (1247)

The original of the papal letter *Quae honorem Conditoris* of Innocent IV, dated October 1, 1247, is lost as well. True: several copies of this text are in circulation, but a critical edition based on these copies has unfortunately still not yet been made available. We are fortunate that a copy of the original has been kept in the Archives of the Vatican.[12]

2.3 Synopsis and translation

On the left page we now present, side by side, the Rule of Albert (from 1206-14)[13] and that of Innocent IV (from 1247).[14] On the

---

[12] *Registrum Vaticanum* 21, ff. 465v-466r.

[13] The provisional critical edition of Albert's Rule which we use in this study has been prepared on the basis of a collation of available manuscripts by Paul Chandler.

[14] The examplar of the Rule in the Vatican Archives has been repeatedly copied: by G. Wessels in *Analecta Ordinis Carmelitarum* 2 (1911-1913) 557-561; M.-H. Laurent, in *Ephemerides Carmelitanae* 2 (1948) 5-16; L. Saggi, in *Constitutiones*, Rome 1971, 15-22; B. Secondin, *La Regola del Carmelo*, Rome 1982. We are following the transcription of Cicconetti in his *La Regola del Carmelo*, 201-205.

right are the respective translations. The differences between the two texts (aside from some orthographic variants) have been italicized.

Textus Albertinus	Textus Innocentianus
Salutatio	*Salutatio*
Albertus Dei gracia ierosolimitane	Albertus, Dei gratia Ierosolimitane
ecclesie vocatus patriarcha,	ecclesie vocatus patriarcha,
dilectis in Christo filiis	dilectis in Christo filiis
Brocardo et ceteris heremitis,	*B.* et ceteris heremitis
qui sub eius obediencia iuxta fontem	qui sub eius obedientia juxta Fontem
in monte	in monte
Carmeli morantur, in Domino salutem	Carmeli morantur, in Domino salutem
et Sancti Spiritus benedictionem.	et Sancti Spiritus benedictionem.
Exordium	*Exordium*
Multipharie multisque modis	Multipharie multisque modis
sancti patres instituerunt	sancti patres instituerunt
qualiter quisque	qualiter quisque
in quocumque ordine fuerit,	in quocumque ordine fuerit,
vel quemcumque modum	vel quemcumque modum
religiose vite elegerit,	religiose vite elegerit,
in obsequio Iesu Christi vivere debeat,	in obsequio Ihesu Christi vivere debeat,
et eidem fideliter de corde puro	et eidem fideliter de corde puro
et bona consciencia deservire.	et bona conscientia deservire.
Narratio	*Narratio*
Verum quia requiritis a nobis,	Verum, quia requiritis a nobis,
ut iuxta propositum vestrum	ut iuxta propositum vestrum
tradamus vobis vite formulam,	tradamus vobis vite formulam,
quam tenere in posterum debeatis:	quam tenere in posterum debeatis:
Caput I	*Caput I*
Illud in primis statuimus	Illud in primis statuimus,
ut unum ex vobis habeatis priorem,	ut unum ex vobis habeatis Priorem,
qui ex unanimi	qui ex unanimi
omnium assensu,	omnium assensu,
vel maioris et sanioris partis,	vel maioris et sanioris partis,
ad hoc officium eligatur,	ad hoc officium eligatur;

cui obedienciam promittat
quilibet aliorum,
et promissam studeat
operis veritate servare.

cui obedientiam promittat
quilibet aliorum,
et promissam studeat
operis veritate servare
cum castitate
et abdicatione proprietatis.

Caput II

Caput II
Loca autem habere poteritis
in heremis,
vel ubi vobis donata fuerint,
ad vestre religionis
observantiam
apta et commoda,
secundum quod Priori et
fratribus videbitur expedire.

Caput III
Preterea
iuxta situm loci
quem inhabitare proposueritis,
singuli vestrum
singulas habeant cellulas separatas,
sicut per disposicionem prioris ipsius
et de assensu aliorum fratrum
vel sanioris partis
eedem cellule cuique fuerint assignate.

Caput III
Preterea,
iuxta situm loci
quem inhabitare proposueritis,
singuli vestrum
singulas habeant cellulas separatas,
sicut per dispositionem Prioris ipsius,
et de assensu aliorum fratrum
vel sanioris partis,
eedem cellule cuique fuerint assignate.

Caput IV

Caput IV
Ita tamen ut,
in communi refectorio
ea que vobis erogata fuerint,
communiter
aliquam lectionem
sacre scripture audiendo,
ubi commode poterit
observari, sumatis.

Caput V
Nec liceat
alicui fratrum,

Caput V
Nec liceat
alicui fratrum,

nisi de licencia prioris
qui pro tempore fuerit,
deputatum sibi mutare locum,
vel cum alio permutare.

Caput VI
Cellula prioris
sit iuxta introitum loci,
ut venientibus ad eundem
locum primus occurrat,
et de arbitrio ac disposicione ipsius
postmodum que agenda sunt
cuncta procedant.

Caput VII
Maneant singuli in cellulis suis
vel iuxta eas,
die ac nocte
in lege Domini meditantes,
et in oracionibus vigilantes,
nisi aliis iustis occasionibus
occupentur.

Caput VIII
Hii qui *litteras* norunt *et legere psalmos,*
per singulas horas eos dicant, *qui ex*
*ins*ticutione sanc*t*orum patrum et ecclesie
approbata consuetudine *ad horas singulas*
sunt deputati.
Qui *vero litteras* non norunt,
xxv uicibus Pater noster dicant
in nocturnis vigiliis,
exceptis dominicis et sollempnibus
diebus,
in quorum vigiliis predictum numerum
statuimus duplicari,
ut dicatur Pater noster
vicibus quinquaginta.
Sepcies autem eadem dicatur oracio in
laudibus matutinis.

nisi de licentia Prioris,
qui pro tempore fuerit,
deputatum sibi mutare locum,
vel cum alio permutare.

Caput VI
Cellula Prioris
sit iuxta introitum loci,
ut venientibus ad eumdem
locum primus occurrat;
et de arbitrio et de dispositione ipsius
postmodum que agenda sunt
cuncta procedant.

Caput VII
Maneant singuli in cellulis suis,
vel iuxta eas,
die ac nocte
in lege Domini meditantes,
et in orationibus vigilantes,
nisi aliis iustis occasionibus
occupentur.

Caput VIII
Hii, qui *horas canonicas*
cum clericis dicere norunt,
eas dicant *secundum con*stitutionem
sac*r*orum patrum et Ecclesie
approbatam consuetudinem.
Qui *eas* non noverunt,
vigintiquinque vicibus Pater noster
dicant in nocturnis vigiliis,
exceptis dominicis et sollempnibus
diebus,
in quorum vigiliis predictum numerum
statuimus duplicari,
ut dicatur Pater noster
vicibus quinquaginta.
Septies autem eadem dicatur oratio in
laudibus matutinis.

In aliis quoque horis
sepcies similiter
eadem sigillatim dicatur oracio,
preter officia vespertina,
in quibus ipsam quindecies dicere
debeatis.

Caput IX
Nullus fratrum
dicat sibi aliquid esse proprium,
sed sint vobis omnia comunia.
Et *ex hiis que Dominus vobis dederit,*
distribuatur unicuique
per manum prioris,
id est, per *hominem* ab eo
ad idem officium deputatum,
prout cuique opus fuerit,
inspectis etatibus et
necessitatibus singulorum.
Ita tamen ut,
sicut premissum est,
in deputatis cellulis singuli
maneant, et ex hiis
que sibi distributa fuerint,
singulariter vivant.

Caput X
Oratorium,
prout comodius
fieri poterit,
construatur in medio cellularum,
ubi mane
per singulas dies
ad audienda missarum sollempnia

In aliis quoque horis
septies similiter
eadem sigillatim dicatur oratio,
preter officia vespertina,
in quibus ipsam quindecies dicere
debeatis.

Caput IX
Nullus fratrum
aliquid esse sibi proprium dicat,
set sint vobis omnia communia
et
distribuatur unicuique
per manum Prioris,
id est per *fratrem* ab eodem
ad idem officium deputatum,
prout cuique opus erit,
inspectis etatibus et
necessitatibus singulorum.

Asinos autem sive mulos,
prout vestra expostulaverit necessitas,
vobis habere liceat,
et aliquod animalium sive
volatilium nutrimentum.

Caput X
Oratorium,
prout comodius
fieri poterit,
construatur in medio cellularum,
ubi mane
per singulos dies
ad audienda missarum sollempnia

convenire debeatis,
ubi hoc commode fieri poterit.

Caput XI
Dominicis quoque
diebus, vel aliis
ubi opus fuerit,
de custodia ordinis
et animarum salute tractetis,
ubi eciam excessus
et culpe fratrum,
si que in aliquo
deprehense fuerint,
caritate media corrigantur.

Caput XII
Ieiunium singulis diebus,
exceptis dominicis,
observetis
a festo exaltacionis sancte crucis
usque ad diem dominice
resurreccionis,
nisi infirmitas vel debilitas corporis
aut alia iusta causa
ieiunium solvi suadeat,
quia necessitas non habet legem.

Caput XIII
Ab esu carnium semper abstineatis,
nisi pro infirmitatis *et nimie*
debilitatis remedio *sint sumende.*

convenire debeatis,
ubi hoc comode fieri potest.

Caput XI
Dominicis quoque
diebus vel aliis,
ubi opus fuerit,
de custodia ordinis
et animarum salute tractetis;
ubi etiam excessus
et culpe fratrum,
si que in aliquo
deprehense fuerint,
caritate media corrigantur.

Caput XII
Ieiunium singulis diebus,
exceptis dominicis,
observetis
a festo Exaltationis sancte Crucis
usque ad diem dominice
Resurrectionis,
nisi infirmitas vel debilitas corporis
aut alia iusta causa
ieiunium solvi suadeat,
quia necessitas non habet legem.

Caput XIII
Ab esu carnium semper abstineatis,
nisi pro infirmitatis *vel*
debilitatis remedio *sumantur.*
Et quia vos oportet frequentius
mendicare itinerantes,
ne sitis hospitibus onerosi,
extra domos vestras
sumere poteritis pulmenta
cocta cum carnibus;
sed et carnibus supra
mare vesci licebit.

Caput XIV
Quia vero temptacio est vita
hominis super terram,
et omnes qui pie volunt
vivere in Christo
persequcionem paciuntur,
adversarius quoque vester diabolus
tanquam leo rugiens
circuit querens quem devoret,
omni sollicitudine studeatis
indui armatura Dei,
ut possitis stare adversus
insidias inimici.
Accingendi sunt lumbi *vestri*
cingulo castitatis.
Muniendum est pectus
cogitacionibus sanctis.
Scriptum est enim,
Cogitacio sancta servabit te.
Induenda est
lorica iusticie,
ut Dominum Deum vestrum
ex toto corde
et ex tota anima
et ex tota virtute diligatis,
et proximum vestrum tanquam
vos*met*ipsos.
Sumendum est in omnibus
scutum fidei,
in quo possitis omnia tela
nequissimi ignea extinguere.
Sine fide enim
est impossibile placere Deo.
Et hec est victoria, fides vestra.
Galea quoque salutis
capiti imponenda est,
ut de solo Salvatore
speretis salutem,
qui salvum facit populum suum

Caput XIV
Quia vero temptatio est vita
hominis super terram,
et omnes qui pie volunt
vivere in Christo
persecutionem patiuntur,
adversarius quoque vester diabolus,
tamquam leo rugiens,
circuit querens quem devoret,
omni sollicitudine studeatis
indui armatura Dei,
ut possitis stare adversus
insidias inimici.
Accingendi sunt lumbi
cingulo castitatis;
muniendum est pectus
cogitationibus sanctis,
scriptum est enim:
cogitatio sancta servabit te.
Induenda est
lorica iustitie,
ut Dominum Deum vestrum
ex toto corde
et ex tota anima
et ex tota virtute diligatis,
et proximum vestrum tanquam
vos ipsos.
Sumendum est in omnibus
scutum fidei,
in quo possitis omnia tela
nequissimi ignea extinguere:
sine fide enim,
impossibile est placere Deo.

Galea quoque salutis
capiti imponenda est,
ut de solo Salvatore
speretis salutem,
qui salvum facit populum suum

a peccatis eorum.
Gladius autem Spiritus,
quod est verbum Dei,
habundanter habitet
in ore et in cordibus vestris.
Et quecumque *a* vobis
agenda sunt,
in verbo Domini fiant.

Caput XV
Faciendum est vobis
aliquid operis,
ut semper vos diabolus inveniat
occupatos,
ne ex ociositate vestra
aliquem intrandi aditum
ad animas vestras valeat invenire.
Habetis in hoc
beati Pauli apostoli
magisterium pariter et exemplum,
in cuius ore Christus loquebatur,
qui positus est et datus a Deo
predicator et doctor gencium
in fide et veritate,
quem si secuti fueritis,
non poteritis aberrare.
In labore, inquit, et fatigacione
fuimus inter vos,
nocte ac die operantes,
ne quem vestrum gravaremus;
non quasi nos non
hab*ere*mus potestatem,
sed ut nosmetipsos formam
daremus vobis ad imitandum nos.
Nam cum essemus apud uos,
hoc denunciabamus vobis,
quoniam si quis non vult operari,
non manducet.
Audivimus enim

a peccatis eorum.
Gladius autem spiritus,
quod est verbum Dei,
habundanter habitet
in ore et in cordibus vestris;
et quecumque vobis
agenda sunt,
in verbo Domini fiant.

Caput XV
Faciendum est vobis
aliquid operis,
ut semper vos diabolus inveniat
occupatos,
ne ex ociositate vestra
aliquem intrandi aditum
ad animas vestras valeat invenire.
Habetis in hoc
beati Pauli apostoli
magisterium pariter et exemplum,
in cuius ore Christus loquebatur,
qui positus est et datus a Deo
predicator et doctor gentium
in fide et veritate,
quem si secuti fueritis,
non poteritis aberrare.
In labore, inquit, et fatigatione
fuimus inter vos
nocte ac die operantes,
ne quem vestrum gravaremus:
non quasi nos non
hab*ea*mus potestatem,
sed ut nosmetipsos formam
daremus vobis ad imitandum nos.
Nam, cum essemus apud vos,
hoc denuntiabamus vobis:
quoniam si quis non vult operari
non manducet.
Audivimus enim

inter vos quosdam ambulantes
inquiete,
nihil operantes.
Hiis autem qui *huius*modi sunt,
denunciamus
et obsecramus in Domino Iesu
Christo,
ut cum silencio operantes
suum panem manducent.

inter vos quosdam ambulantes
inquiete,
nichil operantes.
Hiis autem, qui *eius*modi sunt,
denuntiamus
et obsecramus in Domino Ihesu
Christo,
ut cum silentio operantes
suum panem manducent:
hec via sancta est et bona;
ambulate in ea.

Caput XVI
Comendat autem apostolus
silencium,
cum in eo precipit operandum.
Et quemadmodum propheta atestatur,
Cultus iusticie silencium est;
et rursus,
In silencio et spe erit fortitudo vestra.
Ideoque statuimus, ut
ab hora vespertina usque
ad horam terciam
sequentis diei silencium teneatis,
nisi forte necessitas vel causa racionabilis
aut licencia prioris silencium
interrumpat.
Alio vero tempore,
licet silencii non habeatur
observacio tanta,
diligencius
a multiloquio tamen caveatur.
Quoniam sicut scriptum est,
et non minus experiencia docet,
In multiloquio
peccatum non deerit;
et, Qui inconsideratus est
ad loquendum, senciet mala.
Item, Qui multis verbis utitur,

Caput XVI
Commendat autem Apostolus
silentium,
cum in eo precipit operandum
et quemadmodum propheta testatur:
cultus iustitie silentium est;
et rursus:
in silentio et spe erit fortitudo vestra.
Ideoque statuimus, ut
dicto completorio

silentium teneatis
usque ad primam
dictam sequentis diei.
Alio vero tempore,
licet silentii non habeatur
observatio tanta,
diligentius tamen
a multiloquio caveatur,
quoniam sicut scriptum est,
et non minus experientia docet,
in multiloquio
peccatum non deerit,
et qui inconsideratus est
ad loquendum sentiet mala.
Item, qui multis verbis utitur,

ledit animam suam.
Et Dominus in evangelio,
De omni verbo otioso
quod locuti fuerint homines,
reddent racionem de eo
in die iudicii.
Faciat igitur unusquisque stateram
verbis suis
et frenos rectos ori suo,
ne forte labatur
et cadat in lingua sua,
et insanabilis sit casus eius usque ad
mortem,
custodiens cum propheta uias suas,
ut non derelinquat in lingua sua.
Et silencium, in quo
cultus iusticie est,
diligenter et caute
studeat observare.

Petitio
Tu autem, frater *Brocarde*, et
quicumque
post te institutus fuerit prior,
illud semper habeatis in mente
et servetis in opere,
quod Dominus ait in evangelio,
Quicumque voluerit inter vos maior
fieri,
erit vester minister,
et quicumque voluerit inter vos
primus esse,
erit vester servus.

Vos quoque ceteri fratres,
priorem vestrum humiliter honorate,
Christum pocius cogitantes
quam ipsum, qui posuit illum
super capita vestra,

ledit animam suam.
Et Dominus in evangelio:
de omni verbo otioso,
quod locuti fuerint homines,
reddent rationem de eo
in die iudicii.
Faciat ergo unusquisque stateram
verbis suis,
et frenos rectos hori suo,
ne forte labatur
et cadat in lingua,
et insanabilis sit casus eius ad
mortem.
Custodiens cum propheta vias suas,
ut non delinquat in lingua sua,
et silentium in quo
cultus iustitie est,
diligenter et caute
studeat observare.

Petitio
Tu autem, frater *B.*, et
quicumque
post te institutus fuerit Prior,
illud semper habeatis in mente,
et servetis in opere,
quod Dominus ait in evangelio:
Quicumque voluerit inter vos maior
fieri,
erit minister vester,
et quicumque voluerit inter vos
primus esse,
erit vester servus.

Vos quoque, ceteri fratres,
Priorem vestrum honorate humiliter,
Christum potius cogitantes
quam ipsum, qui posuit illum
super capita vestra,

et ecclesiarum prepositis ait,
Qui vos audit, me audit,
et qui vos spernit, me spernit,
ut non veniatis in iudicium
de contemptu,
sed de obediencia
mereamur vite eterne mercedem.

Conclusio
Hec breviter scripsimus vobis,
conversacionis vestre
formulam statuentes,
secundum quam vivere debeatis.
Si quis autem supererogaverit,
ipse *Deus*, cum redierit,
reddet ei.
Utatur tamen discrecione,
que virtutum est moderatrix.

et ecclesiarum prepositis ait:
Qui vos audit, me audit,
qui vos spernit, me spernit,
ut non veniatis in iudicium
de contemptu,
sed de obedientia
mereamini eterne vite mercedem.

Conclusio
Hec breviter scripsimus vobis,
conversationis vestre
formulam statuentes,
secundum quam vivere debeatis.
Si quis autem supererogaverit,
ipse *Dominus*, cum redierit,
reddet ei;
utatur tamen discretione,
que virtutum est moderatrix

Rule of Saint Albert – Albert's text

Salutatio
Albert, by the grace of God called
to be Patriarch of the Church of
Jerusalem,
to his beloved sons in Christ,
Brocard and the other hermits
who are living under obedience to
him
at the spring on Mount Carmel:
salvation in the Lord and
the blessing of the Holy Spirit.

Exordium
In many and various ways
the holy fathers have laid
down how everyone,
whatever his state of life
or whatever kind

Rule of Saint Albert – Innocent's text

Salutatio
Albert by the grace of God called
to be Patriarch of the Church of
Jerusalem,
to his beloved sons in Christ,
B. and the other hermits
who are living under obedience to
him
at the spring on Mount Carmel:
salvation in the Lord and
the blessing of the Holy Spirit.

Exordium
In many and various ways
the holy fathers have laid
down how everyone,
whatever their state of life
or whatever kind

of religious life he has chosen,
should live in allegiance to Jesus Christ
and serve him faithfully from a pure heart
and a good conscience.

Narratio
However, because you desire us
to give you a formula of life
in keeping with your purpose,
to which you may hold fast
in the future:

Chapter I
We establish first of all
that you shall have one of you as prior,
to be chosen for that office
by the unanimous assent of all,
or of the greater and wiser part,
to whom each of the others
shall promise obedience and
strive to fulfil his promise
by the reality of his deeds

Chapter III
Next,
according to the site of the place
where you propose to dwell,
each of you shall have

of religious life he has chosen,
should live in allegiance to Jesus Christ
and serve him faithfully from a pure heart
and a good conscience.

Narratio
However, because you desire us
to give you a formula of life
in keeping with your purpose,
to which you may hold fast
in the future:

Chapter I
We establish first of all
that you shall have one of you as prior,
to be chosen for that office
by the unanimous assent of all,
or of the greater and wiser part,
to whom each of the others
shall promise obedience
and strive to fulfil his promise
by the reality of his deeds,
*along with chastity and
the renunciation of property.*

Chapter II
*You may have places in solitary areas,
or where you are given a site
that is suitable and convenient
for the observance of your religious life,
as the prior and the brothers see fit.*

Chapter III
Next,
according to the site of the place
where you propose to dwell,
each of you shall have

a separate cell of his own,
to be assigned to him
by the disposition of the prior himself,
with the assent of the other brothers
or the wiser part of them.

a separate cell of his own,
to be assigned to him
by the disposition of the prior himself,
with the assent of the other brothers
or the wiser part of them.

Chapter IV
However, you shall eat
whatever may have been given you
in a common refectory,
listening together to some reading
from Sacred Scripture,
where this can be done conveniently.

Chapter V
None of the brothers may change
his place assigned to him,
or exchange it with another,
except with the permission of
whoever is prior at the time.

Chapter V
None of the brothers may change
the place assigned to him,
or exchange it with another,
except with the permission of
whoever is prior at the time.

Chapter VI
The prior's cell
should be near the entrance to the
place,
so that he may be the first to meet
those
who come to this place,
and so that whatever needs to be done
subsequently may all be carried out
according to his judgement and
disposition.

Chapter VI
The prior's cell
shall be near the entrance to the
place,
so that he may be the first to meet
those
who come to this place,
and so that whatever needs to be done
subsequently may all be carried out
according to his judgement and
disposition.

Chapter VII
Let each remain in his cell or near it,
meditating day and night
on the Word of the Lord
and keeping vigil in prayer,
unless he is occupied with other lawful
activities.

Chapter VII
Let each remain in his cell or near it,
meditating day and night
on the Word of the Lord
and keeping vigil in prayer,
unless he is occupied with other lawful
activities.

Chapter VIII
Those who know *their letters*
and can *read the psalms,*
shall say *for each of the hours*
those which are appointed for those hours
by the institution of the holy fathers
and the approved custom of the
Church.
Those who do not know their letters
shall say twenty-five Our Fathers
for the night vigil,
except on Sundays and feastdays,
for the vigils of which we establish
that the stated number be doubled,
so that the Our Father is said fifty
times.
The same prayer is to be said seven
times
for the morning lauds.
For the other hours the same prayer
is to be said seven times,
except for the evening office,
for which you shall say it fifteen times.

Chapter IX
Let none of the brothers
call that anything is his property,
but let everything be held
in common among you; and *from the*
things
the Lord may have given you,
to each one shall be distributed
what he needs from the hand of the
prior
– that is from *someone*
he appoints to this task –
taking into account the age
and needs of each one,
However, as has already been stated,

Chapter VIII
Those who know *how to say*
the canonical hours
with the clerics
shall say *them according to*
the institution of the Holy Fathers
and the approved custom of the
Church.
Those who do not know their letters
shall say twenty-five Our Fathers
for the night vigil,
except on Sundays and feastdays,
for the vigils of which we establish
that the stated number be doubled,
so that the Our Father is said fifty
times.
The same prayer is to be said seven
times
for the morning lauds.
For the other hours the same prayer
is to be said seven times,
except for the evening office,
for which you shall say it fifteen times.

Chapter IX
Let none of the brothers
say that anything is his property,
but let everything be held
in common among you;

to each one shall be distributed
what he needs from the hand of the
Prior
– that is from the *brother*
he appoints to this task –
taking into account the age
and needs of each one.
You may, moreover

each one is to keep to the cell,
assigned to him
and live there by himself
on what is given him.

have asses or mules
as your needs require,
and some livestock or poultry
for your nourishment.

Chapter X
An oratory,
as far as it can be done
conveniently,
shall be built in the midst of the cells,
where you shall come together
every day early
in the morning to hear Mass,
where this can be done conveniently.

Chapter X
An oratory,
as far as it can be done
conveniently,
shall be built in the midst of the cells,
where you shall come together
every day early
in the morning to hear Mass,
where this can be done conveniently.

Chapter XI
On Sundays, too,
or on other days when necessary,
you shall discuss the preservation
of order and the salvation of your
souls.
At this time also the excesses
and faults of the brothers,
if such should be found in anyone,
shall be corrected in the midst of love.

Chapter XI
On Sundays too,
or on other days when necessary,
you shall discuss the preservation
of order and the salvation of your
souls.
At this time also the excesses
and faults of the brothers,
if such should be found in anyone,
shall be corrected in the midst of love.

Chapter XII
You shall observe the fast every day
except Sunday
from the feast of the Exaltation
of the Holy Cross until Easter Sunday,
unless sickness or bodily weakness
or some other good reason shall make it
advisable to break the fast,
for necessity knows no law.

Chapter XII
You shall observe the fast every day
except Sunday
from the feast of the Exaltation
of the Holy Cross until Easter Sunday,
unless sickness or bodily weakness
or some other good reason shall make it
advisable to break the fast,
for necessity knows no law.

Chapter XIII
You shall *always* abstain from meat,
unless it be taken

Chapter XIII
You shall abstain from meat,
unless it be taken

as a remedy for sickness or *excessive* weakness.

as a remedy for sickness or weakness.

And since you may have to beg more frequently
while travelling, outside your own houses
you may eat food cooked with meat,
so as not to be a burden to your hosts.
But meat may even be eaten at sea.

Chapter XIV

However, because human life on earth
is a trial,
and all who wish to live devotedly in
Christ
must suffer persecution,
and moreover since your adversary,
the devil, prowls around like a roaring
lion
seeking whom he may devour,
you shall use every care and diligence
to put on the armour of God,
so that you may be able to withstand
the deceits of the enemy.
Your loins are to be girt
with the cincture of chastity.
Your breast is to be fortified
with holy ponderings
for it is written:
Holy ponderings will save you.
The breastplate of justice
is to be put on,
that you may love the Lord your God
with all your heart
and all your soul
and all your strength
and your neighbour as yourself.
In all things is to be taken up
the shield of faith,
with which you will be able to quench

Chapter XIV

However, because human life on earth
is a trial,
and all who wish to live devotedly in
Christ
must suffer persecution,
and moreover since your adversary,
the devil, prowls around like a roaring
lion
seeking whom he may devour,
you shall use every care and diligence
to put on the armour of God,
so that you may be able to withstand
the deceits of the enemy.
The loins are to be girt
with the cincture of chastity.
Your breast is to be fortified
with holy ponderings,
for it is written:
Holy ponderings will save you.
The breastplate of justice
is to be put on,
that you may love the Lord your God
with all your heart
and all your soul
and all your strength,
and your neighbour as yourself.
In all things is to be taken up
the shield of faith,
with which you will be able to quench

all the flaming arrows of the wicked one,
for without faith
it is impossible to please God.
Herein lies victory: your faith.
On your head is to be put
the helmet of salvation,
that you may hope for salvation
from the only Saviour
who saves his people from their sins.
And the sword of the Spirit,
which is the word of God,
should dwell abundantly
in your mouth and in your hearts.
And whatever you have to do,
let it all be done in the Word of the Lord.

Chapter XV
Some work has to be done by you,
so that the devil may always find you occupied,
lest on account of your idleness
he manage to find some opportunity of entering into your souls.
In this matter you have both
the teaching and example
of the blessed apostle Paul,
in whose mouth Christ spoke,
who was appointed and given by God
as preacher and teacher of the nations
in faith and truth;
if you follow him you cannot
go astray.
Labouring and weary we lived among you,
he says, working night and day so as not
to be a burden to any of you;

all the flaming arrows of the wicked one,
for without faith
it is impossible to please God.

On your head is to be put
the helmet of salvation,
that you may hope for salvation
from the only Saviour
who saves his people from their sins.
And the sword of the Spirit,
which is the word of God,
should dwell abundantly
in your mouth and in your hearts.
And whatever you have to do,
let it all be done in the Word of the Lord.

Chapter XV
Some work has to be done by you,
so that the devil may always find you occupied,
lest on account of your idleness
he manage to find some opportunity to entering into your souls.
In this matter you have both
the teaching and example of
the blessed apostle Paul,
in whose mouth Christ spoke,
who was appointed and given by God
as preacher and teacher of the nations
in faith and truth;
if you follow him you cannot
go astray.
Labouring and weary we lived among you,
he says, working night and day so as not
to be a burden to any of you;

not that we had no right to do otherwise,
but so as to give you ourselves as an
example,
that you might imitate us.
For when we were with you we used
to tell you,
If someone is unwilling to work,
let him not eat.
For we have heard that there are
certain people among you going about
restlessly and doing no work.
We urge people of this kind and
beseech them
in the Lord Jesus Christ to earn their
bread,
working in silence.

not that we had no right to do otherwise,
but so as to give you ourselves as an
example,
that you might imitate us.
For when we were with you we used
to tell you,
If someone is unwilling to work,
let him not eat.
For we have heard that there are
certain people among you going about
restlessly and doing no work.
We urge people of this kind and
beseech them
in the Lord Jesus Christ to earn their
bread,
working in silence.
This way is holy and good: follow it.

Chapter XVI
The apostle recommends silence,
when he tells us to work in it.
As the prophet also testifies,
Silence is the cultivation of justice; and
again,
In silence and hope will be your
strength.
Therefore we direct that you keep
silence
from after *vespers* until *terce*
of the following day,
unless some necessity or good reason,
or the prior's permission, interrupts the
silence.
At other times, however,
although you need not observe
silence so strictly, you should nevertheless
be all the more careful to avoid much

Chapter XVI
The apostle recommends silence,
when he tells us to work in it.
As the prophet also testifies,
Silence is the cultivation of justice; and
again,
In silence and hope will be your
strength.
Therefore we direct that you keep
silence
from after *compline* until *prime*
of the following day.

At other times, however,
although you need not observe
silence so strictly, you should nevertheless
be all the more careful to avoid much

talking,
for as it is written
– and experience teaches no less –
where there is much talk sin will not
be lacking;
and, He who is careless in speech
will come to harm; and elsewhere,
He who uses many words injures his
soul.
And the Lord says in the gospel:
For every idle word that people speak
they will render account on judgement day.
Let each one, therefore, measure his
words
and keep a tight rein on his mouth,
lest he stumble and fall by his talking
and his fall be irreparable and prove
fatal.
With the prophet let him watch his
ways
lest he sin with his tongue;
let him try attentively and carefully
to practise the silence in which is
the cultivation of justice.

Petitio
And You, brother *Brocard*, and whoever
may be appointed prior after you,
should always have in mind
and observe in practice
what the Lord says in the gospel:
Whoever wishes to be the greatest
among you will be your servant,
and whoever wishes to be the first
will be your slave.

You other brothers, too,
hold your prior humbly in honour,

talking,
for as it is written
– and experience teaches no less –
where there is much talk sin will not
be lacking;
and, He who is careless in speech
will come to harm; and elsewhere,
He who uses many words injures his
soul.
And the Lord says in the gospel:
For every idle word that people speak
they will render account on judgement day.
Let each one, therefore, measure his
words
and keep a tight rein on his tongue,
lest he stumble and fall by his talking
and his fall be irreparable and prove
fatal.
With the prophet let him watch his
ways
lest he sin with his tongue;
let him try attentively and carefully
to practise the silence in which is
the cultivation of justice.

Petitio
And you, brother *B.*, and whoever
may be appointed prior after you,
should always have in mind
and observe in practice
what the Lord says in the gospel:
Whoever wishes to be the greatest
among you will be your servant,
and whoever wishes to be the first
will be your slave.

You other brothers, too,
hold your prior humbly in honour,

thinking not so much of him as of
Christ
who placed him over you,
and who said to the leaders of the
churches,
Who hears you hears me;
who rejects you rejects me.
In this way you will not come
into judgement for contempt,
but through obedience will merit
the reward of eternal life.

Conclusio
We have written these things
briefly for you, thus establishing
a formula for your way of life,
according to which you are to live.
If anyone will have spent more,
the Lord himself will reward him,
when he returns,
Use discernment, however,
the guide of the virtues.

thinking not so much of him as of
Christ
who placed him over you,
and who said to the leaders of the
churches,
Who hears you hears me;
who rejects you rejects me.
In this way you will not come
into judgement for contempt,
but through obedience will merit
the reward of eternal life.

Conclusio
We have written these things
briefly for you, thus establishing
a formula for your way of life,
according to which you are to live.
If anyone will have spent more,
the Lord himself will reward him,
when he returns.
Use discernment, however,
the guide of the virtues.

3. The Opening Words
(*salutatio* or *prologus*)

Every standard letter opens with a salutation or prologue composed of three elements:[1]

The name of the sender (*intitulatio*)
The name of the addressee (*inscriptio*)
The greeting (*salutatio*)

In a hierarchically organized society such as the medieval one, people very carefully saw to it that the proper titles (of the sender) and forms of address (pertaining to the recipient) were used. The sequence, too, required precision: first the name of the more highly placed person, then that of the less highly placed person. Even the formulation of the greeting had to square with the status of the sender. It will be worth our while to take a closer look at the three elements of the opening words. Since the *intitulatio* and *inscriptio* belong together, we will treat them under one heading (3.1). The greeting constitutes a genre of its own (3.2).

3.1 Patriarch Albert and the hermits at the Spring

Albert by the grace of God called
to be Patriarch of the Church of Jerusalem,
to his beloved sons in Christ,
B. and the other hermits who,
are living under obedience to him
at the spring on Mount Carmel.

The opening words of a letter must include the proper forms of address of the sender as well as of the addressees. Every ecclesiastical and worldly status had its own standardized epithets for that

---

[1] Cf. Lanham, *Salutatio Formulas*, 7.

purpose.[2] In his main work *Dictamina rhetorica* (1226-27), master letter writer Guido Faba, shows on the basis of 220 examples how people of different classes ought to write each other.[3] The hierarchical relation between sender and addressee must be expressed as accurately as possible[4] as a way of confirming the sociopolitical network in which they function.[5] For the Rule of Carmel it is interesting to see – as is evident from Faba's model letters – how the pope and his patriarchs constitute the top of the pyramid, while the hermits – *under* the monks – are the bottom.[6] Meeting in Albert's letter, therefore, are the extreme ends of the hierarchical ladder on the rungs of which believers relate to each other in the church.

On top	At the bottom
Albert:	*B. and the other hermits:*
a person mentioned by name	the group, and even the leader, remains anonymous
By the grace of God called to be Patriarch:	*His beloved sons in Christ:*
hierarchically on top, patriarch, "theo"-logically legitimated.	hierarchically at the bottom, sons, "Christo"-logically situated.
The church of Jerusalem:	*The Spring on Mount Carmel:*
a world class city, the center of an episcopal territory; a focal point in a long-established church.	an uninhabited mountain, marginal, where "living" water flows directly from a spring; place of propheticresistance

---

[2] Ibid., 53; 93-94.

[3] C. Faulhaber, *The Summa dictaminis of Guido Faba,* in *Medieval Eloquence,* Berkeley-Los Angeles-London 1978, 95.

[4] Ibid., 96.

[5] For the political and cultural implications, cf. A. Engelbrecht, *Das Titelwesen bei den spätlateinischen Epistolographen,* Wien 1893; H. Wolfram, *Intitulatio,* in *Mitteilungen des Instituts für österreichische Geschichtsforschung,* 21, Graz 1967.

[6] Faulhaber, *Summa dictaminis,* 96.

On top	At the bottom
Patriarch:	*Hermits:*
the central agent of an ecclesiastical jurisdiction; clothed with absolute authority; a distinct role within the church	seclusion in solitude; a liminal position; as lay hermits still without a distinct role

As a result of the sequence and the distinct forms of address two poles delineate themselves as foci in a hierarchical field. On the one side is Albert. He is referred to by name at the top of the letter. He is patriarch of the church of Jerusalem, the center of Israel's religion, the city of kings and priests, the most ancient church community of a long-established church. He fulfils an established role and occupies a permanent position. He is at the center of religious power, a power that operates with accepted norms and proven sanctions. The group addressed, the person B. and the other hermits, remain anonymous. Their leader is nameless. In relation to the patriarch the hermits are called sons. Like Elijah they have secluded themselves in the solitude of an inhospitable mountain range. They make their home near a Spring, the stream of life in which they share.

It is in this polarity that the addressees' spiritual position vis-à-vis the sender comes to expression. We can best understand this position if we look at it through the eyes of Victor Turner, a cultural anthropologist who distinguishes between structure and antistructure.[7] By *structure* he means a coherent whole of role patterns and established positions. It is the one pole, the pole where power is concentrated. The other pole is constituted by the *antistructure*. This pole is marked by community (egalitarian, personal, informal) and intimacy. At this pole people feel they are at the other end of the power spectrum, devoid of power and influence

---

[7] See *Notes on Processual Symbolic Analysis,* in V. Turner-E. Turner, *Image and Pilgrimage in Christian Culture,* Oxford 1978, 243-255.

(marginal), and exposed to wilderness, all sorts of weather, and death (liminal). As forms of antistructure he mentions: Israel in the wilderness; prophetic circles at odds with the central power of kings and priests; early Christianity on the margins of Judaism and Hellenism; mendicant orders on the margin of official religious life; etc. Antistructure is marked by *flow*: "Flow is the holistic sensation present when we act with total involvement, a state in which action follows action according to an internal logic, with no apparent need for conscious intervention on our part".[8] The spiritual field of tension between Albert and the hermits can be characterized as an ellipse of structure and antistructure. This field of tension has been splendidly depicted by Pietro Lorenzetti (d. 1348), when he portrays the moment at which Albert hands the Rule to the hermits on Mount Carmel.[9] On the left we see a group of colorfully decked-out clergy and knights on horseback led by Albert, patriarch of Jerusalem. Behind them in the background is a fortified castle. On the right we see a group of hermits dressed in black-and-white-striped mantles, kneeling behind a hermit holding a staff, obviously B. Their background is a chapel with the door open. It is a picture of two worlds meeting in the middle: Albert handing the Carmelite Rule to the hermit with the staff.

Structure and antistructure are evenly matched. Together they form a dramatic whole, interwoven and connected by many different threads. By means of the words "grace" and "called" Albert bears the antistructure within himself. Listening to the word "God" through the words "grace" and "calling" we perceive that this word, too, is charged with unsettledness. The hermits, on the other hand, seem already to have structured their community by obedience. At this moment B. does not yet have a name but soon his name will head a list of priors. The hermits are staying in an area which will soon be their place of residence. The Spring will become a conduit of orderly life. Before long the cluster of mountains will be a mountain: a symbol of spiritual power. *Carmel*-ites will gain status of their own.

---

[8] Ibid., 254.
[9] Lorenzetti died in 1348. The painting is kept in the Pinacoteca of Siena.

Albert's Rule situates the addressees in an atmosphere of anti-structure. This position makes them inwardly sensitive to the early prophetism of which Elijah is the prototype. They feel inwardly allied with the mendicants whose lifestyle they will share later on in Europe. A critical question, however, is: do the Carmelites really want this antistructure? In the mystical tradition this anti-establishment structure was really sought and beloved. But there are also forces at work which drive the Carmelites in the direction of the centers of power: to gain privileges and mandates, to defend orthodoxy, and to discredit the marginal positions of others. The opening of the Rule is a dangerous reminder: the position of laymen who, on the margins of the world of that day, opted for the solitariness of an inhospitable mountain range and there drank from the Spring.

3.2. Salvation and blessing

The third part of the opening statement contains the actual content of the greeting. According to the teachers of letter writing, this content is summed up by the two root words which together constitute *salutatio*: *salus* (salvation, wellbeing) and *optatio* (wish). *Salutatio* is the greeting in which the wish for someone's health or salvation is expressed.[10] The classic greeting was simply: Hail![11] In the course of centuries this wish came to have numerous variants.[12] The most subtle was the Christian variant: Hail *in the Lord!* Three meanings come together here. First, the movement of the greeting itself: "Greetings to you in the (name of the) Lord". Next the classic content of salvation: wholeness, health, wellbeing. Third, the Christian meaning of *salvation in Christ*.[13] Gradually this wish became so exclusively Christian that only the more

---

[10] For this element of the greeting, cf. Lanham, *Salutatio Formulas.*
[11] X (dixit) Y *salutem*: *ibid.*, 15-22.
[12] Ibid., 26-68.
[13] Ibid., 22-26.

highly placed clergy were permitted to use it. And only the pope was allowed to add: "and the apostolic blessing". Albert adhered strictly to the prescribed style, greeting the hermits with the customary "health in the Lord", but adding "and the blessing of the Holy Spirit".

> Salvation in the Lord
> and the blessing of the Holy Spirit.

Resonating in this greeting are three distinct spiritual traditions.
1. First there is the *Pauline* tradition, evoked by the style in which Albert's opening words are moulded:[14] the three elements of the opening[15] (sender-addressees-greeting),[16] verbal correspondence ("called", "beloved", "God", "grace", "the Lord", "in"),[17] and the christocentric[18] character of the greeting.[19] By these associations Albert calls to mind his antistructural prototype: Paul who from a liminal position (an apostle without a fixed address, giving up his life for the proclamation of the gospel) writes his liminal churches (non-hierarchical, unlearned; unorganized). All in all a risky association: a patriarch *is* an apostle, "set apart for the gospel" (Rom. 1:1); his office *is* grace; he *is* dependent on "the will of God".[20]
2. Coming through, next, on account of the combination "patriarch-sons-blessing", is patriarchal spirituality.[21] The blessing is an ancient religious gesture. One who blesses seeks to be a

---

[14] It is too sweeping simply to call this *salutatio* Pauline, as we ourselves have done as well (see K. Waaijman-H. Blommestijn, *The Carmelite Rule as a Model of Mystical Transformation,* in *The Land of Carmel,* Rome 1991, 62-66).

[15] See for this: 1 Cor. 1:1-3; 2 Cor. 1:1-2; Gal. 1:1-5; Eph. 1:1-2; Phil. 1:1-2; Col. 1:1-2; 1 Thess. 1:1; 2 Thess. 1:2; 1 Tim. 1:1-2; 2 Tim. 1:1-2; Tit. 1:1-4; Philem. 1:1-3.

[16] In Paul these three elements are not hierarchically structured.

[17] In Paul, however, the words are arranged differently.

[18] Cf. 1 Tim. 1:2; Tit. 1:4; 1 Cor. 1:2; Eph. 1:1; 2 Tim. 1:2.

[19] In Paul the wish constitutes an independent blessing based on the leitmotif of "grace" (*charis,* a word play on the conventional greeting: Chaire!).

[20] 1 Cor. 1:1; 2 Cor. 1:1; Eph. 1:1; Col. 1:1; 2 Tim. 1:1.

[21] K. Waaijman, *De kracht van de zegen,* in *Speling* 36 (1984) 4, 68-82.

channel for the Source of life itself: "May he bear you up and protect you". The blessing accompanies each person, from father to son, mother to daughter, parents to children, from birth to death. Similarly, the blessing of the Holy Spirit accompanies the Carmelites on their spiritual journey. The Spirit helps them discern what the right travel provisions are. The Spirit teaches them rightly to observe these provisions, so that they may gradually become receptive to God's attributes. The Spirit inwardly orients them to the salvation which, though it is still hidden, is already awaiting us from the End. If the salvation in the Lord is to become a *way* in us, then the blessing of the Spirit is indispensable.

3. Salvation (health, wellbeing) is a central motif in *Christian spirituality*.[22] In that one word *salvation* two movements converge. On the one hand the incarnational movement: the incarnation of Jesus Christ brought salvation into the world. By following his example that salvation increases among us.[23] On the other hand, there is the theophanic movement: from within his impenetrable light God encounters us in order to divinize us in Jesus the Messiah.[24] Together the two movements constitute the heart of the spiritual way: the one salvation in the Lord which seeks to find its way in us. At every step two movements interlock: God overcomes us and we seek refuge in God. Albert, in his greeting, directs himself to the core of the spiritual life: growth in virtue in order thus to receive salvation in the Lord.

[22] See *Salut,* in *Dictionnaire de Spiritualité* (hereafter *DS*) XIV, Paris (1990) 251-283.

[23] This is the ascending line in salvation which is especially stressed in Western spirituality.

[24] This descending line is stressed in the liturgical-spiritual traditions of the Eastern churches.

4. The Introduction (*exordium*)

Following the opening, in a standard letter, comes the introduction.[1] The purpose of the introduction is to state the point of the exposition which follows.[2] The expert Guido Faba (ca. 1190-1245), who wrote four treatises on this part of the letter alone, compares the introduction with the foundation of a house.[3] This foundation may be a proverbial saying or a Bible quotation, but whatever it is it has to be euphonious, rhythmic, and graphic. Guido Faba offers no fewer than 330 examples. The introduction somewhat resembles the *major* in a classic syllogism:[4] the foundational framework which serves as backdrop for the concrete exposition (the *minor*) which follows. Together they lead to the request (*petitio*).

Albert opens the *major* of his letter with the initial words of the Letter to the Hebrews. This immediately gives his introduction a monumental air:

> In many and various ways the holy fathers
> have laid down how everyone,
> whatever his state of life or whatever kind of religious life
> he has chosen,
> should live in allegiance to Jesus Christ
> and serve him faithfully from a pure heart
> and a good conscience.

All religious life forms are marked by a *how* in which all members school themself, regardless of the order to which they belong or the kind of religious observance they have chosen. This *how* is one of the reasons why one speaks of an order: it is an orderly

---

[1] The *exordium*, also called the *prooemium* or *prologus*.
[2] Faulhaber, *Summa dictaminis.*, 93-97; Lanham, *Salutatio Formulas,* 93-109.
[3] Faulhaber, *ibid.*, 94.
[4] Ibid., 97-98. Such a major is: "All men are mortal". The *minor* concerns the special case. E.g.: "Gaius is a man". The conclusion, then, is "Gaius is mortal".

whole intrinsically ordered to a goal. This *how*, laid down "in many and various ways" by the Fathers, has taken shape in a richly-hued palette of spiritual life forms. The holy Fathers[5] in the main distinguished three such forms:

1. The *cenobites*. They "live together in one community under the authority of an elder".[6] This community has two core features: the will of the superior which pervasively impacts the will of the monk, a feature by which the latter is drawn away from his egoism; and care for one another's maintenance, a feature which allows evangelical freedom from care to flourish. "They stand away from deciding themselves what to do with what they have earned by the sweat of their brow".[7]

2. The *anchorites*. "They have chosen the hidden life of solitude".[8] In solitude they fight with the devil: "they long to join in open combat and in clear battle with the demons. They are not afraid to push into the great hiding places of the desert".[9]

3. Those who devote themselves to *caring for the poor*. Some of them "like to engage in the holy work of welcoming strangers at hostels"; still others "work for the wretched and the oppressed or apply themselves to teaching or to distributing alms among the poor".[10] Essential to them is the encounter with the Lord in the poor (Matt. 25:34-35).[11]

In this way, citing the holy forefathers, Albert evoked the pluriformity of the religious life. His main focus, however, concerns

---

[5] For the authority of the Fathers, cf. John Cassian, *Collationes* XXI, 12. The *Collationes* are included in the *Corpus Scriptorum Ecclesiasticorum Latinorum*, Vol. VIII, part II, 1886. Nine of the 24 *Collationes* have appeared in an English translation by Colm Luibheid in *The Classics of Western Spirituality: John Cassian, Conferences*, Paulist Press 1985 (abbreviated *CWS*). The remainder are quoted from the translation E.C.S. Gibson in *Nicene and Post-Nicene Fathers*, vol.11, New York 1890-1900 (abbreviated *NPNF*). Those without indication are newly translated.

[6] Cassian, *Conferences*, 18.4, *CWS*, 185.

[7] Ibid., 18.7; cf. also 19.8.

[8] Ibid., 18.4.

[9] Ibid., 18.6.

[10] Ibid., 19.4.

[11] Ibid., 1.9.

the religious core which applies to everyone: "to live a life of allegiance to Jesus Christ and serve him faithfully with a pure heart and
a good conscience". To the discerning reader Albert here verbalizes
the two aims which apply to all forms of religious life: purity of
heart and contemplation.[12]

4.1 Purity of heart

Every religious life form has a programmatic design.[13] Under
this heading falls everything we can do by ourselves: the ascetic
side of the religious life. This is something we can work at
(*praktikè*) and observe (*askesis*): fasting, vigils, reading scripture,
meditation, work, loneliness, etc.[14] They constitute "the steps of
a stairway by which we mount upward".[15] They have a practical
objective of their own: purity of heart. All the exercises are
aimed at this objective: "We must practice fasting, vigils, withdrawal, and the meditation of Scripture as activities which are
subordinate to our main objective, purity of heart".[16] Purity of
heart, in turn, is designed to make us receptive to God. Just as
a farmer cleanses the land of rocks and weeds to make the soil
receptive to the seed, so we must cleanse the soil of our soul of
vices and passions to make it receptive to the divine virtues and
contemplation.

> It is impossible for an unclean soul to acquire spiritual knowledge,
> no matter how hard it labors at the reading of the Scriptures. No one
> pours some rare ointment or the best honey or a precious liquid into
> a foul and filthy container ... So it goes with the container which is
> our heart. If it has not first been cleansed of all the foulest contagion
> of sin it will not deserve to receive that perfume of benediction ...

[12] Cf. ibid., 1.2-5.
[13] For this John Cassian borrowed the Greek word "skopos" and called this
aspect of the religious life "praktikè", something a person can work at.
[14] Ibid., 4.12.
[15] Ibid., 1.4-7.
[16] Ibid., 1.7; *CWS*, 42.

This cleansing must extend to everything, even the memory of our sin:

> Let everyone be well aware that one is not really released from former sins, as long as in all satisfactions and sighings the image of the sins one has committed still hovers before the eyes, and as long as I do not say the pleasure but only the memory of it still infests the innermost part of the mind.[17]

Accordingly, purity of heart is the core of a good conscience.

> When by the grace of a compassionate God the thorn of a gnawing conscience has been removed from the marrow of the soul, one may be assured that one has come to the end of the penance, has received forgiveness, and is purged of the pollution of the sins committed.[18]

This is "perfect and complete purity of heart".[19] Now we understand why – citing from Paul's first letter to Timothy – the Rule in a single breath mentions both purity of heart and a good conscience. Everything that blocks the heart must be removed, down to the innermost part of the conscience.

4.2. In allegiance to Jesus Christ

Purity of heart reaches its fulfilment in the reception of God: contemplation (*theoretiké*). This is its final goal (*telos*) which, however, cannot be reached by works: "... the Lord locates the primary good not in activity, however praiseworthy and abundantly fruitful, but in the truly simple and unified contemplation of himself".[20] This final goal, which lies beyond the practical objective, is called eternal life, the eternal prize,[21] the kingdom of God,[22] being joined to

[17] Ibid., 20.5.
[18] Ibid.
[19] Ibid., 20.7; also 20.9.
[20] Ibid., 1.8.
[21] Ibid., 1.5.
[22] Ibid., 1.3-4.

God, divine contemplation,[23] union with the invisible, ungraspable God.[24] This double goal, handed down since Cassian, was already known to early Carmelite spirituality, for in the *Book of the First Monks* we read:

> The purpose of this life is twofold. The one goal, which we can attain by our own exertion and by practicing the virtues with the help of God's grace is: to offer God a holy heart, purged of every present taint of sin. We reach this goal when we are whole and in *Carit,* that is, in *caritate*:[25] hidden in the love of which the Wise man says: "love covers all offenses" (Prov. 10:12). God, because he wanted Elijah to reach this goal, told him: "Go hide in the brook Carit". The other goal of this life, however, is granted us as a pure gift of God, viz.: in some fashion to taste in one's heart and to experience in the mind – not only after death but in this mortal life already the power of the divine presence and the sweetness of sublime glory. This, now, is to drink from the brook of God's pleasure. God promised this goal to Elijah when he said: "There you will drink of the brook ...". Now by the first of these two goals, i.e. by purity of heart and the perfection of love a person arrives at the second goal, i.e. the experiential knowledge of the divine power and heavenly glory.[26]

The Rule presents the final goal of contemplation in a Pauline key. This is typical for the Rule. Three tones determine the key. 1. By means of the monumental opening quotation from the *Letter to the Hebrews,* tension is created between the times past when "God spoke in many and various ways through the prophets" and these last days "when God speaks through the Son whom he destined to be Lord of all that is" (Heb. 1:1-2). The final goal, then, is the disclosure of the Messianic age in which God will give himself completely to the whole creation. 2. The citation from the *First Letter to Timothy* about purity of heart and a good conscience has

[23] Ibid., 1.8, 13.
[24] Ibid., 1.12.
[25] The author interprets the brook *Carit* (= Cherith) in which Elijah hid as the stream of love (= caritas).
[26] *Decem libri*, 1.2; see also 3.5 and 8; 5.2; 8.4.

a contemplative focus as well. Paul puts it succinctly: "The final aim (*telos*) of all admonition is love from a pure heart, a good conscience, and a sincere faith" (1 Tim. 1:5). Love is not a practical objective. It is received from a pure heart and a good conscience. That is the final goal of all religious life: the love which God works in our heart – reception and contemplation. 3. In this way Albert already prepared us for his actual statement of the final goal: "to live a life of allegiance to Jesus Christ and serve him faithfully". This way of putting it, while biblical,[27] is especially Pauline in tone:

> The weapons of our battle are not of the flesh but are enormously powerful, capable of destroying fortresses. We destroy arguments and every pretension raising itself against the knowledge of God, and take every thought captive *in obedience to the Messiah,* and we are ready to rebuke every disobedience the moment your obedience is complete (2 Cor. 10:4-6).

We have here a splendid description of a shift of focus for the sake of the knowledge of God. Human calculations and imaginations must be dismantled in order that they may be centered in the Messiah, the source of all knowledge of God. Obedience here means complete adjustment to the Other.[28] The circle of I-centeredness is broken. When the Other speaks to me, I listen. When the Other looks at me, I prick up my ears. Like a sacrificial animal, I belong to God.[29] This "belongingness" is reinforced by the parallel: "devote themselves in faithful service to God". In the case of "devoting

[27] In the Vulgate see esp. John 16:2; Rom. 9:4; 12:1; 15:31; 2 Cor. 10:5; Phil. 2:17.

[28] To the ears of the crusaders who as converts (*conversi*) had devoted their life to the patrimony of Christ, i.e. to the Holy Land which was the object of their pilgrimage, there was certainly present in the Latin word *obsequium* ("in obsequio Jesu Christi vivere") the notion that as liege vassals and soldiers they were a part of their Lord's retinue. Still this notion does not seem to me to be dominant in this passage of the Rule; the reference, remember, is to *all religious ways of life.*

[29] Cf. John 16:2; Rom. 12:1; Phil. 1:17.

themselves to"[30] as well the reference, after all, is to complete self-consecration: the Levites devoted their entire lives to liturgical service; creatures completely adapt themselves to their Creator. To "devote oneself to" is to become a devoted servant.[31] And the word *faithful* makes this movement irreversible. We therefore note that all these words – allegiance, faithful, devote oneself – point to one and the same thing: placing the center *outside of* human activity. And this is precisely what *beyond* purity of heart – but *from the perspective of* the pure heart – is seen as the final goal of every religious life form. With this insight the mystical perspective has been opened.[32]

---

[30] For this *deservire*, cf. in the Vulgate: 1 Chron. 9:33; Wisdom 14:21; 16:21, 24, 25; 19:6; 2 Macc. 11:26; Mk. 3:9; Acts 24:14; 26:7; 27:23; 1 Cor. 9:13; Heb. 8:5; 13:10.

[31] Precisely like the Latin *de-servire*.

[32] See K. Waaijman-H. Blommestijn, *The Carmelite Rule as a Model of Mystical Transformation*, in *The Land of Carmel* (ed. P.Chandler and K.J.Egan), Rome 1991, 66-73.

5. Exposition (narratio)

Following the introduction which in a standard letter provides the fundamental framework comes the exposition (*narratio* or *argumentatio*). The requirements for the exposition are that it is written lucidly, marked by clear language signals, connects logically with the introduction, and is not lacking in any essential element.[1] Guido Faba, whom we have mentioned before, compares the exposition to the four walls of a house, built upon the foundation of the introduction.[2]

Just as this is done in a well-written letter, Albert clearly marks the transition to his exposition: "*However,* because you ...". The particularity of the *minor*, after all, must stand out clearly against the general background of the *major*.

> However, because you desire
> us to give you a formula of life
> in keeping with your purpose
> to which you may hold fast in the future:
> We establish ...

In spirituality a formula of life is one which both arises from and leads to experience. Both aspects are present in the form Albert presents to us. On the one hand it is bound up with the life which had already assumed form among the hermits. The hermits submit to Albert a plan[3] embodying long-practiced conduct.[4] On the other hand, this formula leads people into the experiential life – the reason why Carmelites do well to adhere to it. It involves a

---

[1] Cf. Lanham, *Salutatio Formulas,* 61-63; Faulhaber, *Summa dictaminis,* 88; 98.

[2] Faulhaber, *ibid.,* 94.

[3] In ancient Christian literature *propositum* frequently serves as a translation of the Greek askèsis: the ascetic level of the monastic way of life.

[4] See the *conclusion* of Albert's letter. *Conduct* (= conversatio), too, often serves as a translation of the Greek *askèsis*.

steady, ongoing process of transformation. Ever new layers of a person's being are caught up in the process: one must adhere to the external ground plan of commitments and customs; one must stick to the purification intended in the ground plan; one must keep oneself ready for God's coming. Through this process as a whole one becomes a "God-keeping" being.

Guido Faba, as stated above, compares the exposition to four walls. This image is applicable to the Carmelite Rule for more than one reason. For Albert's exposition consists of four parts which together – two-by-two – form a whole. The design of the first diptych aims at purity of heart (I-XIII): it explains how the basic provisions (I-VI) must be observed (VII-XIII) with a view to this practical objective (*skopos*). The design of the second diptych aims at contemplation (XIV-XVI): it unfolds how the attributes of God, which are received on the deep level of the receptive heart (XIV), can make an ongoing, permanent and profound impact in our life (XV-XVI). Accordingly, in his exposition Albert literally sets forth the twofold purpose of the Carmelite formula of life which he had earlier posited as the point of departure for a religious life of every kind.

5.1. The basic provisions (I-VI)

In chapters I-VI one is struck, even on a first reading, by a number of points. There is first of all the striking repetition of the term "to have" (*habere*): "We establish first of all that you shall *have* one of you as prior ... you may *have* places ... Each of you shall *have* a separate cell of your own ...". "To have" here does not mean to have in one's possession but to have at one's disposal. The priorate as a means of structuring the community, the place as potential living space for the community, and the cell as living space for each member of the community are all provisions.[5]

---

[5] The same verb "have" occurs one more time: "You are permitted to *have* as many donkeys or mules ..." (IX). Here, too, the idea is not ownership but use. Donkeys, mules, lifestock and poultry are provisions. Ownership of these is permitted "insofar as necessity demands" (IX).

Striking as well is the word "place" (*locus*), which occurs five times: "You may have *places* ... according to the site of the *place* ... the *place* assigned to him ... near the entrance to the *place* ... those who are coming to this *place*". In this context *place* must be understood to mean the place of residence for all of them together and each individually. In addition we must think of the ground and location of the place in the surrounding area. The reference, therefore, is to place as a basic part of the setup.

Finally, one is struck by the two polar tensions exhibited by the Carmelite community. The first one lies curled up in the pronoun "you" (*vos-vester*): "that *you* shall have one of *you* as prior ... *You* may have places where *you* are given ... for the observance of *your* religious life ... whatever may have been given *you*". This pronoun *you* has two sides to it: a communal side (the unanimous assent of all; the prior and the brothers; the prior with the assent of the other brothers; a common refectory; listening in common) as well as a personal side (each of the others; each one individually; one of the brothers; to exchange it with another person's). This is the first polar tension: individual-community. The second is that between the prior and the brothers. This field of tension springs into being as a result of choosing a *prior*: "that you shall have one of you as prior" (I). In the following chapters the elected prior acts three times in conjunction with the brothers: the *prior* and the *brothers* choose the right place (II); the *prior*, with the assent of the other *brothers*, assigns the cells (III); the *brothers* may not exchange cells except with the permission of the *prior* (IV). The entrance to the place, finally, is the prior's cell (VI).

5.1.1 Having a prior (chapter 1)

Albert starts the exposition of his formula of life with the priorate: first the provision itself (*having* a prior), next, the way it comes into existence (the choice of prior), then the confirmation of the prior (the promise of obedience), and finally the manner in which this institution is maintained (obedience to the prior). Innocent IV, in 1247, added the vows of chastity and poverty to that of obedience.

We establish first of all:

A that you shall have one of you as prior,

B to be chosen for that office by the unanimous assent of all, or of
the greater and wiser part,

C to whom each of the others shall promise obedience

D and strive to fulfil his promise by the reality of his deeds,

E along with chastity and the renunciation of ownership.

A. *The priorate.* Albert states first of all that lay hermits must have a
prior. A prior (lit. "one who is before") is not an abbot. The latter
was chosen for life in order, as *pater-familias,* to care for his sons. A
prior is not chosen for life. He is not the head of a family. He is a
brother among brothers. For that reason Albert addresses all of them
as "brother", brother B. as well as the other brothers. The prior is
first among the brothers. By having a prior the brothers structure
themselves in relation to an authority figure so that they become
a religious community.[6] The term "priorate" is a signal for the
cenobitic lifestyle. It is as if Albert – entirely in keeping with the plan
of the Carmelites themselves – wanted to say: from now on the
Carmelite model of life is also cenobitic in nature. We can understand this verbal signal only when we note the structural connection
between the priorate and the cenobitic life, above all in contrast to
the eremitic life. I know of no more striking illustration for making
this clear than the story of the life of Abba John. Having spent thirty
years in the cenobitic life and twenty years as a hermit in the desert,
John returned to his former way of life. His reason? "What I have
lost [in the cenobitic setting of a monastery] in sublimity of contemplation I have gained by subjection to obedience".[7] These words
capture the core of his motivation. In his years of living as a hermit
he was subject to the pressures of finding daily subsistence and practicing hospitality. These pressures are absent in the cenobitic life.
There one's main duty is to live in obedience to a prior.

> This obedience brings about that, as I subject myself to an abbot to
> the very end, I may somewhat emulate him of whom it is said: "He

---

[6] *Domus religiosa, domus orationis, collegium poenitentium, locus sacer.*

[7] Cassian, *Conferences,* 19.5.

humbled himself, becoming obedient to death" (Phil. 2:8) and I may humbly repeat his words: "I came not to do my own will but the will of the one who sent me, the Father" (Jn. 6:38).[8]

B. *The choice of a prior.* The procedure of choosing a prior, formulated and approved by the third and fourth Lateran Councils (1179 and 1215 respectively) included three steps.[9] The first step was that someone would be brought forward and invited by the community to become its leader. The second step was the assurance that the person having spiritual jurisdiction over the community – depending on the status of the community, this could be the local bishop or parish priest – would be monitoring the procedure followed. The third step was the ceremony in which the bishop or parish priest installed the elected person in office. These three steps are simply assumed in the Rule.

The Rule explicitly regulates only the first step: the election. This is governed by a double principle, a quantitative and a qualitative criterion. As for the quantitative criterion, the best election is an election effected by the unanimous assent of all. In that case the prior is simply the choice of all the brothers. When this is not possible, the greater part of the brothers, acting for all, is needed to arrive at the choice of a prior. By the greater part is meant, not a relative majority (a plurality of votes), but an absolute majority (more than half the votes). As for the qualitative criterion: there was a concern to keep an eye on the quality of the person to be elected as well as on that of the voters. To that end a special method was constructed, one which involved the appointment of three scrutineers (*scrutatores*) who – in secret – asked all the brothers: "Whom do you plan to vote for and why?" At the same time, based on functions fulfilled in the past, age, knowledge, merits, prestige, and the like, a list was made of the wiser part of the community. The two lists were laid side-by-side (*collatio*). A discussion then followed about the number of votes each candidate had

[8] Ibid., 19.6.
[9] For this, see Cicconetti, *Rule,* 74-76; 120-125; 268-269.

received; the quality of the votes he had won and the motives advanced for them; the relation between the quantity and the quality of the votes. The choice was finally determined in light of this discussion, after which the abovementioned second and third step followed.

This election procedure not only produces the prior but also exposes the community. All the brothers, after all, have to break out of their shells to bring one of their own group into the limelight. Every one of them will have to disclose and motivate his choice to another. Everyone will have to break out of his shell by formally giving his vote to another. This breaking out of one's shell not only pertains to one's external voting behavior but also to his intellect, will, and heart. When the voting process unfolds correctly and several layers of a person are set in motion outwardly to "one of you", the community not only *has* a prior but it has built itself up around a center. All of the members, in making a unanimous choice for "one of you", have united themselves into a single community of brothers.[10]

In giving his rule Albert only had in mind the prior of the Carmel hermitage. However, when at a later time several houses were established which jointly formed a province, the prior intended by the Rule became the general superior, the so-called prior general. The latter is prior over all the Carmelite provinces, as has officially been the case since 1247.

Since at the time the priorate was instituted the issue was the internal structuring of the community, it has traditionally been assumed that in the designation of a leader religious communities are autonomous. All interference from without (a bishop, a sister community, the mother community, the original owners) is rejected. In 1229 this was confirmed in clear language by Pope Gregory IX.

> To insure your tranquillity and peace we add to this the injunction that no one may claim the right to appoint a prior without the

[10] See Waaijman-Blommestijn, *The Carmelite Rule as a Model of Mystical Transformation,* a.c., 73-74.

consent of the majority of the brothers or of the more experienced part of them.[11]

C. *The pledge of loyalty.* After the community has chosen its prior, all the brothers promise to obey him. Also those who have not voted for him now openly declare that they are turning their wills around in his favor. It is always difficult to interiorize and appropriate something that comes from without. In spirituality the goal is always to step outside of ourselves and to admit things into ourselves. Scripture reading and liturgy, cell and silence – all are forms which must be practiced and interiorized, as it were, from without. At the same time I have to enter into them to explore the space which is present in each and to know myself at home there. In the same way also obedience demands that I admit the will of another into my own life and at the same time that I step outside of myself to enter into the viewpoint of that other person.

D. *To obey in reality.* The promise of obedience is a public act performed by words at a specific moment on a certain day of the year. But actually keeping that promise requires continual application and effort. It is work, a work whose truth comes to light only by doing *(opus veritatis)*. Obedience is made valid only by doing. It is only by doing that my I-centeredness is turned inside out. One can only practice obedience "by self-denial and renouncing one's own will".[12] A will-outside-of-my-will breaks open my willfulness and turns it outward: "the aim of the cenobites is to mortify and crucify all their willing".[13] Allegiance to the other constitutes the inner goal of obedience.

> The cenobites continue to show the patience and the discipline with which they persevere in this profession which they once adopted. They never do what they themselves wish. Every day they are crucified to this world and are living martyrs.[14]

---

[11] Cicconetti, *Rule,* 102; cf. also *Religiosam vitam,* ibid., 121.
[12] Letter of Cyril, *Decem Libri,* 8.4.
[13] Cassian, *Conferences* 19.8.
[14] Ibid., 18.7, *CWS,* 190.

E. *The three vows.* In 1247 the vows of poverty and chastity were added to those of obedience. At first blush this addition seems arbitrary and ill-considered. Still, a brief reflection on the three vows shows that the insertion at this point in the Rule is not a bad choice.

Up until the twelfth century the triad obedience-poverty-and-chastity hardly ever occurred, certainly not as a term denoting the religious profession.[15] One made profession by actually joining a certain religious way of life. It was never a matter of making a public declaration, let alone making a vow of obedience, poverty, and chastity. The act of joining was itself the profession. By wearing a certain garment, living in a monastery, and joining in all the appropriate activities, one demonstrated one's intentions and one's sense of what one was committed to. That was the situation when the Carmelite order came into being.

By the beginning of the thirteenth century the triad obedience-poverty-and-chastity came increasingly into vogue as structuring of the religious life. This never meant, however, that monastics began to apply themselves to these three obligations. They were incorporated into the whole as a matter of course and gave expression to it. Accordingly, the question is not whether the first Carmelites took their solemn vows but rather whether the Carmelites had an official religious status one could seek access to. The status of this way of life governed the nature of the profession, which was precisely what the advisers of Pope Innocent IV had in mind. The idea of inserting this addition in the Rule was merely to transform Albert's life formula into a juridical life model for religious. The addition of the three vows as a triad (not distributed over different chapters) makes the Carmelite life formula into an official Rule.

Now what is the connection between this trio of vows and the chapter on the priorate? That connection can be seen in the following: in the Middle Ages the rite of profession was modelled on the rite of obedience, a rite by which a free man subjected himself

[15] For this and the following, cf. Cicconetti, *Rule,* 30-31; 43-48; 65-68; 158-159 and 268-269.

to his liege lord.[16] Kneeling down, he laid his hands in the lord's hands as he pronounced the oath of allegiance. A kiss then sealed the rite. From this perspective let us now take a look at the Carmelite Rule. Just as the institution of the priorate actually meant the structuring of the community, so the vow of obedience sealed a person's passage into this community. In 1200 such a vow of obedience was as much as the definitive commitment: entrance for life. Later on, in 1247, monastics expressed the same definitive commitment in the vow of obedience, poverty, and chastity. Both aim at formal commitment to a religious way of life. To the Carmelites the crucial thing in this connection was that, by the incorporation of the triad obedience-poverty-and-chastity, their formula of life now became an official Rule.

5.1.2. Having places (II-VI)

As we take a closer look at chapters II-VI concerning the place we are struck by a number of points.

1. Chapter II introduces the theme: "You may have *places* ...". Subsequent chapters elaborate on this theme: the place includes separate cells (III); the place accommodates the common refectory (IV); the place is not an object of exchange (V) and offers access to outsiders via the cell of the prior (VI).

2. Missing in the five chapters dealing with the place is the oratory in the midst of the cells. The chapel only comes up a number of chapters later. This hiatus raises questions. Is the place as such perhaps already suitable for the religious way of life of the Carmelites (II)? What, then, is that religious way of life?

3. There is alternation between earlier and later text fragments. Chapter II is a late text (1247), for the brothers are given a choice between a hermitage in a solitary place or a monastery in the city. Then follows an early text (1206-1214): each brother individually has an separate cell of his own (III). A late insertion (1247) is the chapter on the common refectory (IV).

---

[16] Ibid., 65-66.

On the other hand, the chapters on the non-exchangeability of the cell (V) and the location of the prior's cell near the entrance (VI) are early (1206-1214).

4. Striking, too, is the "inside-outside" field of tension. Chapter II has an outward-looking perspective: the place is located in a solitary area or in the city (II). The three following chapters have an inward-looking perspective: the assignment of the cells (III), the common refectory (IV) and the non-exchangeability of the cells (V). Chapter VI again looks outward: it regulates the reception of those who come to the place.

Chapters II-VI all relate to the place.[17] In this connection it must be noted that several meanings of the word *place* are intermingled.

1. The *topographical* place. The first Carmelite monastery was located in what is today the Wadi-'Ain-es-Siah. Excavations have shown that the cell of the prior was near the entrance. Presumably not all the cells lay behind the entrance. A few cells were probably situated nearby. The earliest hermitages outside the Carmel probably looked approximately the same: cells built at some distance from each other in a spacious area with a chapel in the center.[18] The place assumed another architectonic design when Carmelites decided to live as mendicant friars in the cities.

2. The *juridical* place. A place is not consecrated unless a local bishop decides to make it so: "A private person cannot make a place a consecrated place".[19] A bishop's declaration that a place is consecrated implies the recognition that the religious inhabiting it constitute a religious community. The local designation "at the spring on Mount Carmel", therefore, is more than a topographical reference. It is at the same time a canonical legitimation of the religious community.

---

[17] For her hermeneutic approach to the Rule Constance Fitzgerald chooses "the place" as her hermeneutic point of entry. See C. Fitzgerald, *How to Read the Rule: An Interpretation,* in *Albert's Way,* 51-69, specifically 57-60.

[18] Such an external arrangement can still be seen in what remains of monastic villages in Ireland.

[19] Cf. Cicconetti, *Rule,* 48.

3. The *socio-religious* place. Up until deep into the Middle Ages a place in a solitary area was the distinguishing mark par excellence of the religious life. Religious belonged in isolated places. Solitariness is a form of life.[20] Another such form is suggested where the Rule offers an alternative: "or where you are given a site". The alternative offered refers to a mendicant way of life in the city.

4. The *mystical* place. For the earliest Carmelites Mount Carmel was a place of withdrawal from the world, implying a fervent longing to be drawn away into God. In this respect Elijah was their model. In the nature of the case, this contemplative movement is a concrete event occurring at the place where one lives or works, but as such it is not a physical or geographical place. It is the transformation of one's place under the impact of one's search for God. The mystical place is one which moves away from what is fixed, definite, and restricted, from that which is evaluated, prejudged, and calculated; it is movement away into the uninhabited and solitary, deserted and uncultivated, with a view to being drawn away into God's unfathomable goodness and boundless love. This is the place of mystical solitude which the desert monks sought out.[21]

In solitary areas or in the city (II)

In chapter II[22] the Rule prescribes (A) where the Carmelites can have their place of residence, (B) what criterion they should employ in that connection, and (C) who decides the issue.

A You may have places in solitary areas or where you are given a site that is suitable and convenient

[20] Cassian, *Conferences* 18.4.
[21] Ibid., 14.4; cf. 18.6; 19.8; 24.2-3; 19.5; cf. 19.9.
[22] This chapter comes from the advisors of Innocent IV (Cicconetti, *Rule*, 269). They continue their contribution in the next chapter where they make the location of the cells dependent on "the site of the place where you propose to dwell" (III). Albert only had Carmel in mind. For him that was "the site where you propose to dwell" (*ibid.*, 159).

B for the observance of your religious life,
C as the prior and the brothers see fit.

A. The formulation of Innocent IV evokes socio-religious tensions
by letting the Carmelites choose between places in solitary areas
and places wherever they may be given to them. "Places in solitary
areas", after all, evoke the classic religious form of life. Religious
belong in solitary places. Religious life in its purest form is
eremitic. By the end of the twelfth and the beginning of the thirteenth century, however, we see the religious life pulling toward
the city. First it was a half-way move – at night religious stayed
outside the city; during the day they were among the people –
but later they completed the move and lived in the middle of the
city. This movement coincided with the rise of city culture with
its upper class, middle class, the less advantaged and the very
poor. The mendicant brothers joined the latter two categories.
This choice sharply contrasted with the then-prevailing image of
the ideal religious. "If you really want to be a monk, i.e., a solitary
man, what are you doing in the city, which is a place to live for
the masses, but never for the solitary".[23] As a result of the insertion of 1247 the Carmelites were allowed a free choice between
solitude and the mendicant way of life.[24] By giving them this
choice the Rule confronts Carmelites with a tension-filled socio-
religious dilemma which demands resolution. This choice is then
facilitated by the criterion it presents.

B. The criterion provided for the selection of a place is that it
must be "suitable and convenient for the observance of your
religious way of life" (II). But just what does this mean when this
religious way of life is a hybrid? The place, after all, may be
located on Carmel or away from Carmel, in an uninhabited area
or in the city. How can a non-form furnish a criterion for the
selection of a place? Neither do the topographical situation, the

---

[23] *Decretum Gratiani* II, cap. XVI, q. 1, C. 5 (a quotation from Jerome = Ep.58.5;
Pl 22:583).
[24] Cicconetti, *Rule*, 167-177.

church's jurisdiction, or religious preference offer any firm guidance. Of course, by its topography the place must somehow furnish living space for a group of religious people. And the church authorities must approve of such an establishment. Furthermore, one must aim at a suitable religious architecture: a hermitage must be a hermitage, a convent for mendicants must be a convent. In my opinion this leaves only one criterion which, in the case of the Carmelites, can really help them make a choice and that is the criterion of the mystical place.

C. The place which the prior and the brothers end up choosing must be able to support or make allowance for mystical transformation. It must be intrinsically adapted to transformation in God. Only then is it truly "suitable". It must adapt itself to the process of mystical transformation, the process of moving away from the finite in order to be withdrawn into God. Only then is it really "convenient". It must make way for the brothers' intense longing for God. It must not be a barrier to growth toward God. It must be able to develop in terms of the vision of God. It must begin to furnish us God's perspective. Only that is "what is most suitable in the eyes of the prior and the brothers". The Rule could make the *form* of the place a matter of choice because it is aimed at providing a Carmel. The *Rubrica Prima* (1281) puts it sharply: young Carmelites must know where the starting point of Carmel is located.[25] They must be familiar with its original truth.[26] They must know where Carmel originates. They must know where the Spring is located. A Carmel is not a geographical site – the Carmel mountain range, a hermitage in an uninhabited area, a monastery in the city, etc. – but a place where, along with Elijah, we can let ourselves be drawn into God. A Carmel must offer a view of the Place.

One may ask: Is there a place which does not offer that view? Is not every place intrinsically linked with its Creator? Does not

---

[25] "A quo et quomodo ordo noster sumpsit *exordium* . . . a quo et quomodo ordo noster habuerit *exordium*". See: *Medieval Carmelite Heritage*, Rome 1989, 33-43.

[26] "iuxta *veritatem* ... Dicimus enim *veritati* testimonium perhibentes". Ibidem.

every place open up and give way to our movement toward him? This, I am afraid, sounds too easy. A site for the religious way of life of Carmelites is suitable and fitting only when the meaning of that site has not been preempted by some other function or status. The more coercively the meaning of the place has been defined, the less suitable and fitting it is for the Carmelite religious way of life. To the extent the meaning of a place has been defined in advance by its natural topography, historical value, social status, or instrumental function, to that extent the place would seem to be unsuitable and inconvenient. Such a place never works out. Conversely, to the extent a place by its lack of definition and meaning approximates the character of a desert where everything depends on the significance of God, to that extent such a place seems suitable and fitting as a place to live. It works out best. From this perspective even living in a church is not fitting. For in that case the religious meanings are coercively predefined. In my opinion it is a happy circumstance that the oratory only comes up *after* we have had to reflect on our place to live in terms of our religious way of life. Even to define it as a hermitage or city convent is undesirable. The meaning these words convey are relative. Even to define it as a Carmel can be a hindrance. The only thing that matters is that we "find Place".

Separate cells (III)

Individual, separate cells[27] could be grouped in various ways. Sometimes the windows of the separate cells looked out on a single space. In that case the hermits could exhort each other to greater

[27] In general "cell" means larder or pantry, apartment, a small hut. "Cellula" is a little house belonging to a hermit (Cassian). "Cella" is a division of a monastery intended for a specific group of monks, novices for example (Benedict). In the Carmelite context "cellula" means a detached hermitage (Mount Carmel), apartment (Aylesford) or room (monastery). As late as 1271 Nicholas the Frenchman railed against innovators in these words: "But you city-dwellers changed the separate rooms back to a common house" – (*Sagitta ignea* cap. 8).

zeal. At other times the cells were located at some distance from each other. At still other times the cells were connected laterally, each having an entrance of its own.

As far as Carmel is concerned,[28] initially the system of separate cells was maintained. From about 1250 the construction of separate cells around the oratory was abandoned. Also, the function of the cells changed: having a common refectory removed the need for monks to prepare their own food individually. Especially influential was the given situation in or near the cities. Sometimes a building was donated to the brothers who then adapted themselves to it; at other times the size and shape of the site imposed limitations. The Rule allowed for variation: "according to the site of the place", i.e. depending on the ground, the buildings or the immediate surroundings. In some cases cells were built over a common dormitory. Some Carmelites had two cells and commuted back and forth between a hermitage outside the city and a convent inside the city. The hermit types of course preferred the detached cells. The mendicant types were less attached to having separate cells. In practice their views won out. Initially people simply ignored the Rule and the Constitutions. In 1294 the separate cells disappeared from the Constitutions. In the Rule, however, they stayed on as a thought-provoking symbol.

> Next,
> according to the site of the place
> where you propose to dwell,
> each of you
> shall have a separate cell of his own.

The repetition of the phrase "each of you", reinforced by the word *separate*, brings to the fore the meaning of the *cell*: the cell not only isolates us; it also particularizes us. It gathers up out of distraction. The reverse is true when we spend time away from our cell: "thoughts are scattered as it were to the winds. All the concentration of mind and all the keenness of his vision of the aim is lost

[28] Cicconetti, *Rule*, 175-177.

in multiplicity".[29] The cell induces simplicity. It promotes the abandonment of that which is incidental, of what we have been talked into, of comparisons with others, and of that which has been casually deposited in our soul. The cell takes us inside the mystical space of the place, leading us to the liberating solitude which the place provides. It detaches and liberates us in order to take us, free and naked, into the presence of God. The truth is, what the place does for the group as a whole, the cell does for a person individually: it detaches each of us from social controls, from acquired prejudices and judgments, from the stories told about us. Certainly, it hurts to be detached from our status, to have it peeled off layer after layer. At the same time the cell welcomes us; it shares and senses our solitude.

> The Jewish thinker Emmanuel Levinas describes this energy of the dwelling as inviting and welcoming: "To dwell is recollection, a coming to oneself, a retreat home with oneself as in a land of refuge which answers to a hospitality, an expectancy, a human welcome". Levinas calls this welcome the feminine: an alterity which retreats invitingly, where I recollect myself.

> The Other whose presence is discreetly an absence, with which is accomplished the primary hospitable welcome which describes the field of intimacy, is the Woman. The woman is the condition for recollection, the interiority of the Home, and inhabitation.

> Dwelling is a hospitable welcome offered by the other who retreats from me and in so doing creates space for me.[30]

In the background of these reflections is the Indwelling of God, the Shechinah, the Feminine in God.[31] The interiority of the cell is a womb of compassion. Always, whenever I recollect myself I enter my dwelling, I allow myself to experience hospitality at a

[29] Cassian, *Conferences* 24.3.

[30] E. Levinas, *Totality and Infinity: An Essay on Exteriority*, Pittsburgh 1969, 154-156.

[31] See A. Goldberg, *Untersuchungen über die Vorstellung von der Schekinah in der frühen rabbinischen Literatur*, Berlin 1969; G. G. Scholem, *Major Trends in Jewish Mysticism*, London 1955.

fundamental level. I am being welcomed by the Indwelling, by a divine generosity which brings me home. This basic Marian reality is essential to the conception of the world as the Face of God.[32] The inward reception of the Word (VII), the act of stretching out my hands in prayer (VII-VIII), the giving up of all possessions (IX), stepping outside one's cell in order to come together with others in the midst (X), expressing and receiving criticism (XI), purging myself by fasting and abstinence (XII-XIII), working in silence (XV-XVI) – all this is only made possible by Mary, the Indwelling, who accepts me unconditionally, welcomes me before I ask for it, who forgives me, shows me the abyss of solitariness, comforts me, knows my death and weeps. All movements from the outside to the inside are possible only if there exists an Inside and that is the cell. Indeed, even putting on the armor of God is made possible only by the cell, which is the symbol of all reception. The cell is of essential importance to the Carmelite life. Cells touch on the very form of the monastery.[33] For that reason the institution of the cell is invested with the same weight as the institution of the priorate:

> to be assigned to him
> by the disposition of the prior himself,
> with the assent of the other brothers
> or the maturer part of them.

The parallelism between chapters I and II is striking, and all the more so if we recall that in the original Rule chapters I and III were consecutive. In fact, chapter III seems even weightier! Both the priorate and the assignment of a cell require the assent of the other brothers or of the maturer part. But in the case of the cell the action of the prior comes on top of it! The cell is assigned by the disposition of the prior and with the assent of the other brothers. Accordingly, this action is very carefully considered. All aspects of the cell are weighed to ensure that it will suit me. It is assigned to

---

[32] For the symbolic links between Carmel and Mary, cf. Noel Dermot O'Donoghue, *Mary and the Carmelite Imagination*, in *Albert's Way*, 177-206.

[33] *Decem libri*, 8.4.

me by the other(s). The brothers expressly participate in the arrangement and assignment. The arrangement has to be made intelligently. The awarding of a cell calls for cordial assent. There is nothing excessive or exaggerated about this solemn act of assigning a cell, for the cell is the umbilical cord of solitude which connects us with the Place.

The common refectory (IV)

Originally, as it befits hermits, Carmelites remained in their cell night and day. The meals were distributed in accordance with the needs of each, "taking account of the age and needs of each one", in such a way, however, that, as stated, each of them remains in the cell assigned to him and each one individually lives from what is distributed to him (IX in the original version of 1206-14).

The year 1247 saw the introduction by Innocent IV of the common meal. This was nothing exceptional, for in the meantime eating together and praying together had been made obligatory for all monasteries. In this regard the new religious communities followed the Benedictine tradition, and the Carmelites followed suit.[34] In addition there was a practical reason mentioned by Ribot: when the procurator had to deliver the meals to all the cells, on his arrival at the last brother the food was cold! These and other inconveniences led the brothers to eat together.[35] In any case, the common meal meant the relativization of the life of a hermit. By eating together the brothers expressed – among other things – their equality and mutual love. Also the practice of listening to the reading of holy Scripture during the meal went back to an old monastic custom: "Never let the reading be omitted during the meals of the brothers'.[36] By listening attentively to Scripture the brothers avoided talk and excessive concentration on the food. The common refectory (IV) was clearly related, by the advisors of Innocent IV in 1247, to the separate cells:

[34] Cf. Cicconetti, *Rule*, 178-179.
[35] *Decem libri*, 8.6.
[36] *Regula Sancti Benedicti*, 38; *Regula Magistri*, 24.

Each of you shall have a separate cell of his own,
however, you shall eat
whatever may have been given you
in a common refectory,
listening together
to some reading from Sacred Scripture,
where this can be done conveniently.

The refectory seems to have been achieved in competition with
the cells: "Let each of you have a cell, but then in such a way that
it is possible for you to eat and listen together". The contrast is
further heightened by the tension between the words "separate"
and "common". Over against the separate and special (twice in
chapter III) stands the communal (twice in chapter IV). In order to
sharpen our insight into this field of tension we shall first reflect on
what eating is, or, as the original Rule puts it, on "living from ...".

> Eating is a form of "living from ...". We live from eating and drinking,
> from light and air, from the things we see and work at, from dreaming
> and sleeping. We enjoy them in the elementary sense of the word: we
> ingest them, and transmute them into ourselves. "An energy that is
> other ... becomes my own energy, my strength, me". This elementary
> transformation is enjoyment. A happy person is engrossed in his happi-
> ness and precisely thus does he detach himself from the world on
> which, nevertheless, he feeds himself. One who eats forgets the entire
> world. As one who enjoys himself he is solitary and isolates himself in his
> enjoyment: "Separation in the strictest sense is solitude, and enjoyment
> – happiness or unhappiness – is isolation itself. Eating as an act of "tak-
> ing something other to oneself" in its very accomplishment is self-suffi-
> cient. "Enjoyment is a withdrawal into oneself, an involution". Enjoy-
> ment, by the very fact of its recollective movement, effects separation.[37]

The original Rule (1206-1214) situated eating inside the cell:
in such a way that each lives from what is distributed to him.
"Living from ...", something that in itself already means isolation, separation, and solitude, here reinforces the function of the

---

[37] Cf. Levinas, *Totality and Infinity: An essay on Exteriority*, o.c., 110-114;
117-120; 147-151; esp. 117, 118, 148.

individual, separate cell. The solitariness of eating thus deepens the solitariness of the cell. The cell isolates a person and so does the enjoyment of eating. The cell is separate and so is the act of "living from …". The cell isolates me within the place and the consumption of food isolates me in my enjoyment. But just as in essence the cell is an invitation and a hospitable welcome, so – conversely – the act of eating is not doomed to remain sealed off in its isolation either. Just as the isolation by the cell saves me for birth in the Indwelling, so eating permits me to participate in the Creation. And just as the solitude of the cell can lead me to the One and Only, so the "atheism" of enjoyment[38] prepares me for the encounter with God: coming out of my shell to meet the Other.

The definitive Rule (of 1247) moves eating from one's cell to the common refectory where it is accompanied by a reading from Scripture. And what does the Rule mean by this change? The *commonality* of the refectory relativizes *my* eating and gives it its proper place. Humans do not live of bread alone… This relativization is reinforced by *silence*. My eating is related by silence to that of others without being suspended in collective behavior. My eating is fitted into the community without being communalized. While the eaters keep silent, the Scriptures speak. Scripture puts everything in a new light: "Man does not live by bread alone but by every word that comes forth from the mouth of God" (Deut. 8:3). The practice of communally listening to Scripture relativizes the meditation practiced day and night in the cell (VII). Scripture – remember – was read aloud and consecutively *(lectio continua)* during the meal. It – Scripture – appears here as space; there is no selection of specific parts. Listening during the meal is more relaxed than during the meditation and less focused than the liturgy. Because less is done, more can happen. Unheard-of things can begin to speak.

The Rule is non-coercive: "where this is convenient", it says. It is not clear, however, what the word *convenient* refers to: to eating

---

[38] Ibid., 115, 148.

together, to having a refectory, or to reading out loud from Scripture. If it refers to the refectory, the idea is that the existing hermitages were not forced immediately to build a common refectory. It is also possible that the idea of eating together encountered reluctance on the part of the hermits. If the *convenient* refers to the reading from Scripture, the reason can be either that there was no text or that there was no reader. *Convenient* can be interpreted in still other ways as well; the point is the common meal must adapt itself to circumstances.

Both the practice of eating in the cell and eating in the refectory tie in with the architecture of the Rule. Eating in the cell reinforces staying in the cell and the solitude of the place. Eating in the refectory reinforces life-in-community. Solitude and community are the two pillars of Albert's model for the monastic life. The shift from eating alone to eating together is therefore no more than a shift within the parameters of the given architecture. Eating in the cell affords one a possibility of descending more deeply into the solitude. Eating in a common refectory, particularly if done in silence, can become an exercise in communal living.

Not to change place(s) (V)

In the original Rule (1206-1214) the prohibition of exchanging cells immediately followed the prescription that each of the brothers must have a separate cell of his own. This connection is logical. The prescription and the proscription reinforce each other, the first being inclusive and the second exclusive: each must have a particular cell; no one must have another's. Still, the insertion of the refectory between the prescription and the prohibition is not unlogical. It tends rather to release fresh meanings.

We have noted that the refectory relates one's eating, understood as "living from ...", to the other. The simple presence of brothers relativizes the sameness and solitariness of eating. In eating I reduce that which is other to myself. The common refectory breaks the monotony of this reductive and self-referential process. On the other hand, the prohibition of exchanging the cell blocks the opposite tendency: the changing or "other-ing" of the self, the reduction of the self to the other. This happens when – trading my place – I make intimacy an object of exchange. We will try to make this clear with the aid of the text:

> None of the brothers may change the place assigned to him
> or exchange it with another,
> except with the permission
> of whoever is prior at the time.

With regard to content this prohibition contains several possible meanings.[39] (1) A person may change cells within a given monastery; (2) within a given hermitage a person may move into the territory of another hut; (3) a person may move from one convent to another, or from one hermitage to another; (4) a person may become a wanderer. In the early years of the Order the prohibition presumably had reference to intramonastic changes. Later on it probably concerned moving from one place to another, that is, a change of convent.[40] Still another way of reading the text is that moving from one place to another meant a rise in status. By moving, a person might imperceptibly seek a better position. Whatever the concrete particulars may have been, however, the reference is always to changing and exchanging cells. This is strictly forbidden.

As a rule a clause beginning with *unless* introduces some flexibility: "*unless* occupied with other duties ... (VII); "*unless* sickness or feebleness ...". (XII); "*unless* it be taken ...". (XIII); etc. In this case, however, the conjunction *nisi* introduces an element of stringency: "except with the permission of the prior". The authority of the community as a whole is invoked to guarantee the non-exchange-ability of cells. The *permission* of the community is the only exception to the prevailing impermissibility of exchanging cells. The repetition "permitted-permission" (*liceat-licentia*), linked with

---

[39] Cicconetti, *Rule,* 262 and 270.
[40] In the Rule the word *place* (locum) usually refers to the entire hermitage.

the brother-prior field of tension, is significant. It would appear that the brotherhood itself is at issue. Someone active in the field of barter is no longer "one of the brothers". Soon we will see the same thing in connection with property: *"Let none of the brothers say that anything is his property"* (IX). One who changes (that is, "alters") his cell estranges himself from the brotherhood and becomes "not one of the brothers". In the nature of the case this cannot be *permitted*. The only person who can keep a change of living quarters within the brotherhood – and therefore outside the field of barter – is the prior acting on behalf of the brotherhood. For that reason his *permission* is needed.

> Exchange and commerce are rooted in the human intervention in reality by which I acquire something for myself. Every human intervention separates something from the totality of things. At the same time we (literally!) get mixed up with the things separated. My intervention passes into the matter which it shapes, defines, separates, and takes along: "The labor in which the human will exerts itself is visibly inserted in the things ...". Matter swallows up our intervention. At the same time the thing, swollen with what it has swallowed, separates itself from me and posits itself in opposition to me. It begins to lead a life of its own. The thing I crafted falls into the hands of others. It literally "alters" ("others") itself. "The labor which brings being into our possession *ipso facto* relinquishes it, is in the very sovereignty of its powers unceremoniously delivered over to the Other. The thing we make detaches itself from us and begins to rove. It enters the world of trade. It is "traded". "A separation opens between the producer and the product. At a given moment the producer no longer follows up, [but] remains behind".[41]

One who changes ("alters") place or "trades" it with another by that very fact makes the place into a product, a result of human intervention. But it is something originally given to us, not a product! The Indwelling of God was there before I was – beneficently and discreetly. The place where I recollect myself greets me: "A warm welcome to you! Be there, you!" This divine immanence –

---

[41] For all this, see Levinas, *Totality and Infinity: An essay on Exteriority*, o.c., 158-163; 226-232, esp. 226-227.

God's Indwelling – must be absolutely distinguished both from the act of taking into one*self* (eating) and from changing oneself into something *other* (making). One who regards the place as intervention (expression of the self and an object of exchange) destroys the Indwelling. The place itself intervenes: it infinitely withdraws itself and from a depth that is beyond the intrapsychic beckons me; it is a womb of compassion which has always already received and accepted me; it is the solitude which, from beyond any spatial determination by me, leads me into the Desert of Silence.

The place is that which favors me with its generosity and hospitality. Changing ("othering") it and bartering it must not violate the place. The place is my Conception, which can only be received. It is strange how most people want to fashion – even conquer – their place. That is precisely what alienates us from our place! A place freely given us apparently makes us feel so ill at ease that we dare not even think of it. The acceptance of that which is most peculiarly our own at the place on which we are standing is apparently an act of such intimacy that we shrink from its intense joy and escape into barter. We no longer understand the fact that it belongs to the essence of *my* place that it is assigned to me (III), earmarked for me (V), and permitted me (V). The logic escapes us. We no longer let our place do its work. We look elsewhere – in the homes of others.

> Rabbi Bunam used to say to his beginning pupils: "There is a treasure you cannot find anywhere in the world, not even at the zaddik's. Nevertheless there is a place where you can find it: the place where you are standing. That is where your treasure is".[42]
>
> To this Martin Buber adds:
>
> "Where we are standing, where we have been put – precisely there and nowhere else the treasure can be found. My immediate surroundings, which I experience as my natural habitat, the situation allocated to me by fate, that which I encounter day after day – here lies my true task and here awaits me the fulfillment of the existence that lies open before me".[43]

[42] M. Buber, *Werke* 3:735.
[43] Ibid,.736.

The only place where I come to fulfillment is the place which sur-
rounds me. All else is nowhere. All self-willed changes, exchanges,
and barter are roads leading nowhere¾dead-end escape routes.

The cell by the entrance (VI)

Usually monastic rules make provision for a good reception for
their guests: a wise old monk talks to the guests (Benedict); a
doorkeeper escorts the guests to the prior (Humiliati). In the Rule
of Carmel[44] the reception of guests is bound up with a specific location: the prior's cell by the entrance of the place. Of importance in
receiving those who come to the place is not only the person (in
this case the prior) but also the place (in this case the cell by the
entrance). The specification of the place is primary: "The prior's cell
should be by the *entrance* of the *place*". Now the place has a front,
an entrance. This entrance regulates the "inside-outside" relation.

> The prior's cell should be near the entrance to the place,
> so that he may be the first to meet those who come to this place,
> and so that whatever needs to be done subsequently
> may all be carried out according to his judgment and disposition.

First our perspective is from the outside to the inside, looking
at the place with the eyes of those who come to the hermitage. We
can distinguish four groups of guests:
1. *Novices.* In a hermitage every hermit may accept pupils for the
   purpose of introducing them to the spiritual life. Now that
   the Carmelites have become a community, the hermits can no
   longer be independent abbots in relation to the outside world.
   Now it is the *community* which admits new members.

> When someone comes to the door of the monastery, wishing to
> renounce the world and be added to the number of the brothers, he
> shall not be free to enter. First, the father [Abbas] of the monastery
> shall be informed [of his coming].[45]

---

[44] Cicconetti, *Rule,* 270-271.
[45] *Pachomian Chronicles and Rules,* in *Pachomian Koinonia,* Vol. 2, Kalamazoo
1981, 152-153.

2. *Pilgrims.* Pilgrimages belong to an ascetic mode of life. The Carmelites themselves sprang from these pilgrimages. A pilgrim was one who had broken with his settled life and trekked around in an uncomfortable and dangerous world. Within this framework the visiting of holy places *(visitare loca sacra)*, specifically those in the Holy Land, could be an important element.

3. *Fellow hermits.* From the monastic literature we know that hermits made visits to holy hermits for the purpose of learning from them.[46] Only very holy monks could cope with such an influx of guests.

> When an innumerable crowd of brothers flocked to them for the purpose of visiting them and of enhancing their own progress, they endured this almost continuous trouble of receiving them with imperturbable patience.[47]

4. *Believers from the neighborhood.* People living in the vicinity of a monastery sought help from the monks: instruction in the spiritual life, spiritual direction, assistance in difficult situations, prayer.

We do not know what kind of visitors came to Mount Carmel: interested parties, pilgrims, fellow hermits, or believers from the neighborhood. But that does not matter very much: what is certain is that they came *from the outside.* They are guests. Nor does it matter whether the place was a hermitage or a convent. Guests are the same for all places: they knock on doors from the outside and ask for hospitality.

Hospitality, in turn, is a movement from the inside to the outside. The prior's cell near the entrance makes the place hospitable. The place was already unconditionally hospitable to its inhabitants: toward the inside! Now it opens up to the outside as well. In this way it becomes a dwelling in a new way. Actually I only really take possession of my dwelling the moment I open it up to the Other.

---

[46] See Cassian, *Conferences*, 2.25.
[47] Ibid., 19.9; cf. *NPNF*, 493.

The possibility for the home to open to the Other is as essential to the essence of the home as closed doors and windows.[48]

The encounter between the guest and the phenomenon of hospitality is called a "meeting" by the Rule. Neither the guests, nor the brothers, remain anonymous: from both sides they acquire a face. Only after that comes the organization: then everything that needs to be done further proceeds in accordance with the prior's judgment and disposition. For now he knows with whom he is dealing. He knows the motives, the backgrounds, the purpose of their coming. The prior's dwelling near the entrance of the place is a sacrament of encounter. There the prior (the first in order of precedence) first meets the guest. There's consonance for you! In all things the prior will be the lesser, the minister and servant (XVII), but here he is the first – the first, that is, to meet those who come in from the outside. Hospitality generously awards the other a place in my home This more profoundly opens up my home than my recollection can ever do. The guest bestows on me the deepest possible meaning of my dwelling.

> Late at night a man came to the house of Rabbi Liber Berditschew and asked for lodging. Rabbi Liber prepared for him a gracious welcome and began to make up a bed for his guest. The man asked him: "Why do you wear yourself out to make up my bed?" Rabbi Liber replied: "It is not for your sake, but for the sake of my own cause, that I do this".[49]

5.1.3. Connections

Once there were hermits in the no man's land of a mountain range. Albert's letter furnishes them the basic elements of Carmelite housing accommodations. A basic institution is designed which both opens the interior space and regulates the inside-outside relation of tension.

---

[48] Levinas, *Totality and Infinity: an essay on exteriority*, o.c., 172-173.
[49] Buber, *Werke* 3.185.

1. In chapters I-VI we are dealing with the *institution* of the Carmelite architectural ground plan. By this we mean the institution (creation, establishment) of the most important formal elements of a way of life. For this purpose Albert uses the word "establish" (*statuere*). "However because you desire us to give you a formula of life ..., we *establish* ..." and continues this formal language game in the later chapters as well. Also in the selection of a place what the prior and the brothers think of it is formally decisive. The same thing applies to the assignment of the cells: the prior, along with the other brothers, formally assigns to each his cell. In the context of this assignment the same formal phrases are used as in the election of a prior: "by unanimous assent of all, or of the greater and wiser part". To institute a thing is a more fundamental act than to regulate juridically or to form customs. Juridical regulations and customs *pre*-suppose the basic institutions, just as ordinary laws presuppose a nation's constitution. One who institutes lays out the basic structures. He draws up the field and opens margins of flexibility. He establishes the inner and outer limits. Like any ground plan, so also the Carmelite blueprint contains a number of basic elements. The Rule itself indicates the two most fundamental elements in order of precedence: "We establish *first of all* that you shall have one of you as prior ... *Next,* that each of you shall have a separate cell of his own" (I and III). Here, in a single exciting balancing act, the building principles of the cenobitic life (having a prior) and the eremitic life (having a cell of one's own) are united. In 1247 the "place" is inserted between the two as a third building element: "You may have places" (II). This third building element is literally located between the two: the place as religious site (*locus religiosus*) is the bearer of the religious community as well as of each member's separate cell.

2. The *interior space* of the Carmelite architectural ground plan is formed by the tensions between the basic elements. The first tension is that between the place and the community. In "place" the reference is to the site, the milieu, the living space, the housing, the economics, etc. In "community" the reference is to

the people who live there. How many people can the place support and feed? Can *these* people appreciate the place? Does the place offer a view? Can people live there? etc. The relation between place and inhabitant constitutes an architectonic tension par excellence. It will, accordingly, be expressly developed in the following section of the Rule.

The second tension is that between the place and the cell. The place stands for the common living environment and the communal spaces. The cell stands for the personal spaces within the place. Every architect knows how stressful it is to organically relate the place as a whole to the personal spaces within the place, and vice versa. The part and the whole need each other and must be open to each other.

The third tension occurs within the community: between the prior and the brothers. In this relation the brothers structure themselves as a cenobitic community. This architecture becomes visible already in the election process: one of the group as a whole is placed in the midst and all of the brothers position themselves in their choice (with mind, emotions, and in action). This field of tension can assume form in various relational patterns: one-out-of-them-all (choice), one-for-all (task), all-standing-by-the-one (solidarity), etc. These are perspectival variations of the way the community structures itself. Of course there is more to the community than this basic structure shows (think, for example, of the assemblies in the center).

The fourth tension is that between the person and the community. Repeatedly the Rule speaks of "you". Usually the word refers to the community as a whole, the prior together with the brothers. Often the Rule refers also to "each" or "each one separately". Then the reference is to the individual persons, including the brother who at that moment is the prior.

These four fields of tension together constitute the effective space of every local Carmel. They make intelligible the architectonic position of the refectory (IV): a space reserved – in relation to the cells – for the community. Also the oratory becomes architectonically transparent: a space in the midst of the cells where the community assembles because all of them come together there from their own separate cells (X). The ban on the mutual exchange of cells (V) becomes understandable as well: not only does the self-willed exchange of cells violate the nature of the cell (the cell is not an object of exchange) but it bypasses the prior as well as the community. Also the significance of the entrance for visitors (VI) becomes architectonically clear: the "prior" represents the community to the outside world; the cell of the prior serves as the point of access to the place. Thus the four fields of tension (place-community; place-cell; prior-brothers; community-person) open up the space of the Carmelite way of life.

3. Every architectural ground plan, no matter how many windows and doors it possesses, creates an *inside-outside* kind of tension. This polarity was already present on the level of the religious life form adopted: the Carmel formula is only *one form* of religious life amid many others. But in chapters I-VI the inside-outside polarity comes architecturally to the fore: the Carmelites form an autonomous community which chooses its own prior without involvement from without (I), decides on its own where it will live (II), spatially organizes itself taking account of the topographical situation (III-V), and as community receives its own guests (VI). This flexibility in the inside-outside relation would prove to be of great importance in the move to Europe. While the basic *inside-outside* tension would be preserved, the concrete particularization of it (solitude vs. city; given vs. acquired; being more open vs. being more closed, etc.) would prove relative.

We can diagram the Carmelite architecture as follows (p. 85).

The Carmelite architecture is a basic provision: a garment one puts on, a house one inhabits, a book one reads, a rite one performs. It is intended for use. Hence the key word: to have. One *has* a prior in order to learn to live in obedience. One *has* a place to live, to receive the Indwelling there. One *has* a cell to explore the solitude there and to be at home in. They are all provisions. The same applies to the refectory and to communal hospitality.

		I	II	III	IV	V	VI
I	Community	Community structure: prior and brothers	Choice of place by prior and brothers	Cell assignment by prior and brothers	Eating and listening communally	Permission of the prior	Cell of the prior
N							
S	Place		Fitting place		Common refectory		Entrance to the place
I	Cell			Each has his own cell		No exchange of cells	
D							
E	Person					No one	

		I	II	III			VI
O	Church, religious society, immediate surroundings	Autonomous organizations	A given place in solitude or city	Situation of the place			Visitors
U							
T							
S							
I							
D							
E							

This level of the provisions is continued in the Rule. We have the Scriptures; we have the Psalter; we have goods; we have an oratory; we have a chapter; etc. Together these things constitute the basic provisions of the Carmelite life.

The following section (chapters VII-XIII) focuses on the *exercise* and *interiorization* of these basic provisions: by *remaining* in the cell, by *meditating* in Scripture, by *saying* the Psalms, by *communalizing* all things, by *coming together* in the refectory, by *discussing* the well-being of each brother and of the group as a whole, by being *discriminating* in the use of food. Via these exercises these basic provisions are involved in spiritual transformation. Philip Ribot describes the institution as "the form by which prophetic (i.e. *mystical*) perfection and the final goal of the religious eremitical life is realized".[50]

5.2 Elementary Exercises (VII-XIII)

The chapters I-VI concerned the level of the basic provisions. Beginning with chapter VIII the Rule's focus shifts to the level of the elementary exercises which Cassian calls "bodily exercises".[51] They are processes of appropriation on the most elementary level and are directed toward purity of heart as their practical objective. By way of purity of heart these processes of appropriation constitute the foundation for the life of the virtues which is built on it. Their position within the whole of the spiritual way renders these virtues relative, both with regard to their practical objective (purity of heart) and their sequel (the life of the virtues).

To gain some insight into the content of the exercises in question, we will cite Abbot Joseph, where he makes a distinction between commands and elementary exercises.

> With regard to those which we can either relax or hold fast to with-
> out endangering our state, as for instance, an unbroken and strict

[50] *Decem libri* 1.1 and 1.8.

[51] *Exercitia corporalia* or *exercitationes corporales*. Cf., e.g. Cassian, *Conferences* 17.28 and 30.

fast, or total abstinence from wine or oil, or entire prohibition to leave one's cell, or incessant attention to reading and meditation, all of which can be practised at pleasure, without damage to our profession and purpose, and, if need can be given up without blame. But we must most resolutely make up our minds to observe those fundamental commands, and not even, if need arise, to avoid death in their cause, with regard to which we must immovably assert: "I have sworn and am purposed". And this should be done for the preservation of love, for which all things else should be disregarded lest the beauty and perfection of its calm should suffer a stain. In the same way we must swear for the purity of our chastity, and we ought to do the same for faith, and sobriety and justice, to all of which we must cling with unchangeable persistence, and to forsake which even for a little is worthy of blame. But in the case of those bodily exercises, which are said to be profitable for a little, we must, as we said, decide in such a way that, if there occurs any more decided opportunity for a good act, which would lead us to relax them, we need not be bound by any rule about them, but may give them up and freely adopt what is more useful. For in the case of those bodily exercises, if they are dropped for a time, there is no danger: but to have given up these others even for a moment is deadly.[52]

This text affords us insight into the nature of the elementary exercises: fasting, abstinence, remaining in the cell, continual Scripture reading, persistent prayer. Elsewhere there is also mention of vigils[53] and hospitality.[54] We are here dealing with practices which furnish a foundation for the spiritual way and lead to purity of heart.

Looking at the Rule from this point of view we are struck by the fact that chapter VII presents an accumulation of these elementary exercises: remaining in the cell; meditating on scripture; praying and keeping vigil. Saying the Psalms in chapter VIII is a concretization of prayer. Also chapters XII and XIII (on fasting and abstinence) belong to this category. And what are we to think of the intervening chapters IX-XI? Do they fit smoothly in the same

[52] Ibid., 17.28; *NPNF*, 473.
[53] Ibid., 2.16-17.
[54] Ibid., 2.25; 19.9.

perspective? I think they do. These three chapters describe the basic exercises of the cenobitic life. Community of goods (IX), after all, is characteristic for the cenobitic way of life: hermits work for their own maintenance, cenobites work for the community from whose hands they receive the necessities of life.[55] Hermits come together for the Eucharist only once a week. Carmelites assemble daily for the celebration of the Eucharist (X), practicing what Albert had been asked to do: gather them into a single religious community.[56] In the weekly chapter (XI) the welfare of each and the ordering of the whole are discussed – all in all, a tough schooling. "For he is truly and not partially perfect who with equal imperturbability can put up with the squalor of the wilderness in the desert, as well as the infirmities of the brethren in the coenobium".[57] For the time being there is warrant, therefore, for placing the chapters (VII-XIII) in the perspective of the elementary exercises.

Meanwhile the level of the basic provisions simply continues. Thus the chapters VII-XIII furnish an ordering of time: the order of the day (VII-VIII), the week (X-XI), and the year (XII-XIII). Community of goods (IX) and the oratory (X) further structure life-in-community. In addition there are lines of connection between community of goods (IX), fasting (XII), and abstinence (XIII) insofar as these chapters directly pertain to one's bodily life. In any case, in the chapters VII-XI, the elementary exercises predominate: remaining in the cell, reading in Scripture, saying the prayers, having goods in common, assembling for the Eucharist, discussing the well-being of each and the order of the whole, fasting and abstinence.

5.2.1. Remaining in the cell (VII-VIII)

Remaining in the cell ties in with the basic provision which reads "Each of you is to *have* a separate cell" (III).

---

[55] Ibid., 19.5.
[56] Cf. the *Rubrica Prima*: "… in unum congregavit collegium".
[57] Cassian, *Conferences* 19.9.

> Let each remain in his cell or near it,
> meditating day and night on the Word of the Lord
> and keeping vigil in prayer.

Remaining in the cell is the interiorization of the cell. This appropriation is structured in terms of an active as well as a passive component. The *passive* component is directly linked with the cell as dwelling. We saw that the cell affords its inhabitant a hospitable welcome. Even before I myself extend hospitality I have already received a hospitable welcome from the cell I inhabit. My recollection in the cell releases a divine welcome we call Shechinah. It is the marian dimension of the cell which leads us into the solitude of the place where the Place receives us. From this perspective remaining in the cell is letting myself be received, exposing myself to being favored, admitting to myself the energy of the Indwelling. Remaining in the cell is letting myself be brought to my Place. If I am to get to my Place the cell must be allowed to do its work on me. For my part this means that I must remain (*manere*) at the same place or near it. This is not meant juridically or moralistically but spiritually: if the cell is to receive me to take me to my Place it must be given the chance to do so. See to it, therefore, that you are either in your cell or close to it.

We can track down the *active* component by involving the conclusion of the chapter:

> unless he is occupied with other lawful activities.

It is interesting to note that remaining in the cell can be conceived as being parallel to other lawful activities. Apparently remaining in the cell is an activity, for there are still other activities as well. And when the latter are legitimate, they may excuse me from the main activity, which is remaining in the cell. Remaining in the cell and other lawful activities are only superficially opposed to each other; essentially they exist on the same plane and clarify each other. Both weave a space in which divine conception can effect itself in my life. To experience activities as a cell is a Carmelite challenge; it is a spiritual art to let oneself be entertained and welcomed by every activity, to know oneself a guest-participant in it, to inhabit it. Every activity can strip us of our inauthenticity, conceiving us in truth.

Remaining in the cell is an activity, an exercise in concentration. This is something which was already familiar to the desert monks.

> So we ought always to remain shut up in our cell. For whenever we have strayed from it and return fresh to it and begin again to live there, we will be upset and disturbed as though we were novice inhabitants. For if we have let it go, we cannot without difficulty and pains recover that fixed purpose of mind which we had gained when we remained in our cell.[58]

> Nor is it strange for us who live in a cell, and have our thoughts collected in a very narrow enclosure, to be oppressed by a host of anxieties.[59]

The confinement of the cell, which is intended to shape us and gather us up, frightens and oppresses us by its closeness. The only remedy is the persistent will simply to remain in it. Cassian's story of the monks who are accustomed to work in the open air is a fine example.

> Whenever they come [to a district where monks are accustomed to work in a cell], they are annoyed by such harassing thoughts and such anxiety of mind that, as if they were beginners and people who had never given the slightest attention to the exercises of solitude, they cannot endure the life of the cells and the peace and quietness of them, and are at once driven forth and obliged to leave them, as if they were inexperienced and novices. For they have not learnt to still the motions of the inner person, and to quell the tempests of their thoughts by anxious care and persevering efforts, as, toiling day after day in work in the open air, they are moving about all day long in empty space, not only in the flesh but also in heart, and pour forth their thoughts openly as the body moves hither and thither.[60]

The practical objective of remaining in the cell is the formation of an interior which is purged to the very core in order to become receptive to God, the final goal of the spiritual way. Hence first: the formation of the interior. Remaining in the cell structures the

---

[58] Ibid., 6.15.
[59] Ibid., 24.5.
[60] Ibid., 24.4; *NPNF*, 533.

natural human person both physically and spiritually. The cell helps us open up to ourselves so that we can sort out and purge all that is cooking inside us. Remaining in the cell constitutes a shelter.

Now let's look again at the text of the Rule: "unless he is occupied with other lawful activities". Given this exception – which was already made by the original Rule[61] – it would seem at first sight that now all control is lost. For how many things cannot be considered lawful activities? In any case: eating together in a common refectory (IV); going around begging as mendicants (XIII). Beyond all argument is the daily walk to the oratory for the celebration of the Eucharist (X) and the canonical hours (VIII). Work that cannot be done inside the cell: work that has to be done jointly and therefore outside the cell (just think of tending the livestock) (XV). Added later was the care of souls and working at the university: lawful activities as well. Even Nicholas the Frenchman had to concede that the hermits who lived on Mount Carmel went out to preach from time to time! All these lawful activities make heavy inroads in the practice of remaining in the cells.

But one can also view the matter differently. The exceptions to the rule, though embarrassing, can also force us to take a deeper look. In the first place it is striking that the other lawful activities see to it that the Carmelite is *occupied* (VII). This word returns once again at a crucial point: "Some work has to be done by you, so that the devil may always find you *occupied*" (XV). It is interesting to note that work (certainly also an activity!) as it were constitutes a cell here as a result of which the devil can never, "on account of your idleness" manage to find some opportunity of entering our souls (XV). Activities – legitimate activities – can form a cell rendering us occupied. The core of this exercise, therefore, is not remaining in or near the cell; nor either staying in the cell or being engaged in other activities; but being *occupied* in contrast with being *idle*, a state understood as inactivity. Being occupied is the cell. The physical cell is a form of it, as is its nearness and other lawful activities. Remaining-in-the-cell is an exercise in being-occupied,

---

[61] Cf. Cicconetti, *Rule*, 199-200.

as a result of which space arises in us for the Place where we are standing, for the Spring. This, accordingly, is the first thing: the formation of an interior.

Linked up with this is the practical objective: purity of heart. The interior which has come into being must be purged.[62] Carmelites learn to discern the things that frisk around within them,

> … like a splendid fisherman, looking out for food for himself by the apostolic art he may eagerly and without moving catch the swarms of thoughts swimming in the calm depths of his heart, and surveying with curious eye the depths as from a high rock, may sagaciously and cunningly decide what he ought to lure to himself by his saving hook, and what he can neglect and reject as bad and nasty fishes.[63]

In the splendid image of the fisherman fishing from an over-hanging rock the practical objective of the cell swims into view: viz. discerning the movements of the heart and picking out the good ones with a view to one's salvation.

Now the cell can turn into Inhabitation and the hermit remains in the Messiah. This is the final goal: remaining in the Messiah, the foundational form of every religious way of life *(exordium)*. Now the Johannine words become flesh and blood: "Remain in me, as I remain in you. Just as a branch cannot bear fruit on its own unless it remains on the vine, so neither can you unless you remain in me. I am the vine, you are the branches. Whoever remains in me and I in him will bear much fruit, because without me you can do nothing" (John 15:4-5). By remaining in the cell the hermits become "beloved sons or daughters *in* Christ". Albert's greeting is being fulfilled: "Health *in* the Lord".

Meditating on the Word of the Lord (VII)

Reading Scripture, prayer, keeping vigil and saying the Psalms not only put content into remaining in the cell – they are activities which constitute the cell. Remaining, dwelling, reading and saying

---

[62] Cassian, *ibid.*, 24.3.
[63] Ibid.; *NPNF*, 533.

are elementary exercises by which the Carmelite somatically appropriates the cell in which he lives. In the case of reading Scripture that is patently clear.[64] Scripture reading was basically done out loud. In the refectory, in the ministry of the Word during the Eucharist, in the readings during the canonical hours but also in the cell, Scripture was read out loud. Apparently from time to time this was done with such vigor that the cells had to be constructed so that monks, in meditating out loud, could not disturb each other.[65] Reading Scripture is a physical process. One's senses are involved: one's breathing, voice, and ears. By reciting Scripture out loud the words, sentences, and rhetorical structures tend to penetrate one's body, affectivity, memory, intellect and will. This practice was already known in Israel from the time of the exile. People learned the Torah by heart with a view to letting its meaning deeply penetrate their inner selves.[66] A devout Jew "meditated day and night on the Instruction of the Lord" (Ps. 1:2). This practice was taken over by the desert monks as well. For them, too, reading Scripture was a matter of striving "in every way to devote yourself constantly to the sacred reading so that continuous meditation will seep into your soul and, as it were, shape it to its image".[67] The practical objective of reading Scripture is the formation of our interior. Our mind is occupied by Scripture. This activity produces a layer of humus for the reception of God.

> Therefore the sequences of holy Scripture must be committed to memory and they must be pondered ceaselessly. Such meditation will profit us in two ways. First, when the thrust of the mind is occupied by the study and perusal of the readings it will, of necessity, avoid being taken over by the snares of dangerous thoughts. Second, as we strive with constant repetition to commit these readings to memory, we have not the time to understand them because our minds have

---

[64] Cf. Cicconetti, *Rule*, 199-205.
[65] *Decem libri*, 8.4.
[66] K. Waaijman, *Psalmen bij het zoeken van de weg*, Kampen 1982.
[67] Cassian, *Conferences*, 14.10.

> been occupied. But later when we are free from the attractions of all
> that we do and see and, especially, when we are quietly meditating
> during the hours of darkness, we think them over and we under-
> stand them more closely. And so it happens that when we are at
> ease and when, as it were, we are plunged into the dullness of sleep,
> the hidden meanings, of which we were utterly unaware during our
> waking hours, and the sense of them are bared to our minds.[68]

Reflection on the Word of the Lord is an elementary exercise
which ties in with remaining in the cell and performing lawful activities. The purpose of both is that we Carmelites may
be occupied and so open ourself up to the reception and
conception of the Face.

The appropriation of Scripture – somatically, cognitively, affectively, and mnemonically – is literally intended to *transform*. Abbot
Nesteros makes no bones about this: Scripture must "transcode" the
whole of our language into the Word of God. This startles Cassian,
for he is well trained in letters.

> At this point my mind is, as it were, infected by those poetic works,
> worthless stories, tales of war in which I was steeped from the begin-
> ning of my basic studies when I was very young. I think of them
> even when I am praying. When I am singing the psalms or else beg-
> ging pardon for my sins the shameful memory of poems slips in or
> the image of warring heroes turns before my eyes.

Abbot Nesteros's reaction is brief and direct:

> This very thing from which comes your desperate urge to be
> cleansed can actually give rise to a speedy and effective cure. All you
> need is to transfer to the reading and meditation of the spiritual
> Scriptures the same care and the same zeal which, you said, you had
> for worldly studies.
>
> Of necessity your mind will be taken up by those poems for as
> long as it fails to show equal application and zeal in dealing with
> those other matters which occupy it and for as long as it fails to give
> birth to things spiritual and divine instead of profitless and earthly
> thoughts. If it manages to enter deeply into these new ideas, if it

[68] Ibidem.

feeds upon them, these previous topics of thought can be driven out one by one or even expelled entirely.[69]

Reading Scripture out loud ushers in the beginning of a spiritual process which culminates in contemplation.[70] Reading and rereading Scripture I let it seep into my heart until it becomes a Spring in me. Jesus Sirach put it this way: "And lo, my canal became a river, and my river a sea" (Sir. 24:31). That is to say: With whatever verse (canal) I start, this verse invariably leads me to the whole of Scripture (river), which in turn unites me with the infinite (sea).

Praying

Saying the prayers – psalms, Our Fathers, the Jesus prayer, mantras, brief petitions – is an elementary exercise.[71] Prayers constitute the heartbeat of the spiritual life, sustain our spiritual respiratory system, and direct the motions of the heart toward God. They grow right along with our spiritual life.

> Prayer changes at every moment in proportion to the degree of purity in the soul and in accordance with the extent to which the soul is moved either by outside influence or of itself. Certainly the same kind of prayers cannot be uttered continuously by any one person.[72]

Abba Isaac, furnishing an elementary formula as a beginning exercise, hands on a mantra from the Psalms: "Come to my help, O God; Lord, hurry to my rescue" (Ps. 69:2).[73] This is the first step of prayer. Because of its brevity this verse can lead us to all the places of prayer. It gains depth by dint of repetition. By its simplicity it drives away distraction. Of course, such a verse must "carry within it all the feelings of which human nature is capable and be applicable to every situation".[74] We must never cease to recite the verse chosen.

[69] Ibid., 14.12-13.
[70] Cf. K. Waaijman, *The Hermeneutics of Spirituality*, in *Studies in Spirituality*, 4 (1994).
[71] This is the subject of the Tenth Conference of John Cassian.
[72] Ibid., 9.8.
[73] Ibid., 10.10.
[74] Ibidem.

The thought of this verse should be turning unceasingly in your heart. Never cease to recite it in whatever task or service or journey you find yourself. Think upon it as you sleep, as you eat, as you submit to the most basic demands of nature. This heartfelt thought will prove to be a formula of salvation for you. Not only will it protect you against all devilish attack, but it will purify you from the stain of all earthly sin and will lead you on to the contemplation of the unseen and the heavenly and to that fiery urgency of prayer which is indescribable and which is experienced by very few.[75]

Abba Isaac accurately describes the practical objective: the formation of an interior which prevents the devil from gaining access (we are occupied!) and its purgation from all stains and vices. The mantra purifies the interior. For this practical objective no prior training of any kind is needed.

No one is shut off from perfection because of illiteracy. Lack of culture is no bar to that purity of heart and soul which lies quite close by to everyone. Constant meditation upon this verse will keep the mind wholly and entirely upon God.[76]

If prayer – along with remaining in the cell, along with Scripture reading, along with keeping vigil, along with fasting and abstinence – has led to purity of heart, it unites itself with the flowering of the life of the virtues. The life of prayer and the life of the virtues assist each other toward progress.

Indeed, there is a mutual and undivided link between these. For just as the edifice of all the virtues strives upward toward perfect prayer so will all these virtues be neither sturdy nor enduring unless they are drawn firmly together by the crown of prayer.[77]

The virtues are inwardly directed toward God by prayer. Prayer is purified by the practice of virtue.

Therefore if we wish our prayers to reach upward to the heavens and beyond we must ensure that our mind is cleared of every earthly

[75] Ibidem.
[76] Ibid., 10.14.
[77] Ibid., 9.2.

defect and cleansed of all passion's grip and is so light of itself that its prayer, free of sin's weighty load, will rise upward to God.[78]

In the end the pray-er (petitioner) loses himself in God. The desert monks remembered a saying of Anthony, "who was sometimes seen so long at prayer and with a mind so ecstatic that the sunrise would catch up with him …".[79] About the climax of prayer this Anthony voices this opinion: "Prayer is not perfect when the monk is conscious of himself and of the fact that he is actually praying".[80]

Keeping vigil

The phrase "keeping vigil in prayer" is derived from 1 Peter which sets the Christian life in the perspective of the return of Christ: "The end of all things is at hand; therefore be serious and watchful in your prayers" (1 Pet. 4:7). This seriousness and watchfulness are embedded in a life of virtue: constancy in maintaining love for one another (4:8), being hospitable without complaining (4:9), and mutual helpfulness (4:10). This life of virtue, which has to be attained by resisting conduct that is in all respects corrupted (4:1-6), is the setting for keeping vigil, the third elementary exercise: "Three things keep a wandering mind in place – vigils, meditation, and prayer *(vigiliae, meditatio et oratio)*. Constant attention to them and a firm concentration upon them will give stability to the soul".[81] Keeping vigil consists in reducing sleep as much as possible. Some monks literally fought against sleep. Sometimes this battle would be carried to such drastic lengths that they were past the point of being able to sleep.[82] This excess was most severely repudiated. Usually the monks limited the time for their sleep to three hours, or as others have said, to four.[83] For the rest, in ancient times a night's sleep varied from monastery to

---

[78] Ibid., 9.4.
[79] Ibid., 9.31.
[80] Ibidem.
[81] Ibid., 10.14.
[82] Ibid., 2.17.
[83] Ibid., 12.15.

monastery and from season to season.[84] Not only was the period
of sleep cut short, but it was also interrupted by some who got up
in the middle of the night to pray some psalms. The hours won
from sleep were set aside for Scripture reading and prayer. Sometimes the brothers listened to the exposition of a wise monk[85] or
did some work.

Again, the practical objective of keeping vigil is to become free
for God with a pure heart and to seal oneself off from the devil.
The desert monks sometimes took this quite literally, especially in
the early years when as yet only a few monks lived in the desert.

> For such was the fierceness [of the demons] that it was with diffi-
> culty that a few very steadfast men, and those advanced in years
> were able to endure a life of solitude. Since in the actual monaster-
> ies where eight or ten men used to live, their violence attacked them
> so and their assaults were experienced so frequently, and so visibly,
> that they did not dare all to go to bed at once by night, but took
> turns and while some snatched a little sleep, others kept watch and
> devoted themselves to Psalms and prayer and reading. And when
> the wants of nature compelled them to sleep, they awoke the others
> and committed to them in like manner the duty of keeping watch
> over those who were going to bed.[86]

Saying the Psalms (VIII)

In the original Rule (of 1206-1214), as a way of concretizing
prayer, there is a chapter on saying the Psalms.

> Those who know their letters and can read the psalms,
> shall say for each of the hours those
> which are appointed for those hours
> by the institution of the holy fathers
> and the approved custom of the Church.

The reference here is clearly to saying the psalms in one's own
cell. If it concerned choral prayer, it would already be sufficient for

---

[84] Cf. *Sommeil et vie spirituelle* in: *DS* 14 (1990), 1035-1036.

[85] Cf. Cassian, *ibid.*, 7.34; 8.25; 18.1; 23.1; etc.

[86] Ibid., 7.23; *NPNF*, 370.

the brothers to pray the psalms *along with* the rest. For this purpose one need not be able to read, only to memorize.[87] We must distinguish between praying the psalms and praying the Hours, a matter we will discuss later. Peter Damian, for example, stated that when two hermits shared the same cell they must pray the Psalter through twice every day.[88] Albert only prescribed that each brother should pray the Psalms by himself in the solitude of his cell. This fits into the basic structure of the original Rule. In addition, in the early years the brothers were laymen who were not obligated to say the liturgy of the Hours. Added to this is the fact that the Rule links saying the Psalms, not with the refectory (X), but with remaining in the cells (VII).

Saying the Psalms as an elementary prayer practice goes back to the most ancient monastic traditions.

> The most ancient generations of monks in the deserts of Egypt only know of a liturgical gathering on Saturdays and Sundays. They were not yet familiar with fixed hours for daily prayer, but regularly prayed or sang psalms in the solitude of their cell.[89]
>
> About the way this was done little is known beyond this. Only that their prayer was audible even outside their cell: "Around the ninth hour you can begin to listen to the divine psalmody that rises up from every cell".[90]

In the cenobitic monasteries the monks did assemble daily for saying the Psalms. They recited Scripture *(lectio),* including the Psalms, out loud before the whole community. In Cassian we can already discern a certain structure in the cenobitic choral prayer. In the morning and evening the monks assembled for twelve psalms each time. In addition there were a second morning celebration (prime), the little hours (terce, sext, none), and sometimes a vigil.

[87] Cicconetti, *Rule*, 147; 160-161; 179-190.

[88] Letter 18.10; in *Letters 1-30*, transl. Owen J.Blum, Washington D.C. 1989, 164-165.

[89] A. Verheul, *De psalmen in het getijdengebed vroeger en nu,* in: *De Psalmen,* Leuven-Amersfoort 1990, 151-201.

[90] Palladius, *Historia Lausiaca*, 7; cited in Verheul, *ibid.,* 157.

One person recited out loud, while all the others seated on the ground in deathly silence listened. The monks prayed the psalms in numerical order, the psalms being, as it were, a preamble to personal silent prayer. While the psalms constitute the space of prayer, saying them is an exercise in entering this space.

Praying the canonical hours

In 1247 Pope Innocent IV introduced a change in the Rule pertaining to saying the psalms. We can best get a clear view of this change by juxtaposing Albert's original version (1206-1214) with that of Innocent IV (1247). The differences are marked by italics.

Albert (1206-14)	Innocent IV (1247)
Those who know *their letters* and can *read* the *psalms* shall say *for each of the hours those which are appointed for those hours* by the institution of the holy fathers and the approved custom of the Church.	Those who know how to say *the canonical hours with the clerics* shall say them according to the institution of the holy fathers and the approved custom of the Church.

The differences afford a clear picture of the changes which occurred during the first forty years on Mount Carmel.[91] Three changes call for comment.

1. Noteworthy, in the first place, are the clerics. Who are they? In all likelihood the word "clerics" (deacons, priests, bishops) originally did not refer to clerics in their own ranks, but to clerics outside their community who were bound to celebrate the divine office for the people in their parochial or collegiate churches. At that time the Carmelites did not as yet have their own parish

---

[91] Cicconetti, *Rule*, 179-190.

churches. So, for the time being, they had to join the clerics of the parochial or collegiate churches in the vicinity.

2. The word "psalms" is changed into "canonical hours". Concealed behind this modification are several changes. First, in speaking of canonical hours the text is referring to a different *type* of prayer: the type of communal prayer that developed in the churches and cathedrals.[92] This type of prayer gives expression to the recognition of God; it demonstrates God's rule over the holy place. It was a public event in the service of the people of God. The fact that the clerics of the Carmelites prayed the canonical hours along with nonconsecrated Carmelites was – from a pastoral viewpoint – as important as celebrating masses, preaching, hearing confessions, etc. The office is part of the mendicant way of life: to be in the service of the people of God by celebrating the Eucharist, preaching, hearing confessions, *and* praying together. Concealed behind the phrase "canonical hours" is a second change. Doubt had arisen whether Carmelites were obligated to do two things: to say psalms (as they were accustomed) as well as to pray the canonical hours (on account of the clerical consequences of the mendicant state).[93] For the Carmelites the correction in their Rule meant that they were no longer required to pray both the canonical hours and the psalms (in this connection we must bear in mind that monks usually did both of them together).

A third change implicit in the canonical hours is the communal character of this type of prayer. For the souls of hermits this change must have been the most radical of all: they, after all, were accustomed to say their prayers in the solitude of their cell.

3. The third textual change is the shift from "knowing letters" to "knowing how to say the canonical hours with the clerics". The group which can pray along with is of course larger than the group that is able to read. To pray along with is something

[92] A. Verheul, *De psalmen*, 161-163; 168-170.
[93] *Decem libri*, 8.6.

everyone can do who is able to learn the psalms by heart. The change is intended "to obligate all brothers to take part equally". All the brothers had to participate in the public worship services of the local church, along with the (non-Carmelite) clerics who at the local parish or collegiate church were bound, by their consecration, to the divine office.

Saying Our Fathers

Both Albert's Rule (1204-1214) and that of Innocent IV (1247) make an exception for those who cannot fulfil this order – though two different groups are involved: in Albert's Rule those unable to read the psalms and in that of Innocent those unable to pray the canonical hours. In any case, both groups get the same substitutions.

> Those who do not know their letters
> shall say twenty-five Our Fathers
> for the night vigil,
> except on Sundays and feastdays,
> for the vigils of which we establish
> that the stated number be doubled,
> so that the Our Father
> is said fifty times.
> The same prayer is to be said
> seven times for the morning lauds.
> For the other hours the same prayer
> is to be said seven times,
> except for the evening office,
> for which you should say it fifteen times.

For several religious communities saying the Our Fathers by those who could not manage the psalms or the canonical hours was a normal substitution. The number of Our Fathers varied from order to order.[94] For the rest it is important to realize that in the case of saying the Our Fathers we are not dealing with an exceptional provision. Exceptions are introduced in the Rule with

---

[94] Cicconetti, *Rule*, 185-190.

the word "unless ...". (see chapters V, VII, XII, XIII). We are dealing here with two complementary institutions: just as the canonical hours are "instituted by the holy Fathers and the approved
custom of the church", so also the Our Fathers are "established"
and "their number stated". And just as the canonical hours are
"said", so also the Our Fathers. We are dealing here with somatic
prayer exercises. To this all Carmelites, both those who can and
those who cannot read or pray along with are obligated.

Saying the Our Father is the most elementary form of
praying and is on the same level as the mantra verses from the
psalms considered earlier. One who wants to learn how to
pray begins with the alphabet: the Our Father. Saying the
Our Father makes clear what is primarily at stake in the
canonical hours and saying the psalms: the somatic practice
of the basic religious behavior of praying.[95]

In this respect the Our Father has an advantage over the
psalms. Why? In the psalms (as monastic exercise or divine office)
it is very easy to get lost. A stirring testimony to this effect is that
of Germanus, a friend of Cassian, on his journey through the
Egyptian wilderness.

> Our minds think of some passage of a psalm. But it is taken
> away from us without our noticing it, and, stupidly, unknow-
> ingly, the spirit slips on to some other text of Scripture. It begins
> to think about it, but before it gets to fully grasp it another text
> slides into the memory and drives out the earlier one. Mean-
> while another one arrives and there is a further turnabout. The
> spirit rolls along from psalm to psalm, leaps from the gospel to
> Saint Paul, from Paul to the prophets, from there to incidents of
> spirituality. Ever on the move, forever wandering, it is tossed
> along through all the body of Scripture.[96]

The only way in which one may escape this distraction is to
start with the alphabet of elementary prayer exercises. On this

---

[95] Of great beauty are the meditations of Abba Isaac on the petitions of the
Our Father – everyone a prayer mantra (*Conferences*, 10.18-25).

[96] Cassian, *Conferences* 10.13.

elementary level it does not matter whether I take a verse from the
monastic breviary, the canonical hours, or the Our Father. Not
the form as such is important but the function in the spiritual life:
learning to live in prayer, remaining in it and in a cell, breathing
in its atmosphere as in Scripture.[97]

The purpose of this elementary way of praying is to so appropriate prayer that the Spirit of prayer may control us.[98]

> Nourished by this food ... we penetrate so deeply into the think-
> ing of the psalms that we sing them not as though they had been
> composed by the prophet but as if we ourselves had written them,
> as if this were our own private prayer uttered amid the deepest
> compunction of heart. Certainly we think of them as having been
> specially composed for us and we recognize that what they express
> was made real not simply once upon a time in the person of the
> prophet but that now, every day, we are being fulfilled in our-
> selves.[99]
>
> Saying the Our Fathers lifts us up to that prayer of fire known to
> so few. It lifts them up, rather, to that ineffable prayer which rises
> above all human consciousness, with no voice sounding, no tongue
> moving, no words uttered. The soul lights up with heavenly illu-
> mination and no longer employs constricted, human speech. All
> sensibility is gathered together and, as though from some very
> abundant source, the soul breaks forth richly, bursts out unspeak-
> ably to God, and in the tiniest instant it pours out so much more
> than the soul can either describe or remember when it returns again
> to itself.[100]
>
> There follows ... a still more sublime condition which is brought
> about by the contemplation of God alone and by fervent love, by
> which the mind, transporting and flinging itself into love for God,
> addresses God most familiarly as its own Father.[101]

---

[97] This is an essential aspect of the canonical hours. Cf. Verheul, *De psalmen*,
175-199; Waaijman, *De spiritualiteit van het parochieel getijdengebed*, in *Liturgie
en Kerkopbouw*, Baarn 1993, 47-62.
[98] Cassian, *Conferences*, Prologue.
[99] Ibid., 10.11.
[100] Ibid., 9.25.
[101] Ibid., 9.18; *NPNF*, 393.

5.2.2. *Going out to the center (IX-XI)*

Having possessions in common (IX), assembling for the Eucharist (X), and entering into conversation with each other (XI) are three elementary community exercises. They practice the basic movement of every community: coming out of one's own shell to the center of the community.

Community of goods (IX)

There is, in the Rule, no other chapter which exhibits such a mixture of omissions, modifications, and additions as the chapter on the community of goods. We will first place the texts of Albert and Innocent side by side and then briefly discuss the modifications.

Albert (1206-14)	Innocent IV (1247)
Let none of the brothers say that anything is his property, but let everything be held in common among you; and *from the things the Lord may have given you*, to each one shall be distributed what he needs from the hand of the prior – that is from *someone* he appoints to this task – taking into account the age and needs of each one. *However, as has already been stated, each one is to keep to the cell assigned to him and live there by himself on what is given him.*	Let none of the brothers say that anything is his property, but let everything be held in common among you; and to each one shall be distributed what he needs from the hand of the prior – that is from the *brother* he appoints to this task – taking into account the age and needs of each one. *You may, however, have asses or mules as your needs require, and some livestock or poultry, for your nourishment.*

Although the modifications in the text differ in kind, together they reinforce certain "lines of power".

1. The first modification is an *omission*. Originally the possessions they had in common were what "the Lord may have given you".

Just what did this mean?[102] It meant that Carmel renounced houses, possessions, and income accruing from property claims on third parties. Stated positively: aside from their naked existence and the place where they lived the brothers owned nothing and had to depend on alms and gifts. They renounced as a source of income all property apart from the hermitage and revenues accruing from their work, as well as incomes resulting from spiritual activities (stipends, donations, etc.). In short they gave up all assured income. Reflected in this radical standpoint is the original ideal of the lay hermits. They literally sought to live by the words: "Do not worry about tomorrow. Look at the birds …". (Matt. 6:25-26). This is one side of the issue. But there is another side as well: at that time total poverty carried with it certain privileges! For example, people based the right to protection on it. They were relieved of the duty to pay civil and church taxes and tolls. They formed a non-profit institution and did everything in their power to maintain its non-profit status. In a similar way the new religious communities of the day demonstrated as sharply as possible their total poverty in order to be exempted from financial obligations to feudal lords and prelates – and certain popes supported them in this.[103] Bishops, canons, and landowners viewed this with outright disfavor, with popes again inveighing against their greed: "There are prelates of churches and others who, blinded by cupidity, imagine that gifts by the faithful to religious automatically limit their own revenues".[104] Total poverty is closely bound up with the autonomy of the Carmelites which in turn is closely associated with the fact that they formed a *collegium* (a community in the juridical sense of being recognized).[105]

[102] For this see Cicconetti, *Rule*, 107-120.

[103] Cf. specifically Gregory IX's bull *Ex officii nostri* of 1229 in which the Carmelites were strictly prohibited from owning any possessions – and in the same breath allowed to own donkeys and to start breeding livestock and raising poultry on a small scale.

[104] Quoted from an insertion in the decretals of Gregory IV, cited in Cicconetti, *Rule*, 111.

[105] Ibid., 120.

Why, in 1247, did the two Dominicans charged with the revision of the Rule eliminate the clause what "the Lord may have given you"? Did they by this act cancel out the ideal of radical poverty which fitted so well with the new Carmelite mendicant way of life? Did the Carmelites no longer feel able to cope without an assured income? Did they no longer need the non-profit seal? Did they want to remove from the Rule the ambiguity of living from alms – the Lord! – and *at the same time* from the work of their hands later (1229 and 1247) materialized in donkeys, mules, livestock and poultry? According to Ribot, doubts had arisen among the brothers: were they allowed only to divide that which the Lord had provided for them or also that which had been acquired by their own hands or through some other legitimate channel?[106] What architectonic shift is being brought about by the omission of Innocent IV?

In my opinion, somewhat longer reflection on the omission makes one thing clear: the communal element no longer consists in what "the Lord may have given", or Providence. This need not be an immediate loss. The Rule intends to give us basic exercises for our communal conduct. *On this level* the reference to Providence is an evasion. At the end of the Rule – "the Lord at his return will reward him" – Providence returns – just in time! That, however, is for later; now the objective is to make a movement to the center: by ex-propri-ation as well as by communal-ization.

2. The second textual modification is *verbal*: "someone" is changed to "brother". Not a shocking change, to be sure, but certainly meaningful. About this change Ribot writes as follows:

> The brothers objected to the idea that *someone* from outside the order could be appointed by the prior to divide the goods of the order. By this provision, after all, these goods could be more easily purloined than if a *brother* were appointed to perform this task.[107]

The point is: no one from the outside may any longer be charged with the distribution of the possessions of the community. For

[106] *Decem libri,* 8.6.
[107] *Decem libri* 8.4.

this purpose the community must appoint someone from its own midst. The two textual modifications we have so far considered point in the same direction: the *internal* upbuilding of the community. The first modification omits an external factor: alms as a source of income. Attention therefore shifts to the *internal* community: "Let everything be held in common among you and each one shall be given what he needs ...". That which is now distributed is truly communal: it has been produced, brought in and gathered up by the community (including alms).

The second modification sharpens the focus on the internal. Not only is the acquisition communal, also the distribution of what has been acquired belongs to the community: it must be done by a brother.

3. The third textual modification is again an *omission*. In the original formula for life it was expressly laid down that each would prepare and eat his food in his own cell. To "live on ..." needed to occur in the cell. At appointed times, usually weekly, each of the brothers received a certain amount of food and other necessary goods. Processing these edibles again occurred in the cell and was expressly subordinated to the theme of remaining in the cell: everything must be done in such a way that, "as has already been stated, each one is to *keep to the cell* assigned to him". Originally that was also the link between chapters VII-VIII and chapter IX: everything was done in the cell. By the omission this connection is now broken. The Carmelites no longer lived individually from what had been distributed. On the contrary: from now on people will eat the food prepared for them "in a common refectory, listening together to some reading from Sacred Scripture" (IV). Also the third modification strengthens the community. The "goods" are no longer just acquired and distributed by the community: they are jointly consumed as well.

4. Finally, the fourth textual modification is again an *addition*. In 1247 Innocent IV gave the Carmelites permission to have donkeys and mules and to start raising livestock and poultry on a modest

scale. Actually this permission was given already in 1229. That year Gregory IX wrote his letter *Ex officii nostri* in which he prohibited the Carmelites from having any possessions: "You are not allowed to possess anything". But he immediately added: "except donkeys and some livestock and poultry". A remarkable instance of inconsistency: no possessions, yet some possessions. But, as we saw earlier, the prohibition of property was intended more as a privilege, meaning: "You are officially a non-profit institution". Livestock and poultry were intended as "a means of support, in order to consume the eggs and the milk, for the brothers were not forbidden to eat of them".[108] For the rest, the inconsistency of having possessions and not having them is probably the reason why the papal advisors omitted the alms-clause: "From the things the Lord may have given you" (see point 1 above). In any case, from 1229 on Carmelites had permission to own some donkeys and to keep some livestock. In 1247 mules were added to the list. Just how we must picture this animal farm is a question.[109] Mules were meant as a means of transportation "to bring wood, foodstuffs, and other things needed for the maintenance of the brothers to the monastery".[110] Why have donkeys and mules as well? Usually hermits had one donkey among them. It is possible the Carmelites wanted to be of service to pilgrims. In any case, the donkeys were not meant for breeding: only male donkeys and (sterile) mules were allowed. In both cases the idea was to have beasts of burden, hence a basic provision. In raising livestock and poultry the idea was to produce meat, milk, cheese, and eggs as a source of revenue. This form of income was not viewed as a means of exercising power over others on the basis of property. Nor was the purpose of this production primarily to provide food for the hermitage. The livestock was brought to market in exchange for a variety of goods. The monks themselves did not eat the meat, nor, in certain cases, the eggs. They ate fruit, legumes,

[108] Ibid.
[109] Cf. Cicconetti, *Rule*, 114-118, 191.
[110] *Decem libri*, 8.4.

grains and vegetables, mixed with oil; drank water and wine; and wore woolen clothing. By this type of production they, on the one hand, evaded taxes, for it was not based on possessions; on the other hand, they obviated having to beg away from home and stemmed the uncertainty of having to live on alms. In that way they laid the necessary foundation for the community's economy.

The four textual modifications focused on the *internal* organization of the economic community.

−1. The factor of *income*. As regulative principle in this connection the Rule offers: labor shared by beasts of burden, and products acquired through breeding animals, are permitted, provided this is governed by the necessity principle (see point 4 above). Hence the formation of property by labor and production is permitted. This is expressed by the term "to have" (as in the case of the prior, the place, and the cell). Property falls under the heading of basic provisions.

−2. The factor of *possessions*. This aspect of the economy is totally defined in terms of the community, now that the sting of the alms has been removed (see point 1 above). Here the verb "to say" (Latin) is used: "Let none of the brothers *say* that anything is his property". This denotes an elementary exercise like being obedient, remaining in, reading, and praying, etc. We shall return in a moment to this basic exercise of the economic community.

−3. The factor of *distribution*. Goods are distributed to each brother individually by the hand of the prior. It is the community itself which distributes the goods of the community. It is therefore simply logical that someone of the community should distribute the goods on behalf of the prior (see point 2 above). The principle of distribution is each brother's need. The operative criteria here are age and necessity. Not the community, but each individual is the norm here.

−4. The factor of *the users*. Although the economic dynamics no longer issue in the life of each individual brother who remains in the cell assigned to him, still the omitted lines continue to reverberate in the conclusion (discussed a moment ago) of the sentence that was maintained: "according to the needs of each, taking into account the age and needs of each". Although through all these modifications the accent has clearly shifted to the community, the needs are expressly articulated in terms of the age and the needs of each individual brother. Again we observe a tense balance between the eremitic and the cenobitic way of life.

It is now high time to take a look at that which remained essentially the same in those first forty years. Still the same is: "Let none of the brothers say that anything is his property, but let everything be held in common among you". In terms of its essence this basic rule was derived from the Rule of Augustine.

> And you must not *say that anything is your property,*
> *but let everything be held in common among you,*
> and *to each* of you *shall be distributed*
> by your superior food and clothing,
> not the same to everyone,
> because you are not all equally strong,
> but rather to each man as *he needs.*
> For this is what you read in the Acts of the Apostles:
> *all things* were *in common* to them,
> and *distribution* was made
> to everyone as *he had need* (Acts 4:32, 35).[111]

The similarities between Albert's Rule and the Rule of Augustine (printed in italics) follow three lines of agreement: the reference to Acts;[112] verbal correspondences;[113] similarity of atmosphere.[114] Altogether this gives us sufficient reasons to speak of reference to Augustine's Rule.

In Augustine the chapter on possessions comes at the beginning of his Rule immediately after the summons to be "of one heart and

---

[111] *La Règle de Saint Augustin,* Paris 1961, 10.
[112] This reference to Acts is present in several Rules. Cf. Cicconetti, *Rule,* 272-273.
[113] I.e. the words "say" and "property".
[114] An atmosphere in which there is regard for persons as individuals.

one soul" (Acts 4:32). The question is: why does the chapter on poverty so abruptly follow the statement of the ideal of community in Augustine? "The answer is fairly simple: because in Augustine's view community of goods is the primary expression and initial realization of the love of neighbor".[115] True: community of goods is a primary expression and initial realization. It is an elementary exercise of community.

Community of goods is not a basic provision but a basic exercise; not a basic condition but a basic movement.

> In Augustine community of goods is not merely a condition for loving each other. It is integral to the essence of love to communicate itself. Love sees to it that what each possesses individually becomes the common property of all.[116]

In this connection what counts is not solely the communalization of material goods.

> When Augustine speaks in the Rule of community of goods he is referring in the first place to material goods. It would be wrong, however, to restrict the idea of community of goods solely to them. It is obvious that we must make our spiritual goods available to each other as well. The concept of "spiritual goods" is very broad and hard to define. But it surely includes one's own talents, character, temperament, thoughts and ideas, inspiration and faith.[117]

"Everything you have should be held in common" is a dynamic saying. It spurs people on to an elementary exercise: I attempt to move toward the center of the community all that has been given to me. This movement is the diametrical opposite of that other movement: to bend back toward my own self all that has been entrusted to me. One who does the latter is literally "not one of the brothers". He excludes himself from the brotherhood. Hence we are looking at two movements: the movement of the person

---

[115] T. van Bavel, *Augustinus van Hippo, Regel voor de Gemeenschap*, Kampen-Averbode 1991³, 42.

[116] Ibid., 43.

[117] Ibid., 44-45.

who is not one of the brothers because he bends everything back to what is his own, and the movement of the brother who moves everything toward the communal center.

This movement toward the center, however, does not apply to the community! It must move in precisely the opposite direction: seeking out each one individually in the spirit of Augustine. The community may not seek the things which are communal; it must serve the particular. For that reason the distribution of communal goods is realized by the prior – himself a brother! – and by the brother who is "the hand of the prior". The community can only look at each one individually if there are persons in it who are responsible for this, in this case the prior and the "hand" (deputy) of the prior. A most valuable and costly task: to look carefully at each brother's needs and to let oneself be guided by such obvious givens as "age" and "personal needs". These are creative words. *Age* stands for everything a person inevitably is or is becoming. Age is not something one can choose. Neither is his body or his stomach, or his gender, or his dexterity, or his brains, or his eyes, or his heart or his nerves. Age stands for inescapable specificity.

Needs (Necessity) is an equally creative word, but from another angle of vision. To a writer a pen is necessary, and to an organist an organ. Necessary to our psyche is perspective; to our nervous system it is rest. Necessary is that which is inescapably connected with something else. A task requires room to work in. Building requires stones or other building materials. Swimming requires water; breathing requires air. "Age" and "needs" are creative words designed to make one look at the needs of each person individually.

To communalize everything from the vantage point of each individual and then to personalize everything in the direction of each individual – these are the elementary exercises on the level of religious economy. They are exercises of the cenobitic life, like choosing and obeying a prior.

> The cenobites, who earn so much money for their monasteries, hand it over each day, continue to persevere in their utterly humble submissiveness; who stand away from deciding themselves what to

do with what they have earned by the sweat of their brow and who, in this daily renunciation of what they have earned, manage to renew ceaselessly the zeal of their first act of renunciation.[118]

The communalization of everything is an elementary exercise, a basic movement toward the center. That is the reason why this exercise comes so early and is so prominent in Augustine's Rule.

> Integral to the first degree of love is the communalization of material goods. This is an initial realization of openness to others, a primary form of living together. For by it we make known that we no longer wish to live for ourselves or desire to acquire goods only to our own advantage. The surrender of one's own property serves to eliminate our own egoism and greed, our drive toward domination and power; it is these latter things above all which keep people from achieving genuine community with each other.[119]

From this perspective, poverty is liberating. It opens us up. It purifies our hearts and makes them receptive. It relieves us of cares. Abbot John who returned from the desert to a cenobite monastery, says:

> In this life then there is no providing for the day's work, no distractions of buying and selling, no unavoidable care for the year's food, no anxiety about bodily things, by which one has to get ready what is necessary not only for one's own wants but also for those of any number of visitors ...[120]

By relieving ourselves in all respects of all private possessions and moving toward the communal center, we enter upon the space in which things are together where they belong, in their original connectedness. To us every something becomes the symbol of *everything*. We fundamentally dispossess ourselves and by that very fact open to ourselves the experience of the fundamental givenness of things. This in turn reflects back on ourselves: we are gratuitously given to ourselves as well. In that sense the never-ending

---

[118] Cassian, *Conferences*, 18.7.
[119] Van Bavel, *Augustinus van Hippo, Regel voor de Gemeenschap*, 46.
[120] Cassian, *Conferences*, 19.6; *NPNF*, 491.

dispossession of self is a never-ending initiation into being a religious. This is the way of the *nothing* shown us by John of the Cross.

> To reach satisfaction in all – desire satisfaction in nothing
> To come to the knowledge of all – desire the knowledge of nothing.
> To come to possess all – desire the possession of nothing.
> To arrive at being all – desire to be nothing ...
> When you delay in something – you cease to rush toward the all.
>
> The more I desired to possess them, the less I had ...
> The more I desired to seek them, the less I had ...
> Now that I no longer desire them, I have them all without desire.[121]

Coming together each day (X)

The formula of life Albert presented to the Carmelites, in the first place, offers to them as basic provisions: the priorate (I), a place to live (II-III), and communal property (IX). Added now is the oratory (X). Albert not only handed them provisions, however, he also indicated by what exercises they can appropriate these provisions: obeying in actual truth (I), remaining in the cell (VII), and making all things communal (X). In the case of the oratory it is an elementary exercise: coming together (X). Consequently chapter X consists of two layers: the basic provision (A) and the elementary exercise which goes with it (B).

A. An oratory, as far as it can be done conveniently, shall be built in the midst of the cells,

B. where you shall come together every day early in the morning to hear Mass,where this can be done conveniently.

A. The order to build an oratory in the midst of the cells had an *architectural* side to it. The local situation in the Carmel mountain range brought limitations with it. To build a chapel somewhere in that mountain range is always a possibility but to do this in the midst of the cells is much more difficult, particularly if we assume

---

[121] John of the Cross, *The Mount of Perfection*, in *The Collected Works of Saint John of the Cross*, tr. K.Kavanaugh and O.Rodriguez, rev. ed., Washington D.C. 1991, 111.

that some cells were spread out over the mountain as well. The addition "as this can be done conveniently", therefore, refers to this architectural side of the project. The question is not whether an oratory can be built, but whether it can be built in a central location.

Aside from the architectural dimension, the order also had a *juridical* thrust.[122] By offering this formula of life Albert had in mind the creation of a religious community in a juridical sense. As a result of Albert's order to build an oratory in the midst of the cells the community of lay hermits officially became a religious house (*domus religiosa; domus orationis; locus sacer*). When a bishop granted permission to build a chapel for the purpose of celebrating the Eucharist there, this permission was tantamount to an ecclesiastical endorsement of the community as such.

Playing a part in all this there is a *symbolic* meaning as well. Most rules and forms of life required an oratory in the center. The centrally located oratory gives meaning and connectedness to the separate cells, the oratory serving to prevent the separate living spaces from clogging up into egocentric private domains. From a symbolic viewpoint even the architectural relaxation of the clause "as far as this can be done conveniently" gains a deeper meaning. The construction of the sacred building in the center is not callously projected from behind a drawing board into an empty geometric space, but must be fitted into the site just as stones must be fitted into the building of a spiritual temple (1 Pet. 2:4-5). Essentially we are looking at a double dynamic: the cells as it were seek out their center and the center gathers up the cells. A sound reciprocity governing the relation between the whole and the parts is the symbolic radius of the construction of the oratory in the midst of the cells.

Finally there is the *religious* meaning of the oratory in the midst.[123] This meaning lights up when we look at it with the eyes of Scripture. Audible throughout the whole of Scripture is the motif of the religious Center. The Lord is in the midst of his

---

[122] Cicconetti, *Rule*, 74-76 and 273-274.

[123] Cf. Waaijman-Blommestijn, *The Carmelite Rule as a Model of Mystical Transformation*, 80-81.

people: "I will dwell *in the midst* of the Israelites and will be their God. They shall know that I, the Lord, am their God who brought them out of the land of Egypt so that I, the Lord their God might dwell in their midst" (Ex. 29:45, 46).[124] That which is true for Israel applies to Carmel as well: "They shall make sanctuary for me that I may dwell in their midst" (Ex. 25:8).[125] This Presence in the midst of the people is not something which exists in isolation from the approach of everyone toward the Center: the cells seek out the Center, form the Center, build up the Center. The cells, as living stones, fit themselves into the construction of the spiritual temple, joined together by the Cornerstone, the Messiah, whom they bear (cf. John 2:19-23; Heb. 7:1-10, 31; see also John 20:19, 26; Luke 24:36).

B. The basic provision of an oratory in the midst of the cells calls for exercise. This is realized in the elementary act of coming together.

> In that troop of saints ... there was Paphnutius, a holy man, and we saw his knowledge gleaming with the glow of a great fount of light. He was the priest for that group of ours which was in the desert at Scete. Even as a very old man he never moved from the cell occupied by him since the time when he was quite young and which was five miles from the church. He could have come closer, could have spared his old age the weariness of such a long journey every Saturday and Sunday. Nor would he return empty-handed. He would put on his shoulders and carry back to his cell the container for his week's drinking water ...[126]

That describes how physical the relationship is between the cell and the oratory: it is the physical walk to and from. In my going to the oratory the community assumes visible form, just as the tribes of Israel made the people of Israel visible by going up to Jerusalem (Psalm 122). The living center of the community is constituted by the constantly repeated act of coming together

---

[124] See further Ex. 33:1-6; Num. 11:20; Deut. 6:15; 7:21; 20:4; 23:14, etc.
[125] See Lev. 26:11; Ezek. 48:10
[126] Cassian, *Conferences* 3.1.

(convenire). A "con-vent" is a living event. By coming together we build up the community and everyone departs again as a member of that community.

Corresponding to this spatial body of the community there is a temporal body as well. The ancient desert monks celebrated the Eucharist once a week. That was different in the thirteenth century. The majority of religious communities came together for the Eucharist every day.[127] The daily gathering gives a rhythmic structure to life. The act of coming together every day, early in the morning, at the pivotal point between night and day, gives the day its basic rhythm. The rising sun, which conquers the night, must have been intuitively experienced as the Risen One. This is the center of time. Here the hours (VIII), which are spread out over day and night, find their center. Here the liturgical hours are fitted into a single whole.

Coming together in the oratory, in an elementary way, instills the consciousness of belonging to a community with a temporal-spatial character. Precisely because of this elementary physical character of the community this exercise may not be coercive: its occurrence must be in some sense convenient. This, above all, marks the difference between the elementary exercises and the life of virtue. The former can be omitted, indeed *must* be omitted sometimes (fasting on Sundays, for example, is not fitting). The latter can never be interrupted (justice, for example, must always be pursued).

However, the communal act of coming together is more than a temporal-spatial event, or rather it *can* be more than that.[128] Coming together is basically coming into the presence of One and dispersing out of that presence. This One is not visible to the human eye. The One can only be experienced by stepping out of one's own shell. By coming together into the presence of One in the midst the Place where the Eucharist is celebrated comes into being; indeed, on an elementary level the act of coming together into the presence of One is *eucharistia*. The Eucharist, after all,

[127] Cicconetti, *Rule*, 274.
[128] Cf. Waaijman-Blommestijn, *The Carmelite Rule as a Model of Mystical Transformation*, 83-87.

begins where we allow ourselves to be gathered into one people by
the Lord, who invites us to listen to his word so that it moves us,
shapes the desire of our heart, and causes us to look for his
Presence. He invites us to take to ourselves his body and blood, to
remember him in total self-identification with him, so that we
enter death *with* him, and we are found by God himself. The
Eucharist radicalizes the act of coming out of our selves: it is not
we who come; we are drawn, drawn into the width of the Word
and into the depth of Death: to *be* found, to *be* gathered, to *be*
united. This is the mystical perspective of coming together for the
purpose of celebrating the Eucharist. This mystical movement is
beautifully sustained by the words "early in the morning", words
which evoke Mary Magdalene's quiet walk to the tomb: "On the
first day of the week Mary of Magdala came to the tomb *early in
the morning* while it was still dark ..." (John 20:1). Early in the
morning Carmelites come together in the oratory, the Midst that
is filled by no one. Like the bride in the Song of Songs they seek
him whom their soul loves at night – while it is still dark. It is the
quest of love through the darkness of the night; then follows the
Easter-experience of the tender voice: "Miriam", your dearest
name uttered by One whom your soul loves. Comes the answer
that is equally tender: "Rabbouni". This is the Easter of love, the
mystical depth of the Eucharist. Here is the heartbeat of Carmel.

The elementary beginning of this transformation is stepping
outside, stepping out of our cell. Only those who step outside of
themselves into the darkness of the night can be found by the dawn-
ing Light. Forgetting themselves in love they will receive their name.

The weekly chapter (XI)

In virtually all religious institutions chapter was a self-evident part
of the life of the community.[129] In ancient monasticism spiritual
conferences provided the framework of guidance and formation.
Some religious communities, Carmelites among them, held chapter

[129] Cf. Cicconetti, *Rule,* 161; 274-275.

every week (or when it was needed); others, like the canons of the
Holy Cross in Mortara, held chapter every day. The Carmelites,
like the Trinitarians and Carthusians, linked the weekly chapter to
the Sunday – a very meaningful connection, as we will see later.

Generally speaking chapter revolves around three themes: everything that relates to the ordering of the religious life; everything
that concerns the spiritual journey of every community member;
shortcomings and excesses.

> On Sundays, too,
> or on other days when necessary,
> you shall discuss the preservation of order
> and the salvation of your souls.
> At this time also the excesses and faults of the brothers,
> if such should be found in anyone,
> shall be corrected in the midst of love.

Actually the chapter agenda consists of two major points: on the
one hand, the preservation of order and the welfare of souls; on the
other (and in a sense connected with the first) excesses and faults.
Under the first heading the focus is on treatment; under the second,
on observation and correction. We will first examine the separate
agenda points; then the manner in which they are treated.

1. *The preservation of order.*[130] In speaking of order we are dealing
primarily with the institutions of the Carmelite life, the basic provisions structuring the Carmelite life: a prior acquired via an orderly
election (I); a place with cells for each brother individually, a common
refectory and a single entrance (II-VI); communal property (IX); an
oratory in the midst of the cells (X). Expressed in these provisions is
an order: a combination of an eremitic and a cenobitic way of life,
resumed after 1247 in light of the new perspective of mendicancy.

---

[130] "Order" originally had reference to the state of life which a person had
chosen, the class to which he belonged ("medieval orders"). In the Rule this word
is used to designate the actual life of the community to which one belonged.
Later the concept of "order" also gained the meaning of "an organization of
religious officially approved by the church".

The preservation of this order is realized by elementary exercises: the orderly election of a prior and ongoing fidelity to this election in actual obedience (I); inhabiting the place and remaining – meditating and praying – in the cells (II-VII); the communalization of everything (IX) and coming together in the midst (X). Through these ostensibly physical actions we gain access to the mystical perspective at work in the order.

The discussions are aimed at discernment: learning to see through the issues. A fine example is the conference recalled by Abba Moses:

> I remember the years when I was still a boy in that section of the Thebaid where the blessed Antony used to live. Some older men came to visit him and to talk to him about perfection. Their talk [conference] lasted from the evening hours until dawn and the problem we are now discussing took up the greatest part of the night. There was a most searching inquiry into which of the virtues and which observance could always preserve a monk from the snares and the deceptions of the devil and could lead him with firm tread on a sure path to the summit of perfection. Each one offered an opinion in accordance with the understanding he had of the matter. Some declared that by means of zealous fasting and the keeping of vigils the mind would be enlarged and would produce purity of heart and body so as to enable one to come all the more easily into union with God. Others posited detachment from everything in order that the mind, shorn of everything, freed from all the snares which were holding it back, would come more speedily to God. Others thought that what was necessary was to get completely away, to have the solitude and secrecy of the desert where a man, living there always, could converse more intimately with God and where union could be achieved more directly. Some opted for the practice of charity, that is to say, the works of hospitality, since it was to people of this kind that the Lord in the gospel promised especially that he would give the kingdom of heaven. "Come, you blessed ones of my father, come and possess the kingdom which has been ready for you since the beginning of the world. I was hungry and you gave me food to eat. I was thirsty and you gave me a drink", and so on (Mt 25:34-35).
>
> Thus it was that the different virtues were said to give a more certain access to God. And most of the night was spent in this inquiry.

Finally, the blessed Antony spoke. All the things that you have
spoken about are necessary and helpful to those thirsting for God
and longing to reach him. But the countless disasters and experiences of many people do not permit that any one of these virtues
should be said to be the prime influence for good. For very often we
have seen people who have been most zealous in their fasts and vigils, who have lived wondrously solitary lives, who have endured
such total privation of everything that they would not allow themselves to hold on to even a day's food or even a single coin of the
lowest value, who have hastened to do all that is required in charity
– and who have suddenly fallen prey to illusion with the result that
not only could they not give a fitting end to the work they had
undertaken but they brought to an abominable conclusion that
high zeal of theirs and that praiseworthy mode of life. Hence if we
probe the exact reason for their delusion and fall we will be able to
recognize what it is that, above all else, leads us to God. The virtuous activities, of which you were talking, flourished among them.
But the lack of discernment prevented them from reaching the end.
No other cause can be found for their downfall. Lacking the
training provided by older men they could in no way acquire this
virtue of discernment.[131]

Two motifs are intertwined here. First: the motif of coming
together to discuss "order" in the light of perfection. Second: the
motif of discovering discernment as the necessary compass.

2. *The salvation of your souls.* Spiritual wellbeing must not be con-
fused with the preservation of order, however much the two are
intertwined in life as we live it. In the preservation of order, *order*
is the viewpoint from which things are considered. By preserving
this order we secure access to its mystical space. To be drawn into
this order is for the ultimate wellbeing of the soul – that is how
closely the two are intertwined. But, however the two are intertwined, in the case of the wellbeing of the soul the *soul* serves as
the perspective from which things are considered. In every spirituality there is constant tension between the given order (the

[131] Cassian, *Conferences*, 2.2.

transformative *model*) which calls for interiorization, and the soul – with its own biography, its own charism, and its own boundaries – which is searching for salvation within the framework of that order (the transformative *process*). Though the two perspectives continually overlap and interact, they must be distinguished.

Throughout the history of spirituality the soul is the place where union with God occurs in humans.[132] The soul – originally "breath", "wind" – encompasses the whole of the human person: the intimate expression of life, the locus of consciousness, the seat of emotion, will, and intellect, the vulnerable center, the deepest ground and highest summit of consciousness. Which of these aspects predominates depends on the spiritual tradition in which one stands. But always the reference is to the whole of the human being who reaches out to God.

In speaking of the soul the Rule has opted for the perspective of the non-interchangeable human, persons who for reasons of their own agree with the choice of a prior (I); who, by remaining alone in their cell and living in solitude as unique persons, are welcomed by the Indwelling (II-III); who independently reflect on Scripture and allow their longing to be shaped by the prayers (VII); who are committed heart and soul (IX), and who themselves come to the gathering (X). By its reference to the soul the Rule has opted for the perspective of the unique human person who *through* all these exercises embarks on a journey to the Infinite: the mystical perspective of the order.

By referring to the soul the Rule opts for the interior logic of the spiritual life. Abbot Paphnutius gives us a vivid picture of this interior road.

> ... let us be quite clear about the fact that we can never be fully confident in the face of the storms of temptation and the onslaughts of the devil if the only protection of our patience and all our trust lie not in the strength of the inner man but in the closed doors of a cell, in the escape to solitude, in the company of holy men or in some other external source of defense. If He who in the

---

[132] *Âme* in *DS* 1 (1937), 433-469.

gospel said, "The kingdom of God is within you" (Lk 17:21) – if He does not give us strength of soul through His protective virtue, then it is for nothing that we seek to defeat the hostile attacks of the creatures of the air or try to avoid them in far-off places or strive to bar their approach through the protection of a dwelling place.[133]

Clearly in evidence here is what is meant by the wellbeing of the soul as opposed to the observance of order. For Abba Paphnutius order consisted in the shelters of the cell, the isolation of solitariness, the protection of the religious community. This religious order is necessary but not sufficient. For the wellbeing of the soul it only constitutes the necessary foundation. It is essential, however, that within that order the soul is strengthened by the power of the protection of God. In the prologue of his *Conferences* Cassian had already referred to this distinction, a distinction which is so essential for the religious life. This distinction precisely marks the difference between his two main works: the *Institutes* and *Conferences*.

> Let us therefore pass from what is visible to the eye and the exter-
> nal mode of life of the monks, of which we treated in the former
> books, to the life of the inner man, which is hidden from view; and
> from the system of the canonical prayers, let our discourse mount to
> that continuance in unceasing prayer, which the Apostle enjoins, that
> whoever has through reading our former work already spiritually
> gained the name of Jacob by ousting his carnal faults, may now by
> the reception of the Institutes which are not mine but the fathers",
> mount by a pure insight to the merits and (so to speak) the dignity
> of Israel, and in the same way be taught what it is that he should
> observe on these lofty heights of perfection.[134]

Paramount in all the institutions is a goal that transcends them: the vision of God, in which we are born again to the dignity of Israel – our perfection. And this precisely is the salvation of the soul. The Latin *salus* – like the Greek *holos* goes back to the basic meaning of *wholeness*: health, wellbeing, salvation, being unscathed and unimpaired, integrity, welfare. Earlier already (cf. 3.2) we saw

---

[133] Cassian, *Conferences*, 18.16; *CWS*, 198.
[134] Ibid., *Prologue*; *NPNF*, 293-294.

that salvation is a key word in the history of spirituality.[135] Wholeness
or wellbeing contrasts with death, which threatens to destroy our
life by illness, misfortune, and violation. It also contrasts with
slavery and the infringement of one's personal life. The most
profound form of disaster is the break with God. Wholeness,
accordingly, is at bottom: healing, deliverance, and restoration by
God. In the Eastern churches this wholeness is viewed above all as
God's downward movement toward humans; in Western churches
especially as a person's upward movement toward God. Both
traditions are variations on the theme of the one salvation: the
divinization of human beings and the humanization of God. The
salvation of the soul consists in taking and traveling the spiritual
way. At every step of the journey fresh facets are revealed. Salvation
begins already with the elementary exercises (protection by the
place, the indwelling in the cell, being surrounded by the Scriptures, shelter in the brotherhood, conception in the oratory) but
needs a more secure form of protection: the soul must be clothed
with the attributes of God (XIV). And salvation reaches still further: working in silence, the soul awaits its salvation (XV-XVI).[136]
And beyond that: surrender, in complete and blind faith, to God
(conclusio). The salvation of the soul is God himself who draws
the soul out of its enslavement and decline, out of disintegration
and corruption, out of petrification and death, out of violation
and oppression, out of sin and lostness. Albert's salutation pertains
to the core of the Carmelite life: "*Salvation* in the Lord". The helmet
of *salvation,* by which we look for the *salvation* of the only *Savior*
who *saves* (heals) the people from all their violations, rightly constitutes the apex of all our spiritual defense weapons!

3. *Excesses and faults.* So far we have discussed two points on the
chapter's agenda: the preservation of order and the salvation of
souls. Just what could possibly be added to this? Answer: nothing,

<hr>

[135] *Salut* in *DS* 14 (1990), 251-283.

[136] Perhaps this is the reason why the ancient Carmelites associated the salvation
of the soul so closely with praying in the cell (*Decem libri,* 8.4).

from a material viewpoint; everything, from a dynamic perspective. The truth is, the elementary exercises and the soul's movement toward salvation are threatened interiorly by instability: by "too much" and by "too little". Needed is an internal compass by which we keep our exercises and spiritual strivings in balance. It is the ability to discern the spirits, an ability we encountered earlier. One of its primary functions is the detection of excesses and faults. The elementary exercises are subject to *excesses:* reading Scripture so long that one's head spins; locking oneself up in solitude for inhuman lengths of time; staying awake ever longer hours and sleeping ever less;[137] fasting till you drop, and so forth.[138] At the other end of the scale, and contrasting with the excesses, are the faults: sleeping long inside the cell; wandering about outside the cell; making endless calls among fellow monks; attending the Eucharist without paying attention, etc. What counts is knowing how to steer a midcourse between the two extremes.

> We must rapidly ensure that we do not slide into danger on account of the urge for bodily pleasure. We must not anticipate food before the time for it and we must not overdo it; on the other hand, when the due hour comes, we must have our food and our sleep, regardless of our reluctance.[139]

Actually it is not even so much a matter of knowing how to avoid extremes and steering a midcourse; it is more a matter of seeing that excesses and faults are essentially the same: different forms of one and the same thing.

> For there is an old saying: "Excesses meet". Too much fasting and too much eating come to the same end. Keeping too long a vigil brings the same disastrous cost as the sluggishness which plunges a monk into the longest sleep. Too much self-denial brings weakness and induces the same condition as carelessness. Often I have seen men who could not be snared by gluttony fall, nevertheless, through immoderate fasting and tumble in weakness into the very

---

[137] Cassian, *Conferences,* 2.17.
[138] Ibid., 2.5.
[139] Ibid., 2.17; *CWS,* 76.

urge which they had overcome. Unmeasured vigils and foolish denial of rest overcame those whom sleep could not overcome. Therefore, "fortified to right and to left in the armor of justice", as the apostle says (2 Cor. 6:7), life must be lived with due measure and, with discernment for a guide, the road must be traveled between the two kinds of excess so that in the end we may not allow ourselves to be diverted from the pathway of restraint which has been laid down for us nor fall through dangerous carelessness into the urgings of gluttony and self-indulgence.[140]

Discernment, the subject Cassian rightly treats at the beginning of his *Conferences*,[141] is the supreme virtue and the heart of chapter.

In considering chapter we are inclined to think of it as shaping policies and making democratic decisions: discussing a matter jointly and on that basis taking a decision. We may also view it as an opportunity for exchanging experiences. In my opinion these emphases are one-sided; they stress procedure and neglect the deeper dimension. The verbs the Rule uses (treat, detect, correct) point, in part by their context (excesses and faults), to an in-depth reading of the preservation of order and the soul's movement toward salvation traditionally known as discernment. To demonstrate this I will first briefly explain what the treatment of a topic is, what observation means, and what the correction of imbalances entails.

1. To *treat*[142] a subject is to study it in depth, to look at it from all sides, to explore it with care. This intensity may concern the subject matter itself (looking at it from all angles); but it may also describe persons studying: we relate the subject matter to ourselves and take it very much to heart. By intensely occupying ourselves with a matter we may grasp its essence and explain it from the inside out.[143] Now,

---

[140] Ibid., 2.16.

[141] The second *Conference*, which flows naturally from the *whole* of the spiritual life that was the subject of discussion in the first *Conference*, is devoted to it.

[142] *Tractare* is a frequentative form of *trahere*: to pull, to drag; to drag along, to seduce; to relate to; to explain; to drag along; to pull it toward onself; to accept; to grasp, etc.

[143] This is especially the medieval meaning of *tractare*.

looking at the weekly chapter we can say a number of things about
it. (1) Treating a matter means to take a serious and many-sided
look at it, i.e. looking at order or our soul through the eyes of
each person present. (2) We are not interested in an academic
treatment but in a way of looking that is *both* subject-related *and*
person-related. For that reason it is perhaps of some importance
from the viewpoint of method to discuss each pole of the issue
separately: that which is subject-related (the preservation of order
and the soul's movement toward salvation) and that which is person-related (what is happening with every individual person). (3)
The treatment must intrinsically aim at insight and clarification.
Probing, yes; preaching, no. Searching, not knowing, is central.
What we are after is explanation, not persuasion. Jointly we search
for the essential. We want to get *in*sight into things – *see* them.
Connectedness, essence, core – these are the words which offer a
framework of understanding.

2. This brings us to *perception*.[144] For me to perceive a thing is to
grasp, understand, discover it, to bring it out. This can be
threatening when it concerns excesses and shortcomings. It easily
assumes the form of "catching at", but that is not what is
intended. To begin with, we are dealing with matters which have
been *submitted* for evaluation with a view to arriving jointly at discernment. It is analogous to asking someone if you may have a
talk with him or her. In that case I act in perfect freedom as I
myself submit a matter to another for his or her opinion. The
object, then, is that my truth and my value may be brought out.
This inquiry into my truth or my value – the perception of the
progress of my soul – rests on the assumption that I may deceive
myself. The other party can help me "march directly along the
true road of discernment".[145] That is the first reason why "catching a person at" lies outside the horizon of a chapter. The second

[144] *Deprehendere* means to seize upon, to apprehend; to come upon, to discover; observe, perceive, discern.
[145] Cassian, *Conferences* 2.10.

or the generosity of
someone else ...

Hearing these words, the young man was so filled with sadness
and grief that his expression could not hide the bitterness which
had arisen in his heart.

"My son", said the old man, "up to now you were loading yourself with the weight of your wrongdoing. You had no fear that in
confessing such awful crimes you would be much remarked upon. I
have just now given you a little bit of simple advice, which of itself
implies no criticism of you and is prompted by the wish to edify
and to show care. Yet, I ask you, how is it that I see you stirred by
such anger that your expression has not been able to hide it nor
have you been capable of putting on a pretense of being serene?"[146]

Perception has nothing to do with "catching someone at doing
something"; it arises from kindness and love. The Rule is explicit at
this point: "with love as center". Love is the inner compass by which
perception is guided. We will return to this later. But there is a third
reason why this perception has nothing to do with "catching at". The
idea is that everyone will put aside false modesty, making perception
an act by which we will view the excesses and shortcomings of the
other as those of ourselves. The perception is mutual. Of this, too, a
fine instance has been handed down to us by the desert monks.

[146] Ibid., 18.11; *CWS*, 192.

Someone, by no means the least dedicated among the young men, came to an old man whom I knew well. He came for help, and he explained that he was troubled by the urges of the flesh and by the spirit of fornication. He felt sure that the prayers of the old man would ease his troubles and cure his wounds. But the old man berated him in the bitterest terms, calling him an unworthy wretch, exclaiming that he had no right to bear the name of monk ... And he so hurt the other with his reproaches that, as a consequence, the young man left the cell in utter misery and deadly despair. Weighed down with sadness, ... he met Apollo, the holiest of all the old monks. Apollo could see how troubled he was and how fierce a battle he was silently waging in his heart. Observing the depressed look on his face he asked to know the reason for such distress. The other could muster no reply to the gentle persistence of the old man. More and more the old man felt that it was not for nothing that the reason for such wretchedness was being veiled in silence, and the other's expression could not hide what he really felt. So ever more insistently he began to demand to know the causes of such hidden grief. Cornered, the young man told his story and declared that since, according to the old man he had consulted, he was incapable of being a monk, and since he could neither check the urges of the flesh nor get a cure for his temptation he was going to leave the monastery, get married, and return to the world.

The old man soothed him with gentle consolation, claiming that he too was moved each day by the same urges and tossed by the same storms. He urged him not to fall headlong into despair and not to be astonished by the ferocity of temptation. This was something to be conquered, not so much by the thrust of one's own effort as by the mercy and grace of the Lord. He asked the young man to hold off for just this one day and he begged him to go back to his cell.

Abba Apollo then went as speedily as he could to the living quarters of the other old man and . . . prayed. "Lord", he said, ... "Turn the temptation aside from the youngster and on to that old man. Do this so that in his old age he may learn to reach down in kindness to the weaknesses of those in toil and may sympathize with the frailty of the young".

God immediately heard Apollo's prayer and hurled fiery javelins at him. The old man was seized by raging desires. Apollo saw it happen and, going to him, said: "The Lord has allowed you to be hurt so that in your old age you may learn to have sympathy for the weaknesses of others, so that you may learn, as a result of what has happened to yourself, to reach out to the frailty of the young. A young man came to you struggling with the torments of the devil, and not only did you offer him no consolation but you actually gave him over in his deadly despair to the hands of the enemy. It was your fault that he was to be lamentably devoured by the enemy". With these words and others like it Apollo spoke to the old man. After that they prayed together begging God to quench the fiery javelins which he had permitted the devil to hurl at him.

The old man's one prayer was enough. The Lord took away the temptation as speedily as he had inflicted it and that very obvious experience taught the lesson that not only must we not denounce the fault which someone has admitted but we must also avoid despising any pain, however slight.[147]

3. Treating and observing a matter in depth have now set the stage for the third verb of the weekly chapter: *to correct*.[148] Excesses and faults are literally *one*-sided-nesses. Something is a departure from the golden mean. To correct it means to so effect a change in course that we are again going down the center of the road – to so adjust things that the proportions are right again. Order is a delicate complex of provisions; preserving it is an equally delicate matter. One may hold another too fanatically to it, or too carelessly release him from it. The soul, too, is a extremely delicate thing. To realize this we need only for a second look inside ourselves. While salvation beckons, how will I, the unstable one, be able to receive it? This is reason enough, following the loving perception of our excesses and faults, for us to make adjustments and to correct a matter.

The three verbs (to treat, perceive, correct) with which chapter approaches the three agenda points (the preservation of order; the salvation of the soul; the excesses and faults) can all be reduced to

---

[147] Ibid., 2.13; *CWS*, 71-72.
[148] *Corrigere* is to make right; to adjust; to make the crooked straight; to lead in the right direction; to compensate for; to improve, to correct.

one denominator: discernment. Just as Albert discusses the subject of "chapter" while refraining from the use of the word, so he clearly assumes "discernment", though again he refrains from using the word. In the history of spirituality discernment is an immensely important factor because it illuminates the entire progression of the spiritual life, as it were, from within. It searches for the essence, attempts to see through appearances, observing the truth of a person and makes adjustments at all levels of the spiritual process.[149]

In designing a life the discernment of spirits furnishes balance: balance between the interior and the exterior, body and soul, reflection and work, person and community. In praying and watching, fasting and working, silence and solitude it sees to it that excesses in both directions (too much *and* too little) are avoided. It helps us to see clearly the source of a given attitude or action; the good or the evil spirit. It is the compass needle of correct intuition and a good conscience. It helps us make the right choice. It teaches us to see through facts and events – to decode complex situations. It teaches us to tell the essential from the incidental, the end from the means, the final goal (*telos*) from the intermediate objective (*skopos*). Like a lamp it illumines the interior of our house. It picks up the ambiguities present in our motives. It distinguishes between reliable and unreliable inspirations. At all stages of the spiritual journey and in all the situations of life discernment is a trustworthy guide. It continually shows a different face but is always present as a source of guidance. For that reason Antony – and all the other desert monks with him – called discernment the supreme virtue.

> Hence it is very clear that no virtue can come to full term or can endure without the grace of discernment. And thus it was the agreed opinion of the blessed Antony and of all those with him that it is discernment which with firm step leads the enduring monk to God and which holds utterly intact together all the virtues referred to above. With discernment it is possible to reach the utmost

---

[149] For a survey of "discernment" (*diakrisis*) within spirituality, see both *Discernement* (*DS* 3 (1957) 1222-1291) and *Discretion* (*DS* 3 (1957) 1311-1330).

heights with the minimum of exhaustion. Without it there are many who despite the intensity of their struggle have been quite unable to arrive at the summit of perfection. For discernment is the mother, the guardian, and the guide of all the virtues.[150]

Among Carmelites the formation of discernment (*discretio*) occurs at the weekly chapter. This makes chapter a very special observance, just as discernment is a very special virtue. Actually discernment is not really a virtue: it is the inner light by which we practice virtue. Similarly, chapter is the exercise of all exercises. At chapter we lovingly consider our formula of life and the manner in which we observe it. We listen to the movement of each soul in search of salvation. Chapter is an exercise in taking soundings. We sail the sea of experience in the fulness of its breadth and sound its depths, all the while hoping for a good mind. I get this image from Abba Serenus. After one night's conversation he looks forward to the following night to continue the exploration of the breadth and depth of the religious life.

> Serenus: Although your proposals would rob us of our whole night's rest, so that we should not notice the approach of the rising dawn, and should be tempted greedily to prolong our conference till sunrise, yet since the solving of the question raised, if we began to trace it out, would launch us on a wide and deep sea of questions, which the shortness of the time at our disposal would not permit us to traverse, I think it will be more convenient to reserve it for consideration another night, when by the raising of this question I shall receive from your very ready converse some spiritual joy and richer fruit, and we shall be able if the Holy Spirit grants us a prosperous breeze to penetrate more freely into the intricacies of the questions raised.[151]

"Chapter" and "discernment" are interlocking realities. Chapter deals with order – i.e. attempts to penetrate to its core – with a view to discerning how that order can be preserved. It listens intensely to the movement of the soul, searching for

---

[150] Cassian, *Conferences,* 2.4; CWS, 64.
[151] Ibid., 7.34; *NPNF*, 375.

the God of the souls; salvation. It gives to perception a sharp
nose for excesses and faults. It puts things in their proper
place and perspective.

in the midst of love

Although, strictly speaking, the words "in the midst of love"
only apply to correction, as concluding words they have retroactive
force for the interpretation of the entire chapter. Chapter as a
whole must be carried out from within the center of love. But love
as center reaches back even further. For it forms an inclusion with
the preceding chapter which speaks of "the midst of the cells" (X).
This inclusion is reinforced by Mary Magdalene who on the first
day of Easter, while it was still dark, went to the tomb (John
20:1). Now, then, on the evening of that same first day of Easter,
Jesus appeared to his disciples "while the door of the house where
the disciples met was locked, Jesus came and stood *in their midst*"
(John 20:19). In great love, standing in their midst, Jesus taught
his disciples the essence of all chapters: "Receive the Holy Spirit!
Whose sins you forgive are forgiven them, and whose sins you
retain are retained" (John 20:22-33; cf. vs. 26). Just what are we
to understand by "love as the center"?[152]

1. In the first place, the reference is to this love's *identity of focus*.
According to Abba Joseph this love is even the strongest form of
love in existence.

> Among all these then there is one kind of love which is indissolu-
> ble, where the union is owing not to the favour of a recommen-
> dation, or some great kindness or gifts, or the reason of some bar-
> gain, or the necessities of nature, but simply to similarity of
> virtue. This, I say, is what is broken by no chances, what no inter-
> val of time or space can sever or destroy, and what even death
> itself cannot part. This is true and unbroken love which grows by
> means of the double perfection and goodness of friends, and

---

[152] See Waaijman-Blommestijn, *The Carmelite Rule as a Model of Mystical Transformation*, 82-87.

which, when once its bonds have been entered, no difference of liking and no disturbing opposition of wishes can sever.[153]

Love as center, meaning: love looking for ways which bring the soul closer to its Source; love observing that someone threatens to fall from grace; love putting each other straight; love in all things seeking the Center. It is the compass needle directing discernment itself.

2. Immediately bound up with this love's identity of focus is *reciprocity*. One who speaks, listens as well, one who listens, speaks as well – at least that is the case in a conversation that is guided by love.

> A dispenser of spiritual matters makes a twofold profit: he not only furnishes great profit to the one who listens to him but also – by his own exposition – to himself. For because he instructs his listeners he no less excites his own desire for perfection. Thus your zeal is to my advantage, your concern a stimulus to me. For I myself would now remain dull in mind and in my heart refrain from considering any part of the things you ask of me, if your zeal and expectation did not arouse me as out of my sleep to think of spiritual things.[154]

This is real shalom: giving in receiving and receiving in giving. We already noted this in the discussion of perceiving excesses and faults: the true perception of an excess in someone else evokes the memory of one's own excesses, and these are not concealed. The same is true of faults.

3. Identity of focus and reciprocity resonate most deeply when placed in the context of the love of *the Risen One*. The Eucharist on the day of Resurrection, the reference to the love of Mary Magdalene, and the meeting of the apostles on the first day of the week, the appearance of the Risen One in their midst – all these things put chapter in the context of the love of the Risen One who gives himself in his Word, in his Body and Blood, who tenderly utters her name "Miriam", who grants and

---

[153] Casian, *Conferences*, 16.3; *NPNF*, 450-451.
[154] Ibid., 22.1.

teaches forgiveness and breathes on them the spirit of Shalom. This love is Carmel's Center: it unites the cells into a living temple and brings the Carmelites together in prayer and sacrifice. It teaches us insight into everyday life and society. It teaches us to perceive what is going on inside ourselves. It is our compass and keeps us centered on the way.

As we look back on the chapters on communal property (IX), coming together in the Eucharist (X) and the weekly chapter (XI), we are struck by two interlocking lines of thought.

The first is the *realization* of community. This occurs by communalizing all goods and giving to every Carmelite what is due to them from within the community; by coming together in the oratory in the midst of the cells; by speaking to each other about the things that pertain to order and to each individual's wellbeing.

The second line of thought concerns the *reception* of community: by our giving up private property the All can become our portion; by our coming together in the midst, the One can come into our midst; because we listen and talk to each other intensely, Love gets a chance to do its work in our midst.

Communal possessions, coming together in the Eucharist and the weekly chapter are all exercises in community: stepping outside of ourselves and out toward the center to be built up by the Center.

> The true community does not arise through people having feelings for one another (though indeed not without it), but through, first, their taking their stand in living mutual relation with a living Centre, and, second, their being in living mutual relation with one another. The second has its source in the first, but is not given when the first alone is given. Living mutual relation includes feelings, but does not originate with them. The community is built up out of living mutual relation, but the builder is the living effective Centre.[155]

---

[155] Martin Buber, *Ich und Du*, Köln 1958, 45.

5.2.3 The purging of the body (XII-XIII)

The chapters on fasting and abstinence (XII-XIII) could be called *bodily* for two reasons. In the first place they are bodily because these practices are "bodily exercises", like remaining in one's cell, reading Scripture, saying prayers, etc. In the second place they are bodily because they immediately concern the body. Eating and drinking pertain to the upbuilding and maintenance of the body. Fasting and abstinence are a form of influencing oneself on the physical level. In this connection we are dealing with two purgations. Fasting is a form of self-evacuation designed to make room for the life-giving Other. Abstinence is a form of self-evacuation designed to admit life in its holiness.

Fasting (XII)

Fasting is an ascetic practice which over the centuries took many forms and was construed in various ways.[156] Strictly speaking, fasting is the practice of completely abstaining from food for a specific length of time. But people also speak of fasting when a person consumes only a small amount of food, like the desert monks who recommended eating once a day and limited themselves to two rolls (monophagy).

> Moses: "I know this was something often dealt with by our elders. They used to talk about the practices of self-restraint among many, those who lived solely on vegetables or herbs or fruit. They thought that what was better than this was the use of dry bread and they reckoned that the best measure was two small rolls, amounting in weight to barely one pound".[157]

As for the times, the different religious orders all adhere to more or less the same times of fasting. The longest period of fasting lasted from the Exaltation of the Cross (September 14) to Easter. In general fasting was suspended between Easter and Pentecost, the

---

[156] Cf. *Jeûne,* in *DS* 8 (1974) 1164-1179.
[157] Cassian, *Conferences,* 2.19; *CWS,* 77.

period in which the Risen One repeatedly met with his disciples. The scope, nature, and time of fasting were determined in line with the religious tradition in question.

> You shall observe the fast
> every day except Sunday
> from the feast of the Exaltation of the Holy Cross
> until Easter Sunday,

Fasting belongs to the category of things which "are clearly neutral, such as marriage, farming, riches, isolation in solitude, vigils, reading and pondering the holy books, and also fasting".[158] Fasting is a means. Just as a doctor, a goldsmith, or an artist uses his or her instruments, so the monk employs fasting.[159] To keep this instrument sharp we must "fairly and impartially keep indulgence and fasting in balance and correct excesses in either direction".[160] This is an insight born of discernment.

> There is an old saying: "Excesses meet. Too much fasting and too much eating come to the same end ... Often I have seen men who could not be snared by gluttony fall, nevertheless, through immoderate fasting and tumble in weakness into the very urge which they had overcome".[161]

Fasting aims at the purgation of the body and thereby at purity of heart.[162]

> Fasting is useful only if we adhere to the time, the quality, and the measure which is fitting, and not if we set the end of our hope on fasting itself. Our object has to be that through fasting we may attain to *purity of heart* and apostolic love.[163]

[158] Ibid., 21.4.
[159] Ibid., 21.15.
[160] Ibid., 21.22.
[161] Ibid., 2.16; *CWS*, 76.
[162] Ibid., 21.16; cf. 1.10.
[163] Ibid., 21.17.

Accordingly, purity of heart is not the final goal, only the practical objective. The final goal is Love, the sum of all virtues: the reception of the Other.[164]

> Purity of heart is subservient to the reception of God's attributes. Indeed, mercy, patience, love, or the other virtues in which there clearly lies an essential good must not be maintained for the sake of fasting, but fasting for the sake of those virtues. For our endeavor must be to gain those virtues which are really good by fasting and not make the practice of those virtues subordinate to fasting.[165]

Fasting is a form of physical self-evacuation aimed at receiving the Living One. In this respect fasting resembles the practices of maintaining silence, shaving one's head, rolling naked in the dirt, etc. They are all self-abasement rituals which take us into the sphere of death in the hope that the Living One himself may build us up.

> When humans are hungry they stretch themselves; when they stretch themselves, they expand; when they expand, they become receptive; when they are receptive they will in due time be filled.[166]

Within Christianity this process of transformation is depicted in the Messiah. The great period of fasting brings home to us the suffering and death of the Messiah while the great time of non-fasting between Easter and Pentecost serves to interiorize the joy of the Resurrection. For the same symbolic reason fasting is omitted on Sunday, the day of the Resurrection.

The ritualization of death and life, of dying and rising again in the Messiah, has a bottom limit emphatically indicated by the Rule:

> unless sickness or bodily weakness
> or some other good reason
> shall make it advisable
> to break the fast,
> for necessity knows no law.

---

[164] *Jeûne*, in: *DS* 8 (1974) 1172.
[165] Cassian, *Conferences*, 21.15.
[166] Augustine, *De utilitate ieiunii*, 1.1 in *CCL* 46.231.17-19.

Within the Jewish-Christian tradition self-abasement rituals are only permitted up to a point. Self-abasement may never injure a person or exceed that which is reasonable. To fast is to begin to realize, by the active interiorization of death, the overwhelming power of the Living One. This self-abasement relates to the reception of divine Life. Precisely because of this focus on Life it is forbidden to exploit sickness or bodily weakness as self-abasement. Fasting is an exercise! It is a means to be forged and used with discretion. That, too, is the reason why fasting may be suspended for good reason. Such a good reason may be hard work, intensive study, extreme pressures, fast bodily growth, loss of blood, etc. But also hospitality. Guests may not be burdened with the elementary exercises of a Carmelite, certainly not when it concerns forms of asceticism like fasting and abstinence. But whether the reason is sickness or weakness, or particular situations demanding hospitality, all these exceptions flow from the one juridical principle: necessity knows no law. When real necessity is present (sickness, weakness, excessive workloads, physical growth, hospitality) the law on fasting must yield.

Abstinence (XIII)

Abstinence is an ascetic practice which has been observed throughout the entire history of spirituality in all sorts of forms and gradations.[167] In the most rigorous form of abstinence practitioners abstained from meat, fish, eggs, milk, butter, cheese, oil and wine. They lived off bread, with a little salt, water, and some vegetables and fruit. In the less rigorous form people abstained from meat, gravy, fat, and all things made of blood. In fasting the issue was the *amount* of food, in abstinence the *kind* of food, one refrained from eating. One keeps away from the body foodstuffs of which one thinks that they exert a negative influence on the spiritual processes one aims for. In general it can be said that one stays way from all foodstuffs which have a highly arousing or stimulating effect.

[167] *Abstinence* in *DS* 1 (1937) 112-133.

The ancients proceeded on the assumption that there are certain human drives which directly arise, as it were, from the body, e.g. gluttony and sexual passion: "They spring up without any arousal of the mind". In this respect they contrast with anger or gloominess which arise from the mind and "can only be overcome by an effort of the mind". The desert monks made a twofold division between the two for the purpose of determining precisely the nature and method of curing certain passions. Passions immediately arising from the body "need a special treatment of bodily abstinence". The goal of this method of influencing the self is purity of heart, the practical objective of all elementary exercises: "Whence it is extremely useful for those who aspire to purity to begin by withdrawing from themselves the material which feeds these bodily passions".[168]

All religious communities are familiar with practices of abstinence, even though the material content and degrees of stringency are rather divergent. Some do not regard fowl as meat, others do. Some even exclude fish. Sometimes people abstain from all things which in one way or another spring from animal sperm, hence milk, cheese, and eggs.

As for the exceptions, sickness and weakness were accepted by all as grounds for dispensation; hospitality, too, prompted people to suspend the rule;[169] in the period after Easter meat was often allowed. Carmelites fit well within this general picture. Among them abstinence from meat is the rule. Exceptions are sickness and weakness. Innocent IV added still two more exceptions: while travelling as mendicant and being at sea. We will discuss these exceptions in a separate section (5.2.3.3).

You shall *always* abstain from meat, unless it be taken as a remedy for sickness or *excessive* weakness.	You shall abstain from meat, unless it be taken as a remedy for sickness or feebleness.

[168] Quotations from Cassian, *Conferences,* 5.4.
[169] Ibid., 8.1.

Abstinence is an elementary exercise, that is, a practice which is part of the infrastructure of the spiritual life. That is its power. For apart from this method of influencing the self, a method which frees us from that which is inauthentic and estranging, purity of heart cannot be attained. But it is its spiritual limit as well. Elementary exercises – however elementary – never achieve the status of virtue, something that must by definition be practiced uninterrupted. For that reason the subtle modification introduced by Innocent IV in 1247 is not a mitigation but an improvement. Albert's Rule (1206-14) read: "You are *always* to abstain from meat". Innocent IV dropped the "always". The reason is that he did not wish to contradict the addition about eating meat while travelling (about which later). The spiritual reason, however, is no less stringent: in the context of elementary exercises the word "always" is misplaced in principle. After all, by definition they can be, and sometimes have to be, suspended – Albert himself already indicated when (in cases of illness and feebleness!). For that matter, the Carmelites in 1247 wanted nothing more than to cancel abstinence altogether. Did not Elijah and the Old Testament Carmelites eat meat? The Dominican advisers objected that though Elijah and the Old Testament Carmelites ate meat, they did not drink wine! Since New Testament Carmelites *were* allowed to drink wine, they must abstain from eating meat.[170]

Abstinence is geared to the wellbeing of the soul. Harmful processes resulting simply from the admission of wrong substances into our body must be averted. The fact that this is the practical objective of this exercise is made clear in the bottom limit indicated by the Rule: "Unless it is taken as a remedy for sickness or weakness". Accordingly, abstinence is not aimed against a given substance *as such* but against its ingestion *into the body*. However, if at a certain time and in a certain quantity it proves to be curative in case of sickness or weakness, it may of course be taken. A little poison, when used as a remedy, may turn an illness around. Sometimes poison works very well! The exception shows with

---

[170] *Decem libri* 8.4.

splendid clarity the intent of the Rule: to be a remedy that wards off illness or weakness!

This intention again shows up in another minor modification in the text. Albert wrote (1206-14): "Unless it is taken as a remedy for sickness or excessive weakness". Innocence omits the adjective "excessive" (1247). At the time this relaxation of the rule was not unusual.[171] The Carmelites wanted to see this qualifier ("excessive") deleted altogether because they found it hard to tell what was "excessive" and some therefore allowed things to get out of hand.[172] But the modification also has a spiritual reason: it should by no means ever get out of hand! All abstinence aims after all at purity of heart. And it is muddied by all inauthentic and estranging processes, not only by addictions, which are directly opposed by abstinence, but by illnesses and processes of debilitation, whatever may be causing them. Abstinence aims at the wellbeing of the soul, specifically the decisive intermediate step: purification extended to the heart. Some substances are simultaneously arousing and addictive. With them one slips into a vicious circle, one that is harmful to the soul. If we do not intervene, we are permanently soiled by alien processes which imperceptibly creep into our bodily patterns through our culture.

Begging while travelling

The original Rule (of 1206-1214) contained two dispensations from abstinence: sickness and feebleness. The definitive version of the Rule (of 1247) added two more grounds for dispensation: to have to beg while travelling and to be on a journey by sea.

> And since you may have to beg more frequently
> while travelling, outside your own houses
> you may eat food cooked with meat,
> so as not to be a burden to your hosts.
> But meat may even be eaten at sea.

[171] Cicconetti, *Rule,* 198.
[172] *Decem libri* 8.4.

The second ground hardly needs explanation once we realize what the Carmelite order was like at the moment of the addition (1247). At that time the mother house and a few other convents were still located in Israel. But between 1238 and 1249 a number of houses had been founded in Europe as well: Cyprus, Messina, Hulne, Aylesford, Les Aygalades, and Pisa. To maintain mutual contact between such far-flung areas as Cyprus, Sicily, Southern England, the Provence and Italy, travel by boat was a necessity. Apparently sea travel was quite common, for the constitutions of 1281 stipulated that the prior or senior brother on board was allowed to break the silence during meals. This dispensation was probably based on two grounds: the rigor of the journey and the paucity of food options.

The first ground for dispensation derives from the *Constitutions* of the Dominicans. But there is a small difference. The Dominican *Constitutions* read: "In all our houses all our meals must be prepared without meat except in places where the sick are cared for. In order that our brothers may not be a burden to their hosts they may, when away from their houses, eat foods cooked with meat". Missing here are the words which so pointedly describe the changing situation of the Carmelites: "And because you must beg more often when you are travelling ...". But what does this clause mean? We will first briefly take note of the words, then look for the connection between them.

1. *Begging*.[173] Originally, receiving alms and gifts was integral to the life of hermits on Mount Carmel. Albert after all had advised them to live "from the things the Lord may have given you" (IX in the original version). In 1229 this was expressly confirmed by Gregory IX: "Inasmuch as you renounce all forms of accumulating possessions and may therefore claim the title of poverty, you may receive alms, which cannot be taxed by any outside authority". In 1245 this privilege was once more confirmed and even expanded by Innocent IV: from then on Carmelites were permitted to go out and beg. We must

---

[173] Cf. Cicconetti, *Rule,* 107-136 and 191-198.

remember that such questing was not limited to the later mendicants. From the beginning all hermits renounced property on principle. One could see them go around two-by-two, clothed in a recognizable habit, singing of the love of God and asking for alms *in natura*. Moreover, begging is only one facet of the mendicant way of life. Although mendicants owe their name to begging, more essential to them than begging was the fact of travel.

2. *Travelling.*[174] One might be tempted to think that mendicant monks travelled because they had to beg. Nothing is further from the truth. The opposite was the case: the main thing was travel. The monks travelled to give expression to their being disciples of Jesus. He himself after all went around preaching in Israel and had no fixed abode. Going around and preaching were inseparably bound up with each other. The brotherhood was part of this picture as well. Did not Jesus go around with his apostles in Israel? This is the so-called apostolic life. As early as the beginning of the eleventh century this form of life developed. Hermits exhibited a variant of it, and also the later mendicants were the result of it. To be on the road is a form of proclaiming the gospel. The mendicants in question did not seek remuneration, as was customary, but received alms in the form of food in exchange for preaching. Possessionlessness was an element within the ministry of preaching.

3. *More frequently.* Actually to what does the expression refer? Is it that the monks must beg more often if they travel more often, or vice versa? Is not begging always a necessity when they travel? Or must we look at the expression from another angle: more often than before when you lived on Mount Carmel; more often than when Albert's formula of life was still in force? Or is it a mistake to read the expression comparatively? For the moment we will leave these questions unanswered.

4. *Have to.* To *have to* beg: does this imply a command to beg? Or is it simply a statement of fact? A self-evident or inevitable

---

[174] Ibid., 193-198.

thing? Just what kind of necessity are we talking about when we speak of the necessity of begging? "To have to" (*oportet*) implies that this activity flows from a principle; it is logical.[175] Begging is logically connected with travel. When as brothers they went around preaching, the inevitable concomitant was begging. Begging is not just a factual activity; it is above all a way of acting that is intrinsically bound up with itinerant preaching in evangelical poverty. Now then, because this mendicant manner of life was in fact approved by implication in the new version of the Rule of 1247, Carmelites would automatically travel more often, the logical implication being that they would have to beg more often as well. This implies that from that time on they would *more often* have occasion to eat their meals in the homes of others. Now then, when they were away from their own houses and eating in the homes of their hosts, they were not allowed to be a burden to them. They must accommodate themselves to what was set before them, even if it was foods cooked with meat.

The two grounds for dispensation – being guests or on a sea journey – depict clearly the intent and limits of abstinence. Abstinence is a form of influencing the self, more precisely: of physically distinguishing oneself. One keeps away from one's body those materials of which one thinks that they adversely affect the spiritual way. This method of exerting influence is not intended for others. Carmelites do not wish to be a burden to their hosts. They accommodate themselves to the people whose guests they are. The boundary line of their practice, therefore, is the host! To be a mendicant traveller is to be a guest in the home of another. By abstinence we set ourselves apart. The former (influencing the self) posits a boundary for the second (the role of guest). That is inherently logical. All elementary exercises aim at the purity of heart that is receptively oriented to the other. Now then: being a mendicant guest in the home of another *immediately* takes us to receptivity to the other. In actual deed we practice not burdening

---

[175] Cf. *Oxford Latin Dictionary*, Oxford 1976, 1254-1255.

the other with our methods of influencing the self. However good these methods may be, vis-à-vis exercises which more directly lead us to our practical objective, they must yield.

The same motivation was operative in the second ground for dispensation: sea travel. In any case one of the things it implied was spending a considerable length of time within a limited space with a limited group of people and a limited supply of food-stuffs. A journey at sea as such already forces us to orient ourselves to others, take account of others' feelings and interests, and to be positively tolerant toward the other. A sea journey is an elementary exercise which directly leads to the goal to which abstinence attempts to take us indirectly: to become receptive to the Other.

If now we look back at the chapters on fasting and abstinence we can do that from two angles: from the angle of the exception and from the angle of what is said about it positively.

1. Viewing them from the angle of the exceptions one is struck by the number of grounds given for the suspension of fasting and abstinence. It is worth our while to briefly review them. (1) As day of the Resurrection, Sunday is exempted from fasting. (2) As the time of the Resurrection, the post-Easter time is exempted as well. (3) Sickness or weakness set a limit to fasting. (4) A lawful reason sets a limit to fasting. (5) Abstinence is limited by sickness or weakness. (6) Necessary begging limits abstinence because the host may not be burdened. (7) Abstinence is suspended on a sea journey: meals spoil quickly; there is little choice; and we are guests on board.

These restrictions have in common a single basic motive: *Necessity* overrides the law. The law of fasting ends where necessity begins. Necessity is that which is unavoidable, inescapable, and therefore urgent.[176] Necessity is very clear in the case of physical illness or feebleness (nos. 3 and 5). Logical necessity is clear in the

---

[176] The Latin *necesse* comes from *necedere:* that which cannot be avoided (Oxford Latin Dictionary, 1164-1165).

case of *having to* beg (which arises naturally from the work of an itinerant preacher (no. 6). A similar logical necessity is present in a lawful reason (no. 4): the necessity of dispensation has to be demonstrated. Also the necessity inherent in a sea journey (no. 7) is self-evident: the limitations of life aboard a ship are inescapable the moment one has embarked. The necessity implicit in the regular exceptions – Sundays and the Easter period (nos. 1 and 2) – seems harder to demonstrate. But we get a little closer to it when reading how the monks in the Egyptian wilderness "watched with great care to make sure that no one ventured to fast" in the fifty days after Easter.[177] Why? Out of respect for the core mystery of the faith: the Resurrection. "During these days we observe in all things the same festive character as on Sunday – a day on which, as the Fathers have taught us, we may not fast, nor bow our knees, out of reverence for the Lord's Resurrection".[178]

The necessity which overrides the rule teaches us that fasting is *contingent,* i.e. does not have an independent value of its own.

> The properties by which one recognizes a thing that is good in itself cannot possibly be attributed to fasting, it is not good of itself, nor *necessary* for its own sake, for it is rightly used as a means of gaining purity of heart and body.[179]

The same necessity further teaches us the *relativity,* i.e. the relatedness to what is absolute: life. Life is that which is preeminently necessary: resurrection, healing, a safe arrival at home.

Necessity, finally, suggests an atmosphere of freedom, for if fasting and abstinence do not belong to the sphere of necessity they belong to that of freedom. They are freely chosen by craftsmen with a view to practicing their craft.[180]

2. By pondering the exceptions we have implicitly explored the space within which fasting and abstinence fulfil their role. What is

[177] Cassian, *Conferences,* 21.11.
[178] Ibid., 21.20.
[179] Ibid., 21.16.
[180] Ibid., 21.15.

their regular function? We have repeatedly remarked earlier that both fasting and abstinence are designed to gain purity of heart as their practical objective. Both of them are methods of physically influencing one's self with a view to breaking out of the circle of obsession and passion. This breakthrough further aims to create openness and receptivity for the attributes with which God clothes us: the armor of God. The difference between the two physical exercises confirms their common practical objective. Fasting is a movement of self-abasement aimed at the reception of Life. Abstinence is a form of self-distinction aimed at one's sanctification by the Holy One. In the chapter on the armor of God both aspects will resonate along with the chastity and sanctification of our thoughts. The difference confirms the agreement between them: both are designed to let the Living and Holy One do his work in us unhindered.

5.2.4 Connections

The chapters VII-XIII are inherently connected by the fact that they all deal with the elementary exercises – something that is clearly evident from the language used in the Rule. These elementary exercises are an appropriation of the religious provisions on the physical level,[181] a process of transformation which takes place in time and whose practical objective is purity of heart. We will now explain this point by point.

1. One can tell that chapters VII-XIII deal with the elementary exercises from two language signals. The first such signal is the use of certain verbs. These chapters center around verbs which, from a traditional perspective, point in the direction of elementary exercises: remaining, meditating, keeping vigil, praying (VII), saying the Psalms, saying the Our Father, praying the canonical hours (VIII), having all things in common (IX),

---

[181] It is not correct to view chapters VII-XIII as the "living foundations of the brotherhood" (B. Secondin, *What is the heart of the Rule?* 110). They are not foundations but exercises. And the brotherhood is not central but the tension-filled quadrangle of "community-place-cell-person".

coming together, celebrating the Eucharist (X), discuss, observe, correct (XI), fast (XII), abstain (XIII). These verbs together evoke the semantic field of the "bodily exercises".

The second language signal corroborates this fact. Typical for the "bodily exercises" is their relativization. Physical exercises can be omitted and are fenced in by exceptions, restrictions and alternatives. The brothers must remain in their cell *unless* occupied by other duties (VII); they must fast *unless* sickness or physical weakness prevents it (XII); eating meat is prohibited *unless* it is taken as a remedy (XIII); fasting is to be practiced every day *except* Sundays (XII); saying the Psalms is the rule *but* those who cannot read pray Our Fathers (VIII); goods are distributed *according to* everyone's need (IX); an oratory should be constructed in the midst of the cells *as conveniently as possible*; the Eucharist is celebrated every day *where this can be done conveniently* (X); an extra chapter is conducted *if necessary* (XI); faults and excesses are discussed *if any are found* (XI). All these exceptions, alternatives, and adaptations are indications of a genre, not expressions of a flexible mindset. They point to the genre of "bodily exercises", as the detailed exposition of these chapters showed.

2. These elementary exercises aim at *transformation* in the literal sense of the word: the old form is decoded and the new form is practiced. Remaining in the cell creates an interior which is closed to demonic destruction and open to the divine presence (VII); by reciting Scripture, saying the prayers and saying the psalms, we abandon our old language forms and put on the language form that is directed toward God (VII-VIII); the transformation of the brothers into communal human beings takes place as everyone holds all things in common, everyone comes to the center of the oratory and everyone participates in the weekly discussion (IX-XI); fasting and abstinence make clear that we are talking about transformations on the bodily level.

3. Striking is the use of time indications in chapters VII-XIII: each one *remains* in his cell, meditating *day and night* (VII)

and praying at appointed *hours* (VIII); *every day, early in the morning,* everyone attends the Eucharist (X); *every Sunday* a chapter is held (XI); *every day* except in the *Easter period* there is fasting (XII); throughout the *whole year* abstinence is in force (XIII). The "bodily exercises" have their *time.* In the previous section (I-VI) indications of *place* predominated. That makes sense: then the elements of the transformational *model* were introduced; now the first steps of the transformational *process* are indicated.

4. The practical objective of the elementary exercises is *purity of heart.* Of this objective chapters VII-XIII give us the following picture. The reference here is, first of all, to a heart, i.e. an interior that is being transformed by Scripture, the psalms, the Our Father, and the prayers. This interior runs parallel to the interior of the cell. Next: this heart must be transformed. It must be opened up as it were from without. Our corporeality has to be laid open down to the level of the heart by Scripture and the prayers. This open space must be purified: that which is excessive is kept out and that which alienates is repelled. Third: the heart is directed *outward*: it keeps vigil in prayer; it seeks out the center of the community; it reaches out from within a sense of deprivation. Finally: the heart is made *receptive* to being clothed with God's attributes (XIV). The *Book of the First Monks* in all simplicity formulates this practical objective as follows:

> That a love may freely emerge so fervent and intense and yet so peaceful and wholly uniting your heart with mine – unhindered – that your heart feels nothing within itself that runs counter to or hinders my heart but rests, undisturbed, completely in my love.[182]

If we now take the two sections we have up until now explained and put them side by side we get the following picture.

---

[182] *Decem libri* 1.7.

PROVISIONS

	I	II	III	IV	V	VI
Community	Community structure: prior and brothers	Choice of place by prior and brothers	Cell assignment by prior and brothers	Eating and listening communally	Permission of the prior	Cell of the prior
Place		Fitting place		Common refectory		Entrance to the place
Cell		A separate cell for each brother individually		No exchange of cells		
Person	Everyone chooses and obeys				No one	

EXERCISES

	VII	VIII	IX	X	XI	XII
Community		Praying the hours	Having all things in common	Celebrating the Eucharist; coming together in the midst	Communal discussion	
Place		Fitting place		Common refectory		Entrance of the place
Cell	Remaining in the cell					
Person	Scripture reading; praying; keeping vigil; being occupied	Saying the psalms; praying the Our Father				Eating less; emptying the body Eating differently; purging the body

Purity of heart

5.3 Being Clothed with God's Attributes (XIV)

The chapter on the armor of God (XIV), is different from the preceding chapters, but besides the contrasts between them there are lines of continuity as well.

1. *Contrasts.* The *first* contrast concerns content. Up until now the Rule dealt with the exercise of basic provisions. That is a setting in which the figurative language of cinctures, breastplates, shields, helmets, and swords does not fit. The prior does not dispense helmets, cinctures or breastplates. And at the beginning of the day I cannot say to myself: "Let me put on the breastplate of justice a minute". The *second* contrast is literary. A new beginning is made that is marked by the contrasting opening phrase: "*However* because ...". Albert evoked such a contrast only once before: when he made the transition from the religious life in general *(exordium)* to the Carmelite life in particular *(narratio)*: "*However,* because ...". A *third* contrast emerges in the copious use of Scripture. This profusion arises in part from the biblical imagery of the armor of God but also from the subject to which the imagery applies: being clothed with the attributes of God. These three contrasts flow from a single source: we are no longer dealing with the exercise of provisions but with the practice of virtues. The provisions given (I-VI) and observed (VII-XIII) until now are obviously no match for the trials, persecution and annihilations threatening us from the world of demonic powers.[183] Only being clothed with God's attributes can keep us standing firmly in the struggle.

The transition from provision to virtue becomes visible in yet a *fourth* contrast: in the chapter on the armor of God all the relativizations which up until now were so characteristic for the Carmelite form of life are missing. We no longer encounter such words as suitable, convenient, unless, those who do not know, to each according to his need, with regard to, where this

---

[183] Cf. Cassian, *Conferences*, 1 and 21.16-17.

is needed, etc. On the contrary: there are no exceptions, no modalities whatever. In the meantime we have learned from Cassian that we are *therefore* now dealing with a principal good as opposed to such instrumental goods as fasting, Scripture reading, staying in the cell, etc. From now on we are dealing with virtues, and virtues allow for no exceptions, modifications, time provisions, and the like.

2. *Lines of continuity.* A first such line is that both in the case of the provisions and in the case of the virtues we are dealing with exercises. The provisions are appropriated in the so-called bodily exercises (VII-XIII); the virtues by the effort and extreme care with which one puts them on. A distinct line of continuity is present in the chapters on fasting and abstinence: in the case of fasting and abstinence there is a strong focus on the body. In the chapter on the armor of God this physical aura is evoked by words like loins, chest, head, and hand, while here these words, evoked as they are by the imagery of armor of God, do not refer to parts of the human body, they still jointly evoke corporeality as the sphere in which the life of virtue must incarnate itself as well. There is a third line of continuity: the chapter on the armor of God begins with the statement that human life on earth is a trial. Trials – like fasting and abstinence! – are designed to effect purity of heart. Now then, the armor of God begins with chastity and holy thoughts, both of which follow naturally from purity of heart.

What is the meaning of these contrasts and lines of continuity? Answer: they make visible an important spiritual junction in the Rule. The preceding chapters VII-XIII describe how the basic givens of spirituality – staying in the cell, meditating on Scripture, coming together in the midst, etc. – can be internalized. We also saw that these bodily exercises are all aimed at purity of heart as their practical objective. This purity of heart in turn is aimed at the reception of the virtues, God's powers for human beings. Now then, the reception of God's attributes, that is: putting on the whole armor of God, is precisely what is being discussed in chapter XIV. Given this development the transformational process now lays hold of a further layer: the foundations of the psychic structures. It goes without saying that with this development the deeper forms of resistance and the more dangerous pitfalls come into play as well.

5.3.1. The motif of the armor of God

The armor of God is a widespread motif.[184] We will explore this motif by taking four snapshots. The first is the most ancient: the representation of God as warrior. Then we will take a great leap in time: the Qumran community, armed by God, fights an eschatological war with Belial. Then follows the church of Ephesus which in its own way fights against demonic powers. Its spiritual armor is the immediate background of the Rule. Finally we will look at the desert monk fighting his solitary battles against diabolical subversions.

God fights for his people

The most ancient song traditions in Israel represent God as the warrior who liberates his people from oppressive forces (Ex. 15:2-5; cf. Judg. 4:23). God is the inspiration of his people in time of military conflict.[185] Within these traditions it is not at all strange to represent God as archer. "He *shot* Egypt into the sea" (Ex. 15:20-21).[186] In the course of Israel's history, this basic feature of God's liberating pathos in the midst of his people, like a magnet, attracted a variety of images. Especially within the prophetic tradition the notion developed that God's struggle is essentially a contest among the gods in which the non-Israelite

[184] J. Gnilka, *Der Epheserbrief,* Freiburg-Basel-Wien 1971, 309-314.

[185] For examples of and literature about, this ancient liberation spirituality, cf. K. Waaijman, *Betekenis van de Naam Jahwe,* Kampen 1984, 65-69 and 85-86.

[186] The song of Miriam is generally viewed as part of the most ancient song material of Israel. In this song God is represented as archer, hunter, or slinger, in any case as an armed warrior. On this, see K. Waaijman, *Psalmen over de uittocht,* Kampen 1984, 9-17.

deities are definitively defeated.[187] "God put on justice like a *breast-plate,* and a *helmet of salvation* on his head; he clothed himself in the garments of vengeance, and wrapped himself in fury as in a mantle" (Isa. 59:17). Fighting for his people he makes known that he alone is God.

> Admit then that I, I alone, am he,
> there is no Power besides me ...
> I will sharpen my flashing *sword,*
> my hand lays hold on judgment.
> With vengeance I will repay my adversaries
> and requite those who hate me.
> I will make my *arrows* drunk with blood
> and my *sword* shall gorge itself with flesh (Deut. 32:39-42).

Shortly before the exile the Mighty One is pictured as a gigantic warrior who in a single movement reconquers all of Israel (Psalm 60).[188] In this connection Ephraim is his *helmet* and Judah his *scepter* (Ps. 60:9). As champion of Israel's freedom we see God wearing all parts of a soldier's armor: helmet and breastplate, sword and soldier's boot, arrow and javelin, cincture and shield (Is. 34:5-6; cf. Jer. 12:12). This imagery remains fruitful right into the late Wisdom literature.

> He shall take his zeal for *armor*
> and he shall *arm* creation to punish the enemy;
> He shall don justice for a *breastplate*
> and shall wear sure judgment for a *helmet;*
> He shall take invincible holiness as a *shield*
> and whet his relentless anger for a *sword,*
> And the universe shall war with him against the foolhardy.
> Well-aimed *shafts* of lightnings shoot downward,
> and from the clouds as from a well-drawn *bow* shall leap to the mark;
> and as from his *sling* heavy hailstones shall be hurled (Wisdom 5:17-22).

---

[187] On this see: "the contest between the gods" on Mount Carmel, won unambiguously by God, so unambiguously even that in retrospect it proves not to have been a contest! For this, see K. Waaijman, *De profeet Elia,* Nijmegen 1985, 43-52.

[188] Cf. K. Waaijman, *Psalmen vanuit de ballingschap,* Kampen 1986, 84.

From these traditions we learn that the armor of God is the armor
God himself wears. The attitudes recommended by the Rule are
the attributes of God. Chastity, holy thoughts, justice, faith,
hope and the Word are all qualities with which God defends
himself. He does this, not in a sheltered part of the world, but
in the actual field of religious-political forces of a specific historical situation. This last fact will certainly have resonated for
the Carmelites who lived, as we recall, in a context which was
extremely combative. Living in allegiance to Jesus and wearing the
armor of God certainly meant a specific religious-political position as well: fighting as vassal under the command of the Lord,
for the liberation or protection of the holy places, the patrimony
of the Lord.

Humans fighting God's endtime battle

The Qumran community, consisting of priests, levites, and other
pious folk belonging to the temple faithful, seceded from it around
130 B.C. It withdrew to the desert by the Dead Sea to prepare
itself for the end that was near. Then the sons of light would fight
the final battle against the sons of darkness. The latter would be
led by the diabolical Belial who, with countless ruses,[189] would lure
the pious to destruction. This war between the sons of light and
the sons of darkness is recounted in the so-called *War Scroll*.[190]
The account tells of an eschatological battle in which ancient
holy-war themes are incorporated. This eschatological war, realis-
tically represented, was staged with liturgical texts, prayers, hymns
and priestly invocations: the cultic community understood itself
as an eschatological army in battle array. Hierarchical ordinances,
faithful adherence to the Torah and extreme purity rituals together
made up the fortified sanctuary which would in the end stand
firm against Satan.

---

[189] See 1 QH II, 16; IV, 13-14.
[190] *The Scroll of the War of the Sons of Light Against the Sons of Darkness,* tr. by
Batya and Chaim Rabin, Oxford 1962, 282-286.

When the [priests and levites and all men of the Serekh] are on the spot, they shall array themselves into seven formations, one behind the other ... After these, three skirmishing battalions shall go forth and take up position between the lines. The first battalion shall hurl into the enemy line seven battle darts. On the blade of the *first* dart they shall write: Flash of a lance to the might of God, on the second weapon they shall write: Sparks of blood to fell the slain by the anger of God, on the third dart they shall write: Glitter of a sword devouring the sinful slain by the judgment of God. Each of these shall throw seven times and then return to their position. After these, two skirmishing battalions shall go forth and take up position between the lines, the first battalion being armed with lance and shield and the second with shield and sword to slay through the judgment of God and to vanquish the line of the enemy by God's might, to exact retribution for their wickedness upon all nations of vanity, and the kingdom shall be of the God of Israel, and He shall do valiant deeds through the saints of His people.[191]

From Qumran we learn specifically that the armor of God functions within an eschatological situation, that is to say, a situation of being tested to the limit. The demonic schemes are extremely dangerous. The end time in which the community now finds itself is a time of purification and testing in which there occurs a "separation of spirits": truth and falsehood, light and darkness go their separate ways.[192]

The church of Ephesus

The immediate background of the Rule is the Letter to the Ephesians. The writer of this letter seeks to bring home to his community that it is involved in a life-and-death struggle with superhuman powers (Eph. 6:11-13) and that it must therefore put on the panoply of the heavily-armed warrior (Eph. 6:14-17).[193] First the enemy is depicted: not mortals but superterrestrial powers

---

[191] 1 QM VI, 16-VII, 6.
[192] *Die Text aus Qumran,* Darmstadt 1986[4], Einführung XV.
[193] See Gnilka, *Der Epheserbrief,* 303-319.

headed by the devil (6:11). Against these only the armor of God can offer protection.

> Finally, draw your strength from the Lord and from his mighty power. Put on the armor of God so that you may be able to stand firm against the tactics of the devil. For our struggle is not with flesh and blood but with the principalities, with the powers, with the world rulers of this present darkness, with the evil spirits in the heavens. Therefore, put on the armor of God, that you may be able to resist on the evil day and, having done everything, to hold your ground. So stand fast with your loins girded in truth, clothed with justice as a breastplate, and your feet shod in readiness for the gospel of peace. In all circumstances hold faith as a shield, to quench all [the] flaming arrows of the evil one. And take the helmet of salvation and the sword of the Spirit, which is the word of God. With all prayer and supplication, pray at every opportunity in the Spirit. To that end, be watchful with all perseverance and supplication for all the saints (Eph. 6:10-18).

It is striking that in this passage the armor is expressly conceived in metaphorical terms. As a result all the emphasis lies on the spiritual armor which graphically depicts the messianic system of values. And this system of values, in contrast to the warlike imagery, is irenic in nature. The girded loins evoke watchfulness rather than militancy. "Gird your loins and light your lamps. Be like servants who await their master's return" (Luke 12:35-36). Defensive weapons (cincture, breastplate, shield, helmet) predominate. Non-military components like the cincture and the shoes take up more than their share of space. All this is related to the fact that concealed behind the heavily-armed soldier there is an evangelist whose feet are shod to prepare him to proclaim the gospel of peace throughout the world: "How beautiful upon the mountains are the feet of the messenger who announces *peace* and brings *good news*" (Is. 52:7)!

In the Letter to the Ephesians the divine attributes with which God clothes humans with a view to life-and-death trials have two functions.

1. In the armor referred to, God gives himself to humanity in order to *build human beings up inwardly.* This motif is known

to us from the Psalms: "But you, Lord, are a shield around me, my weightiness" (Ps. 3:4; cf. Ps. 5:13; Deut. 33:29). God is the space in which the core of my personhood can shine. God is not only a shield-around-me but my strength-within-me: "My God, my rock of refuge, my shield" (Ps. 18:3). God's protection permeates David down to his very essence (Ps. 18:26-27). Abraham, too, experienced this: "Be not afraid, Abram, I am your *shield*" (Gen. 15:1). It is not strange, therefore, that this mystical-messianic[194] meaning resonates in Pauline spirituality as well (Col. 3:12-14). The armor of God is God's own power: "The weapons of our warfare are not weak; they are charged with divine power, able to destroy strongholds" (2 Cor. 10:4). We are clothed with divine power to be strong in the struggle for *life*. With this we have arrived at the second point.

2. God equips us with his attributes *with a view to battle*. In mythology this is a familiar motif: Hephaistos, in the war against the Trojans, forged a new shield for Achilles;[195] In Ugarit Kothar-en-Hasis made a bow for Aqhat.[196] In biblical spirituality we see the same phenomenon:

> By you I can crush a troop,
> by my God I can leap over a wall.
> This God – his way is solid,
> the promise of the Lord proves true.
> He is a *shield* for all who take
> refuge in him (Ps. 18:29-31).

The armor which is our essence, by its own inner propulsion, becomes an active force in our life. Paul has in mind this function of our armor as well. To be able to withstand eschatological ruin

---

[194] Cf. F. Beare, *The Epistle to the Ephesians,* New York-Nashville 1953, 597-749; J. Gnilka – incorrectly in my opinion – rules out this nuance: "A 'mystical' interpretation according to which the warrior must fight with the armor of God, i.e. with the armor God himself uses when he goes out to battle his enemies, is to be rejected" (J. Gnilka, *Der Epheserbrief,* 305); at the same time Gnilka states "that it is God who furnishes the weapons and hence the ability to fight" (*Ibid.*)

[195] *Ilias,* 18.478-480.

[196] II Aqhat 5.12-13.

God has armed us with "the *breastplate* of confidence and love and the *helmet* of the hope of salvation" (1 Thess. 5:8). It is clear: to put on the armor of God is to be clothed with God's power and might (Eph. 6:10) to be able to stand firm against (Eph. 6:11, 13) the anti-divine powers of evil (Eph. 6:12-13).

The desert monk

Cassian devotes an entire section to "the kinds of weapons and their characteristics with which, if we so desire, we can fight the Lord's battles".[197]

> *Take the shield of faith,* [says the apostle], *with which you are able to quench all the fiery darts of the evil one.* Faith then is that which intercepts the flaming darts of lust, and destroys them by the fear of future judgment, and belief in the heavenly kingdom. *And the breastplate,* he says, *of charity.* This indeed is that which going round the vital parts of the breast and protecting what is exposed to the deadly wounds of swelling thoughts, keeps off the blows opposed to it, and does not allow the darts of the devil to penetrate to our inner person. For it "endures all things, suffers all things, bears all things". *And for a helmet the hope of salvation.* The helmet is what protects the head. As then Christ is our head, we ought always in all temptations and persecutions to protect it with the hope of future good things to come, and especially to keep faith in Him whole and undefiled. For it is possible for one who has lost other parts of the body, weak as that person may be, still to survive: but even a short time of living is extended to no one without a head. "And *the sword of the Spirit* which is the word of God". For it "is sharper than any two-edged sword, and piercing even to the dividing of soul and spirit, and of the joints and marrow, and is a discerner of the thoughts and intents of the heart": as it divides and cuts off whatever carnal and earthly things it may find in us. And whosoever is protected by these arms will ever be defended from the weapons and ravages of the foes, and will not be led away bound in the chains of spoilers, a captive and a prisoner, to the hostile land of vain thoughts.[198]

---

[197] Cassian, *Conferences* 7.5; *NPNF,* 364.
[198] Ibid.

The setting of the monastic life bestows a color of its own on the armor of God. In the previous "snapshots" we saw depicted entire communities: God fighting in the midst of the people, the community of Qumran positioned like an army in battle array and the church of Ephesus bringing the gospel in the last days. In Cassian we see depicted the solitary warrior. We must not, however, exaggerate this point. This solitary warrior was aware of being part of an invisible army. All of life in the desert, for that matter, was a concentrated protest against Christianity's assimilation to the state following the Constantinian turning point.[199] In reality any military battle is fought out in person-to-person combat!

The armor as spiritual model

The central feature of the armor of God is its fundamentally *polemical* character, which does not rule out that the battle is fought with irenic means. At the heart of this polemic is a life-and-death struggle between the power of evil which systematically destroys life and the power of God which systematically extends an invitation to life in God. This polarity has many faces (light-darkness; God-devil; God-idols; salvation-demonism; redemption-lostness; etc.) and several layers (social, political, religious, cultural), but at bottom it is one-and-the-same polemic: the systematics of death versus the systematics of life.

If we turn to the pole of evil, we see the unreality of a power which, in all sorts of ways but never openly, penetrates into human life and society down to the most intimate places of the human spirit. This unreality alternatively assumes divine, human, and natural traits but these are never more than a facade. Legitimations claiming the highest authority of God are legion and hard to see through. This unreality manifests itself invariably – and not without reason – in eschatological and apocalyptic contexts, for its influence is extremely great, unlimited in its range, and a nightmare for those who must endure it.

[199] O. Stegginck, *Spiritualiteit was nooit zonder tijdgeest,* in: *Speling* 37 (1985) nr. 1, 75-76.

The armor of God is a layered phenomenon. Fundamentally it denotes the armor which God himself wears. The God of Israel opposes the systematics of death and systematically promotes life. This is his Name. God gives this armor to humanity so that we can resist the system of death. In giving his armor God is basically giving not just an attribute but himself. As a result of this mystical self-communication of God we are able to resist evil.

5.3.2. Three reasons for putting on the armor of God

Albert offers three interrelated reasons for putting on the armor of God. The first is:

> However because human life on earth is a trial.

This motif comes from the book of Job. The whole of human life is one unbroken time of trial. This is so, in the first place, because we experience over and over that we do not control this life (Job 7:14). Second, because this life is marked by illness and transience (Job 7:5-10). Finally, because the Infinite constantly disturbs us (Job 7:11-12). Wise people know that human life on earth is a trial. For Christians all trials come together in the three temptations of Jesus in the wilderness. By way of the desert fathers this motif became a central given in spirituality.[200] Just what is meant by being tried? In light of biblical spirituality it has two aspects: a theoretical and a practical.[201]

The *theoretical* aspect: one who would become a "person of God" must realize how things are with us. We will have to learn to look inward[202] to fathom our own conduct down to what it really is (Lam. 3:40; cf. Job 5:27). We must also learn to look

---

[200] For a survey see: *Tentation* in *DS* 15 (1990) 193-251.

[201] For an analysis, see K. Waaijman, *Temptation* in *Journal of Empirical Theology* 5 (1992), no 2. 86-94.

[202] Scripture calls this *fathoming* (chqr): checking in depth beneath the surface; seeing through the facade; plumbing the depths (see Theologisches Wörterbuch zum Alten Testament (herafter *TWAT*) III, 157-160; and Theologisches Handwörterbuch zum Alten Testament (hereafter *THAT* I, 274).)

outward: toward the ultimate destiny for which we have been
made[203] by the One "who tests heart and mind" (Jer. 11:20; 12:3;
17:10; 20:12) in keeping with the divine intention with us. Both
perspectives – inward and outward – are related to who we are
as creatures: created in God's image and for God's likeness. The
experience of being tried is designed to bring out the image of
God in us in order that our lives may increasingly become more
like him.

Being tried also has a *practical* aspect: to shift our boundaries
by experience. It has an inward dimension: a "person of God" lets
God have his way with us so that the possibilities and limits of
our trust may be revealed through experience.[204] For this reason
these trials or testings take place in boundary situations (Gen.
22:14; Ex. 17:1-7; Wisdom 3:5; 11:9-10; Sir 2:1-18; 39:4). God
moves into my life for the purpose of determining by experience
the width and scope of my heart. But it also has an outward
dimension: likeness to God draws me out of myself.[205] My final
destiny in relation to God leads me away from myself (Prov. 1:1-
4; Ps. 19:8; Prov. 8:21).

The theoretical and practical testings are connected. I learn to
examine myself in depth *as* I am being expanded. I learn to assess
myself *as* I am being lured away in God's love. Theoretically as
well as practically *that* takes place with me *which* is the end of it
all: the actual emergence in me of the image of God. The silver of
my existence is refined out of the mixed, ambivalent and muddy
materials which mark my ordinary daily life.[206] It is God who as

[203] Scripture calls this *testing* (bchn): to illumine and assess a condition in
light of its final destination (see *THAT* I, 272-275).

[204] Scripture calls this *trying* (nsh): to explore the possibilities and limits of a
thing or person by experience (*TWAT* V, 473-487; *THAT* II, 69-71).

[205] Scripture calls this *luring* (pth) in a positive sense (*THAT* II, 495-498;
TWAT, VI, 820-831; cf. *HAL* (Hebräisches und Aramäisches Lexikon zum Alten
Testament I-II) 925-926 and 929).

[206] Scripture calls this *smelting* (tsrf): precious metal is separated under high
temperatures from other materials and purified of foreign alloys (*THAT* I, 273;
TWAT VI, 1133-1138).

the crucible (cf. Pr. 17:3) smelts out in utter purity the image of God which lies concealed in me.

and all who wish to live devotedly in Christ suffer persecution,

The second reason for putting on the armor of God comes from the Second Letter to Timothy. "In the last days distressing times will come" (2 Tim. 3:1), "in which people will brutalize each other" (2 Tim. 3:1-5). These people do not only exist outside the Christian communities, however, but also inside the circles of the evangelists themselves (2 Tim. 3:6-9). Timothy, by contrast, remained faithful to Paul in all respects, specifically during times of persecution. Paul adds: "Indeed, all who want to live a devoted life in Christ Jesus will be persecuted" (2 Tim. 3:10-13). Paul then urges Timothy to remain true to what he learned by adhering to the holy Scriptures (2 Tim. 3:14-17).

The persecutions to which Paul refers are familiar to us from various testimonies of the early Christian communities.[207] They refer to persecutions by Jewish and Roman authorities for religious reasons, interpreted by Christians in the context of the last days: "But before all this occurs they will arrest you and persecute you; they will hand you over to synagogues and prisons, and you will be brought before kings and governors because of my name" (Lk. 21:12). The early Christian communities saw these persecutions as "testings" [to be expected] in the messianic faith (Matt. 13:21; Mark 4:17; cf. 2 Thess. 1:4). Persecutions are testings which permit the power of the messiah to manifest itself: "Therefore I am content with weaknesses, insults, hardships, persecutions, and calamities for the sake of Christ" (2 Cor. 12:10). The reality of being in Christ is brought to light as it were through persecution; union with the Messiah is realized more deeply through the crucible of suffering: "Who will separate us from the love of Christ? Will hardship, or distress, or persecution, or famine, or nakedness, or peril, or sword?" (Rom. 8:35).

[207] See Matt. 5:10-12; 10:23, 30; Lk. 11:49; 21:12; Rom. 12:14; 1 Cor. 4:12; 15:9; Acts 8:1; 13:50, etc.

Within the Rule Paul's statement acquires a meaning of its own which can best be made visible by comparing it with the motif from Job.

| Human life on earth is a trial (Job 7:1) | All who wish to live devotedly in Christ must suffer persecution (2 Tim. 3:12) |

Comparing the two we see both similarity and difference at three points.

1. The first point concerns the repetition of the word "life" (*vita ... vivere*). There is a verbal similarity but as a result of the difference in context there is also dissimilarity. For in Job – and this is true of the whole of the spirituality of wisdom – the reference is to life from the cradle to the grave. But in Paul the reference is to a devoted life. By juxtaposing the two the Rule creates tension between human life *as such* and the human life that is shaped by *devotion*.[208] In doing this the Rule addresses two layers in our life: the *natural* existence given us at birth and taken away from us at death, and the *cultured* life we can choose by transforming our existence into a life that is full of respect and fidelity to duty. The Rule considers the armor of God important for *both* levels. One gets the impression it might like to take us from the one way of life to the other!

2. The second point confirms the above and makes it concrete. Human existence as such is realized on earth, the devoted life is realized in Christ. To the wise the earth is the element in which we live our life: we are taken from the earth (Gen. 2:7)

---

[208] The Greek *eusebeia*, like the Latin *pietas*, denotes devotion toward relatives and gods. *Sebo* means to honor, worship, reverence. The devotion is to a shrinking sense of awe before men and gods. *Sebas*, accordingly, means respect, awe, diffidence. This usage was taken over in the early Christian writings (see *sebadzemai, sebasme, sebasmios, sebo* and *eusebeia, eusebeo, eusebès, eusebos,* in W. Bauer, *Griechisch-Deutsches Wörterbuch zu den Schriften des Neuen Testaments und der übrigen urchristlichen Literatur,* Giessen 1928, 508-509 and 1197-1198) and circles around the semantic field of *being reverent, pious, godly, honoring,* something conveyed by the Latin *pius/pietas* in the Vulgate.

and return to it (Gen. 3:23). The culture of devotion, by contrast, permeates life in Christ. This is a typically Pauline expression. Paul uses the expression numerous times[209] to indicate that the Messiah is his element. In baptism we are literally incorporated (Rom. 12:5; Gal. 3:28) in the Messiah (Rom. 6:3; cf. Acts 2:38; 10:48; Gal. 3:27). From now on, says Paul, "I live to God in Jesus the Messiah" (Rom. 6:11; 6:23; 8:2; Gal. 2:17). "Our life is hidden with the Messiah in God" (Col. 3:3).

3. The third point of similarity-in-difference is the field of tension: "testing-persecution". In *testings* we are dealing with a lifelong process of purification in which the image of God is "smelted out" so that it shines in full likeness to God in our life. In *persecutions* what matters is that we become conformed to the Messiah and bear his likeness in ever deepening ways. Persecutions are a specific kind of testing: they bring to light in the concreteness of life the power of the Messiah, ritually put on in baptism. Precisely for that reason Paul took delight in persecutions (2 Cor. 12:10): they gave him a chance to become more intimately incorporated in the Messiah.

The word of Job and the quotation from Paul place us in a field of tension that is typical for messianic spirituality. Transformation in God not only concerns our natural life on earth but also our supernatural life in Christ. The two layers intersect precisely at the point where what matters is the liberation of God's image in us.

> ... and moreover since your adversary, the devil,
> prowls around like a roaring lion,
> seeking whom he may devour,

The third reason for putting on the armor of God comes from the First Letter of Peter (1 Pet. 5:8). Peter views everything from the perspective of "the end of all things which is at hand" (1 Pet. 4:7). Squarely looking at this end he wants people to be sober, loving,

[209] See Rom. 8:1; 9:1; 15:17; 16:3, 7, 9, 10; 1 Cor. 1:4, 30; 3:1; 4:10, 15, 17, etc.

and ready to serve (4:7-11). He teaches his fellow Christians the
value of being tested through gaining insight into suffering (4:12-
19). Suffering belongs to the end. From within the perspective of
that same end older people as well as younger people must "clothe
themselves with humility" in their dealings with one another (5:1-
7). He sums up all his admonitions in the words: "Be sober and
watchful. Your adversary the devil prowls around like a roaring
lion, looking for someone to devour" (1 Pet. 5:8). It is a temptation to read Peter's statement in the Rule as a simple climax: from
being tested (Job) via persecution (Paul) to being devoured (Peter).
But there is more than that going on.

In the first place the mention of the devil evokes a supernatural
power. The testings are integral to human existence as such (pow-
erlessness, transience, unrest); persecutions are the work of human
agents and are processed with a view to becoming conformed to
Christ; the devourings by the devil are the work of superhuman
powers which attempt to destroy our very core.

> Put on the whole armor of God, so that you may be able to stand
> against the wiles of *the devil.* For our struggle is not against enemies
> of *blood and flesh,* but against *the rulers,* against *the authorities,*
> against the *cosmic powers* of this present darkness, against the *spiri-
> tual forces of evil* in the heavenly places. *Therefore* take up the whole
> armor of God (Eph. 6:11-12).

The special nature of the higher powers is that they insinuate their
way into human life without showing their face. By the agency of
this diabolical adversary[210] the system of death enters the world
(Wisdom 2:24). He goes about on earth just as he did in the days
of Job (Job 1:7; 2:2).[211] Prowling around is characteristic of him.
He avoids the open confrontation of testings and persecutions but
favors the surprise attack by way of "hidden schemes" (1 Tim. 3:7-
9; 2 Tim. 2:26) or "ambush" (Eph. 6:11). When at the end of the
times the devil will be released from his prison – and according to

---

[210] Cf. Ps. 108:6 in the Vulgate; see also 1 Tim. 3:6.
[211] The Vulgate here uses *circumire,* as in Peter's letter.

Peter we are living at the end of time – he will go about to deceive the nations and along with his henchmen "surround the camp of the saints" (Rev. 20:7-10).[212] The destruction of the self steals into our life and does its devouring work there.

Aside from a superhuman dimension – in the figure of the devil – Peter also attributes a subhuman dimension to testings and persecutions: the roaring lion which prowls around looking for someone to devour. This lion found his way into Peter's letter from Psalm 22,[213] reinforcing the secretive[214] and all-devouring nature of the devil. At the same time the lion introduces subhuman destruction. In Psalm 22 animals graphically represent this subhuman dimension: bulls, lions, wild oxen and dogs all carry on against me, one who is no longer "a human" but "a worm" (Ps. 22:7).

Peter's statement lays bare two new dimensions in the testings and persecutions: the *super*human evil which, operating out of a collective delusion, strikes out at the core of people's personhood, and the *sub*human evil which with merciless bestiality devours human lives. Both dimensions are marked by faceless penetration into the core of personhood.

The three reasons the Rule mentions for putting on the armor of God together form a dramatic whole. Both the natural life and the supernatural life are exposed to degradation and destruction issuing from the anonymous power of faceless superhuman and subhuman forces. It seems that in this connection the devil especially has it in for all who want to live a reverent life in Christ while bestiality threatens the life of humanity on earth.

5.3.3. Being clothed with the armor of God as mystical transformation

The armor of God is a symbol for the attributes of God. God, who himself wears armor, gives this armor to us humans. He gives

---

[212] Again the Vulgate uses *circumire* here.

[213] Vulgate: "sicut leo rapiens et rugiens" (Ps. 21:14); cf. also Ps. 104:21; Prov. 28:15.

[214] See, for example, in the Vulgate Ps. 10:9; 16:2; Eccl. 27:11, 31; Cf. L. Goppelt, *Der erste Petrusbrief,* Göttingen 1978, 335-345.

himself to us humans. This self-communication is a divine power expressed in human strength. The Rule counsels Carmelites to put on this armor.

> You shall use every care and diligence
> to put on the armor of God,
> so that you may be able to withstand
> the deceits of the enemy.

What does it mean to put on the armor of God? And, in this connection, what do diligence and painstaking care mean?

1. *Putting on.* Putting on God's attributes is a biblical metaphor[215] used particularly to convey transformation in the Messiah by baptism (Gal. 3:27-29; Rom. 13:14; Col. 3:10; Eph. 4:24; 2 Cor. 4:16). This transformation in Christ, if it is to be realized in our life, calls for daily practice. It is with this as with the armor of a soldier: only those who regularly practice are really able to fight the battles of daily life (1 Thess. 5:8; Eph. 6:11, 14; Rom. 13:12; Col. 3:12). This practice is aimed at acquiring an attitude. By my practicing respect and esteem chastity enters my life. By my thinking honestly the spirit of integrity begins to permeate my thoughts. By my doing deeds of love, love enters into the architecture of my life. By my fastening an attachment to God, to the other and to myself, I myself become securely fastened and solid. Hope becomes more deeply rooted in me as I watch and pray, look forward to, and refrain from filling in the details. By my speaking sincerely and acting authentically the word of God begins to indwell my existence.

2. *Care and diligence.* Care and diligence, in the first place, refer in very general terms to the artisanship of the exercise.

> My sons, when we wish to acquire the skills of a particular art we need to devote all our possible care and attention to the activities characteristic of our chosen profession.[216]

---

[215] See A. Oepke, *duo* ktl, in: *Theol. Dict. of the N.T.* Grand Rapids 1964, Vol. II, 318-321; H. Paulsen, *enduo*, in: *Exegetisches Wörterbuch zum Neuen Testament*, Stuttgart-Berlin-Köln-Mainz 1980, 1103-1105.

[216] Cassian, *Conferences*, 18.2; *CWS*, 184.

This artisanship has a structure of its own for we are discussing the subject of being clothed with God's attributes. In this case the pains we take must continually be kept at a point midway between intense hope and relaxed confidence; between an attentive love which does not hesitate and restraint in speech and thought; between the diligent practice of the Word and a sustained tolerance of our inadequacies. In this painstaking work, work which is characterized by the slow pace and concentration of a noble craft, carefulness attends diligence. For carefulness is fervent in love but patient in chastity, tender in its attentiveness but watchful in hope, intensely expectant, both vigilant and confident. Carefulness is without self-mutilation and tactful, sensitive and clear. It even sees through its own anxiety.

The process of being clothed with God's attributes achieved its goal when the realization dawns that it is God himself who is at work in all *our* exercises. In that light putting on the armor of God means letting ourselves be girded by chastity; allowing ourselves to be consecrated down to the very roots of our thinking; it means hospitably admitting love into our life; becoming deeply persuaded that we are lovable "for nothing"; letting ourselves be sustained by confidence; awakening in the wide-open spaces of salvation; letting ourselves be totally leavened by the Word. This phase in our transformation calls for a diligence and painstaking care of its own. Sensitivity exerts itself in wonder. The eagerness of love is restless like the bride in the Song of Songs but simultaneously tactful like Tobias. The zeal of the prophet Elijah is palpably present but also the total freedom from care felt by the weaned child on its mother's back (Psalm 131). This understanding is inquisitive like a child and clairvoyant like Daniel.

The mystical movement in transformation breaks through when, outside of ourselves, we are led into the interior of God's own armor. We are purified in the Source of chastity itself. Unforgettable! For a moment we are wrapped up in God's boundless thoughts, unhindered by any prejudice, seeing ways to go where we imagined the end to be. Incomparable! For just one breath we entered into the divine saving love. The fire reached the core of the wood; now it is in the fire. Incomprehensible! Here we find security in the dark but this darkness is light enough for us. Here we are reduced to quiet expectation, a guest at the banquet of life, for only an instant. But it goes on forever! Here we are born in the moment of God's speaking to us. Just one word but that one word is our name. Indelible! Painstaking care and diligence have melted into the zeal of love. We have been made zealous by God's own zeal, the zeal of the divine love. Indeed: You are a love-zealous God in whom, in complete stillness, without any effort of our own, we abandon ourselves; in whose flames we are consumed, no longer seeking any voice apart from You, the fire of love in whom our illusions are burnt away; here we are all there, in quiet attentiveness, for You, You who will to be there for us.

It is this "being clothed upon" which makes us able to resist the ambushes of the Enemy, the Un-friend. The Rule deliberately changes the original devil *(diaboli)* who is in Scripture into the un-friend *(inimici)*. In the case of the un-friend *(in-amicus)* we are dealing with a personal enemy.[217] The unfriend betrays me, ignores me, denies me, breaks me down; the unfriend is against and tries to devour my personhood. This does not occur frontally, however, but from the concealment of an ambush.[218]

Levinas has keenly expressed the connection between this person-aimed violence and an ambush. Person-aimed violence is the attempt "to overpower the other by surprise, from an ambush". This violence is characterized by the fact that it views the Other "merely as mass, does not look him in the eye; to be precise: does not see any face on him". Here the satanic link between "unfriend" and ambush becomes visible.[219]

Strictly speaking, the un-persons who have it in for our personhood can only make their un-friendliness felt by making us a faceless

---

[217] *Inimicus* is the personal enemy; *hostis* the impersonal one.
[218] The Greek *methodeia,* in the Letter to the Ephesians, denotes craftiness, hidden snares, ambushes.
[219] E. Levinas, *Het menselijk gelaat,* Bilthoven 1971², 101.

mass, i.e. by overpowering us from an ambush – from behind or from the side, but never frontally! We are lost the moment we capitulate to this *way* of approaching people, for then we have already adapted ourselves to the "style" of the ambush: we have become a faceless mass. The Rule – following Paul – advises us to put on the whole armor of God in the interest of resisting these tactics of the devil.

5.3.4 The six parts of the armor of God

Albert has designed a panoply of this own. Footwear – compare the Letter to the Ephesians (6:15) – has been omitted, perhaps because this would tend too much to evoke the life of evangelists. The tunic has been inserted as an addition, perhaps because the Rule attaches great value to a pure heart and a good conscience. By comparison with Cassian, both the cincture and the tunic have been added. Furthermore, the motivation differs. It is noteworthy that the Rule consistently adheres to the transformation described above. Each part of the panoply is founded in God and directed toward actual conduct. We will show this to be true for every part of the panoply.

For all the parts the instructions are stated in the form of a Latin gerundive: "... are to be girt ... is to be fortified ... is to be put on ... etc.". The grammatical form of the gerundive, by being repeated, evokes an atmosphere of its own. Two aspects are important there. First: we are placed in the field of tension between present and future. The gerundive, after all, indicates what we must *do*:[220] we must put on the cincture of chastity; we must protect our chest with a tunic, etc. Second: we have no other choice; we are to do it. Those who wish to survive are to put on the whole armor of God: they are to be girt, protected, etc.[221] The two

---

[220] This aspect comes into play when grammarians describe the gerundive as "the future passive tense" (*Living Latin,* Massachusetts 1967, EM-2). In their onesidedness they stress the things to be done. When combined with "sum" (the so-called passive periphrastic) they express necessity. See Allen and Greenough, *New Latin Grammar,* New York 1975, 106-107.

[221] For the scope of this meaning, cf. H. Throm, *Lateinische Grammatik,* Düsseldorf 1970⁵, 194.

aspects have to be related to each other: those who have seen the
life-threatening character of the testing, the persecution and the
demonically destructive know with complete clarity what they *have
to* do: apply themselves with the greatest possible care to putting
on (all the parts of) the armor of God. The accumulation of
gerundives reflects the potentially lethal character of the situation
and compellingly indicates what our inescapable duty is. This
chapter breathes a very different atmosphere than the preceding
ones. Then there was a downpour of exceptions and relativizations. Here the gerundive creates an atmosphere of inexorable
seriousness and situates us within the fundamental tension essential to the armor of God: the polar tension between life and death,
good and evil, the One who is and unbeing.

The cincture of chastity

In classical antiquity the cincture was an essential part of a soldier's armor.[222] It consisted of one or more leather straps fastened
around the waist with a buckle. In that way it supported and protected the more vulnerable parts of the body, the stomach and
abdomen. Fastened to the one strap was the sheath for the dagger,
to the other the sheath for the sword, to the third a kind of apron
made of leather strips embossed with metal for the protection of
the stomach and abdomen. The straps reinforced each other and
formed a single whole: the cincture. Consequently, in the case
of the cincture it is hard to distinguish its function as an item of
clothing from its function as a piece of armor. A soldier always
wore his cincture, not only in battle but also when working or
in training. The cincture was so essential to a soldier's identity that
to be "girded" was synonymous with becoming a soldier. Accordingly, to take off one's cincture meant to desert or to neglect
oneself.

[222] For a description see C. Daremerg-E. Gaglio, *Cingula*, in: *Dictionnaire
des Antiquités Greques et Romaines* 1:2, Graz 1969, 1176-1182; *Paulus Realencyclopädie der classischen Altertumswissenschaft* 3:1, Stuttgart 1897, 375-378, and
3:2 Stuttgart 1899, 2561.

Your loins are to be girt
with the cincture of chastity.

The rule does not employ the "cincture" metaphor in a general military sense, but cites from the letter to the Ephesians: "Stand therefore, and *fasten the cincture* of truth *around your loins*" (Eph. 6:14). In so doing it places this motif within the perspective of Scripture as a whole.[223] This broadens and deepens the scope of the image at three points. First: in Scripture the loins are the vulnerable and tender part of the body.[224] Girding it with a cincture means protection of this area of vulnerability. Second: the loins are the area of the unbound, not only because the cincture ties up one's clothes but also because it firms up the waist between the chest and the hips. Such girding with a cincture is necessary not only for a warrior,[225] but for anyone preparing for a journey, a task, or heavy labor.[226] Third: the loins are the seat of deep emotion,[227] and the cincture gives expression to it. Just as we may gird ourselves in sackcloth to give expression to sorrow,[228] so we may gird ourselves with a cincture of gladness to show joy. The cincture expresses feelings of pride, of readiness for battle, of strength, of a desire to show off. It protects that which is vulnerable, binds up the unbound, and expresses emotions. These qualities all serve to make the cincture suitable as an image for chastity.[229]

The chastity recommended by the Rule is the chastity of God, just as the armor as a whole is the armor of God. The cincture of

---

[223] The phrase "girding your loins" occurs 19 times in the Vulgate. The "loins" occur 41 times. We will cite the Bible references from the Vulgate.

[224] Gen. 35:11; 2 Par. 6:9; Acts 2:30; Heb. 7:5, 10.

[225] Nah. 2:1; Eph. 6:14.

[226] 3 Kgs. 18:46; 4 Kgs. 4:19; 9:1; Jer. 1:7; Job 38:3; 40:2; Prov. 31:17; Luke 12:35, 37.

[227] Isa. 21:3; cf. Ez. 21:6.

[228] 3 Kgs. 20:31-32; Isa. 32:11.

[229] For an overview of chastity from the perspective of spirituality, see *Chasteté* in: *DS* 2 (1950) 777-809.

God's chastity can best be approached in the light of two citations from Scripture. The first Scripture text can be heard (via Eph. 6:14) directly: "Justice shall be the *cincture* around his *waist* and faithfulness the *cincture* around his *loins*" (Is. 11:5). The divine Power which in the case of idolatrous powers arbitrarily gives free rein to itself means preservation in the case of Jahweh. In the Name the divine does not carry on wildly but binds itself and adheres to justice. The Name does this with enduring constancy and intimacy, as has become evident in the history of Israel. This is the context of the second citation from Scripture: "For as the cincture clings to a man's loins, so I made the whole house of Israel and the whole house of Judah cling to me" – says the Lord – "in order that they might be for me a people, fame, praise, and glory" (Jer. 13:11). To give expression to his most intimate emotions God has bound himself intimately to his people, the people among whom he made visible what he had in mind for all people.

It is this cincture of God's chastity which has been given us as in former times it was given to kings.[230] Every morning anew God gathered up his king, brought him into the light of day "out of the womb of the morning" (Ps. 110:3). Without intermingling with him he bound him together, "cast" him in his image (Ps. 2:6; cf. Hos. 13:2; Job 31:27; Prov. 8:23), granted him the integrity which was God's own. It is striking how often the words *sound* ("blameless") and *pure* occur in the royal psalms.[231] The cincture of God's chastity makes the king sound, pure, authentic, whole, good through and through like 24 karat gold, unspoiled, uncorrupted (see especially. Ps. 101). During the Exile this royal spirituality was democratized and integrated into messianic spirituality. Every human shares in God's chastity: in his protection of that which is delicate and tender, in his gathering up of that which is unbound, in his purifying action down to the essential. This is the cincture of God's chastity which Carmelites are instructed to put on.

[230] Cf. K. Waaijman, *Psalmen rond bevrijdend leiderschap*, Kampen 1984.
[231] Cf. Ps. 2:12; 18:21, 24-27, 31; 72:16; 101:2-4.

1. Chastity protects in us that which is *vulnerable*. This vulnerability has many faces: the delicate and shameful, the soft and unformed, the unbalanced and manipulable, the needy and seducible. The cincture of chastity provides protection: strength and ability to fight, balance and respect, restraint and abstinence. Chastity forms in us an attitude which keeps us from violating the vulnerable, the intimate, the tender parts of ourselves and others. Chastity is the opposite of shameless behavior. Chastity is an attitude of deference toward everything in ourselves and others that is vulnerable. What it comes down to is that we adopt an attitude of reserve and restraint toward that which is delicate and tender in ourselves and others.[232]

2. Chastity binds up that which is *unbound*. Also the unbound has many faces: to be disordered and distracted, to be drifting and getting lost. The cincture of chastity gathers up: brings concentration and order, control, moderation, regulation, and recollection. Chastity keeps us from going under in ourselves, from getting lost in uncontrolled impulses, from being swallowed up by our own activities and going astray in our diversions.

3. Chastity purges away the *unreal*. Also the unreal shows itself in many ways: muddled feelings, shallow conduct, artificial needs, imposed patterns, prejudices, estrangement from our real self. Chastity purges away these imposed and accepted blots. It seeks to smelt out the soundness and genuineness of the core of one's personhood and letting it shine through in our conduct. It seeks to bring out the true nature of our personhood, unalloyed, unestranged, and pure.[233]

This cincture has its roots in God and is given us by him. This does not mean, however, that it drops from the sky. We must gird ourselves with it. By practice we make this gift our own. This

[232] This aspect of distance and restraint comes through literally in the etymology of *castitas*, derived as it is from *careo*, which means *to lack, to be devoid of, to be free from, to go without* (Oxford Latin Dictionary).

[233] *Castitas* in Latin and *chasteness* or *chastity* in English denotes moral, sexual, ceremonial, and esthetic purity.

requires sensitivity and patience. All self-mutilation is fatal here. Patience and sensitivity themselves are our chaste helpers in putting on this cincture!

It is no accident that the Rule has given first place to chastity. For chastity is (ever) the beginning of the spiritual life. This is also underscored by the image of the cincture. Soldiers who gird themselves begin their military career. In Scripture when persons gird themselves, they start out on something.[234] That which is true of the image is true of the reality as well: chastity starts us out on the practice of virtue. It leads us away from the muddled, the unbalanced and unbridled in order to lead us into the real, the solid and the concentrated in us, in others, and in our association with God. But this cincture of chastity which is (ever) the beginning of the way is itself in turn a way.[235]

The tunic of holy ponderings

By comparison with the cincture the undergarment called the tunic lies closer to our skins. The men's tunic[236] was usually short. When tucked up by a cincture it reached nearly to the knee. It could be worn by itself or under a cloak or suit of armor. In the last case the tunic furnished protection not only against the cold but also against the roughness of the armor. The tunic is the most intimate article of clothing and as such is not part of the armor. It lies under it, under the cincture, under the suit of armor, and directly covers the skin.

> Your breast is to be fortified
> with holy ponderings,
> for it is written:
> Holy pondering will save you.

---

[234] 3 Kgs. 18:46; 4 Kgs. 4:29; 9:1; Jer. 1:17.

[235] For chastity as a phased process in the spiritual authors, see *Chasteté*, *DS* 2 (1953) 784-787.

[236] C. Darenberg – E.Gaglio, *Tunica* in *Dictionnaire des Antiquités*, 5:534-540; *Chitoon* in *Paulus Realencyclopädie*, 3:2:2309-2335.

The tunic protects the chest, which is here the symbol of the emotions (heart and conscience, character and inmost self), the intellect (mind and memory), and the core of personhood (the self).[237] It is the seat of the ponderings. Just what are they?

Within the framework of Scripture[238] ponderings revolve around two core ideas: the first is to count-value-calculate and the second is to think out-plan-devise. The two core ideas are closely related: one who devises a plan must calculate the possibilities, has a strategy in mind and works within a framework. On top of all this, ponderings are marked by a certain restlessness and movement. This is logical for it concerns an activity that is aimed forward: making plans, pursuing goals based on evaluated possibilities by way of carefully pondered strategies within a preconceived framework.[239]

The ponderings of God are very agitated as well, agitated as they are by us humans. God devises plans for our good (Ps. 33:11). Indeed, against the evil intentions of some he makes plans for good (Gen. 50:20). God's ponderings are based on an infallible estimate of possibilities, perfect understanding of strategy and the boundlessness of his conceptual framework. For that reason God's ponderings completely transcend our ponderings (Is. 55:8-9; cf. Mic. 4:12).

Add to this that God's ponderings are holy, i.e. not subject to corruption. They are perfectly attuned to reality. Their agitation is not muddied by self-interest. They go their way through the world and through time as a holy fire (Lev. 10:3) which smelts out that which is authentic and consumes the inauthentic, like holy water which brings out the purity of the core and flushes away that

[237] Corresponding to the most significant fields of meaning of *pectus* (Oxford Latin Dictionary).

[238] W.Scholtroff, *chsjb* in *THAT* 1:641-646; K. Seybold, *chsjb* in *TWAT* 3:243-261.

[239] The word *ponder* suggests movement, the movement of an object being weighed (*pondus*) on a pair of scales. The same is true of the Latin *cogitatio* (= coagitatio). The *cogitatio* is intrinsically marked by *agitatio*: movement, activity, practice, busyness, the violent moving or being moved of anything.

which soils and stains us. The Name is the expression and sum of all
that moves God: I shall be there! I be there! I Be-er! In the Name
we humans are the recipients of the purest pathos which exists in the
Mighty One. The Name makes us resourceful, opens our eyes to
the essential, unfallibly points out to us the way to go and calls the
future into the present. Those who admit the Name into the deepest
core of their heart and into the farthest reaches of their conduct are
sanctified by him. "Keep my commandments and do them – I am
Be-er! Do not soil my holy Name that I may be sanctified in the
midst of Israel – I am Be-er who sanctifies you" (Lev. 22:31-32). By
letting the holy Name pass through my pondering as a purifying
force they receive the import of God's holy ponderings.

This is an enormous transformation. For those who examine
Scripture on this subject[240] discover that the restlessness of human
ponderings is deeply rooted in the human heart.[241] These ponderings have their roots in the depths of our needs, desires, and
motives, depths which only God can plumb.[242] Ponderings form
the inner dynamics of our behavior: they determine our attitude[243]
and direct our conduct from within.[244]

Accordingly, ponderings have a great range: they are rooted
in the unfathomable depth of the heart and impact the farthest
reaches of our conduct. This range is inversely proportionate to
their stability. As we said earlier: ponderings are intrinsically
marked by mobility. They are readily disturbed,[245] extremely vulnerable and volatile,[246] subject to corruption and very susceptible

---

[240] In the Vulgate we find *cogitatio* in 146 instances. The Scripture passages
cited hereafter follow the Vulgate.

[241] Gen. 8:21; Jer. 23:20; 30:24; Ezek. 11:5; 20:32; Prov. 6:18; 19:21;
Matt. 15:19; Mk. 7:21; Lk. 2:35; 24:38; Acts 8:22.

[242] Cf. Jer. 29:11; Ezek. 11:5; Dan. 2:30; Ps. 93:11; 138:3; Heb. 4:12;
1 Cor. 3:20. Jesus, too, completely sees through the ponderings of the heart:
Matt. 9:4; 12:25; Lk. 5:22; 6:8; 9:47; 11:17.

[243] Cf. Jer. 49:30; 51:29; Lam. 3:60-61; Dan. 13:28.

[244] Cf. Is. 65:2; Jer. 18:12; Ezek. 21:24; Eph. 2:3.

[245] Cf. Dan. 4:2, 16; 5:6, 10; 7:28.

[246] Cf. Isa. 59:7; Job 17:11; Prov. 15:22; Ps. 145:4; Wisdom 9:14; 1 Macc.
2:63: Rom. 1:21.

to meanness and malice.[247] It is therefore essential that our ponderings be inwardly transformed[248] in the ponderings of God. The Holy One of Israel[249] is the only One who can teach the true depths of our ponderings, can reinforce and influence their inner dynamic with God's holy passion – without destroying their spontaneity. Letting the mobility of our ponderings be transformed in God is one of the first concerns of a monk. Their mobility must calm down so that the Face can mirror itself in them down in the deepest depths of the heart.[250]

The transformation of our ponderings in those of God means our salvation. We are kept from corruption and imbalance, from self-seeking thoughts and illusions, from unreliable strategies and false expectations. The Rule rightly repeats after Scripture: "Holy pondering will save you".[251] In Scripture salvation[252] among other things means preservation and the storage of seed and grain,[253] keeping children and firstborn alive,[254] the protection of soul and body,[255] in short the preservation of life.[256] Holy ponderings are intrinsically aimed at the preservation of life. They weigh the present with a view to the generation of new life and look for ways to advance it. Over and beyond the dead points of existence they carry the life of God into the future. For that reason Judas

[247] Cf. Gen. 6:5; 8:21; Deut. 15:9; Is. 1:16; 29:16; Jer. 4:4; 23:22; 25:5; Ezek. 38:10; Sef. 3:7; Prov. 15:5; 15:26; Ps. 55:6; Acts 17:29; Eph. 2:3.

[248] Cf. Prov. 5:2

[249] This is Isaiah's favorite name for the Lord (Is. 1:4; 5:19, 24; 10:20; 12:6 etc.).

[250] See Cassian, *Conferences*, 1.16-17; 7.4; 9.7; 10.7; 23.9 and 19.

[251] The citation in the Rule is a reference to two Scripture passages; to Proverbs: "Prudence *will save you*" (Pr. 4:11) and to Maccabees. "Judas the Maccabee considered that a splendid reward is laid up for those who fall asleep in godliness. Indeed, a *holy* and pious *consideration*" (2 Macc. 12:45).

[252] *Servare* occurs 124 times in the Vulgate.

[253] We are quoting from the Vulgate: Gen. 19:32; 41:35; 1 Kgs. 9:24.

[254] Ex. 1:18; 12:6.

[255] Sir. 7:26; 10:31; Tob. 3:16; Job 2:6; Prov. 4:23; 16:17.

[256] Deut. 19:4; Judg. 8:19; 1 Kgs. 22:23; Is. 27:3; 42:6; 49:8; John 17:11, 12, 15; 1 Thess. 5:23; Rev. 3:10.

Maccabeus calls the thought of resurrection-in-the-power-of-God "a *holy* and pious *pondering* (2 Macc. 12:45).

The breastplate of justice

The breastplate[257] was originally made of leather partly covered with metal plates. Later a breastplate was made of metal, sometimes entirely closed, at other times constructed of ringlets, chains, scales, filigree and the like. A breastplate not only had to protect as well as possible the warrior's back and chest but be flexible enough for a soldier to move about in. We therefore see a succession of inventions designed to make the breastplate as flexible and light as possible and as much as possible adapted to the shape of the body.

> The breastplate of justice
> is to be put on.

In biblical spirituality[258] justice is full of tension. Three lines of thought converge in it. In the first place justice is *preservative*; it implies a constructive atmosphere solidified in just relations; aims at what is true, valuable, and worthy; and is actualized in constructive conduct. However, how can the sea of preservation be fitted into the thimble of judicial verdicts? It is possible only when the judicial verdicts are at every moment checked against the ideal of preservation. That brings us to the third line: justice is skilled in righteousness. Every judgment calls every moment for direct appraisal in light of the goal of preservation.

The only one who is proficient in *justice* is God. He is capable of leading the entire flock without letting a single sheep get lost. He has arranged everything in his creation in such a way that ultimately it is preserved as well. Of God *alone* it can be said: "*Savingly just* You are, God, and your *judgments* are *righteous*" (Ps. 119:137).

---

[257] See *lorica* in *Paulus Realencyclopädie*, 13, 2, 1444-1449; in *Der kleine Pauly*, Stuttgart 1969, Band 3, 737-738; in *Dictionnaire des Antiquités Grecques et Romaines*, 3, 2, 1302-1316.

[258] K. Waaijman, *Gerechtigheid in de Schrift: een spannend gebeuren*, in *Speling* 41 (1989) nr. 2, 79-89.

According to the New Testament,[259] this justice is embodied in Jesus Christ. In the Messiah the justice of God has become visible. He saved that which was lost. In him has become visible what it means to give everyone his due (Rom. 3:21-24). God *is* justice and in Jesus Christ this justice has been revealed in order that we should seriously attach ourselves to it.

Thus the breastplate of justice is primarily and most authentically worn by God: "God put on justice as a breastplate" (Is. 59:17; Wisd. 5:18). God is the preserver of truth, value, and worth. He brings all things to the truth of his own being (Is. 51:6).

Putting on the breastplate of justice is first of all an act of pure receptivity. Paul calls it faith: attaching oneself to God's justice, to totally trust oneself to it (Rom. 10:6; Phil. 3:9). Of us it is only required that we learn to consent to this justice: "Present the parts of your bodies to God as *weapons for justice*" (Rom. 6:13). Being equipped with weapons does not happen without deeds of justice; on the contrary, by doing, in an attitude of faith, we *receive* what we do (1 John 2:29). Doing, receiving, and divine being are communicating vessels: "Everyone who does what is right is righteous, just as God is righteous" (1 Jn. 3:7; cf. Phil. 1:11; Rom. 14:17; Eph. 5:9; etc.). We become righteous as God is righteous by fighting with the aid of the weapons of justice in the right hand and in the left (2 Cor. 6:7).

The strange thing is – at least at first sight – that in the Rule justice is linked with love: the love of God, the love of neighbor, and the love of self.

> that you may love
> the Lord your God
> with all your heart
> and all your soul
> and all your strength
> and your neighbor as yourself.

[259] K. Kertelge, *dikaiosunè*, in *Exegetisches Wörterbuch zum Neuen Testament*, Stuttgart-Berlin-Köln-Mainz 1 (1980) 784-796.

This link is biblical. Justice includes love. Justice is a matter of letting ourselves really come to the truth of our being, saving, affirming, authenticating us. This process involves at least three agents: God, my neighbor, and my soul. Those who cannot receive themselves cannot save their neighbor. Those who do not see their neighbor standing near them do not see anything – certainly not God. Those who do not see God diminish everything, first the other, then themselves, or vice versa. In the Sermon on the Mount (Matt. 5-7) Jesus shows us that love is justice which overflows (Matt. 5:20). This love is Abba who is undiscriminatingly good (Matt. 5:48). Abba is pure love which demands being received down into the core of desire (Matt. 6:33). Those who have received this overflowing justice will almost automatically – in secret, unobserved by themselves – let that same love flow out in action. "Be undividedly good as Abba is undividedly good" (Matt. 5:48) – that is the body-armor with which the body is covered from now on.

In the New Testament[260] love is the heart of God's justice. John and Paul are tireless in testifying that God is Love (Romans, 2 Cor., 1 and 2 John). The synoptics show how this Love assumed flesh and blood in Jesus, the basic pattern of messianic love.

The Rule's design is that the justice which is Love takes shape in the love of God, of neighbor, and of the self. It has often been attempted to unite these three dimensions of love in a higher synthesis. But all attempts at synthesis have failed. The reason is plain: the tension-filled triangle of the three love-dimensions does not call for an intellectual synthesis but for the experience of thoroughly living it. In the concreteness of our lives these three dimensions are a harmony. It is interesting to see how the *Book of the First Monks* relates the three dimensions of love to each other.

> You must love God for his own sake, not yourself for your own sake, but for the sake of God. And because you must love your neighbors as yourself, you must not love them either for their own sake, nor for your own sake, but for God's sake.[261]

---

[260] G. Scheider, *agapè* ktl, in *ibid.*, 19-29.
[261] *Decem libri* 1.6.

With respect to the love of neighbor the love of God teaches
me that love is unconditional, forces nothing, regards people
creatively, does not freeze them in categories, is infinitely merci-
ful. With respect to the love of God the love of neighbor teaches
me that love is mutual, sees-in-being-seen; that love is a face,
physical and tangible. With respect to the love of God self-love
teaches me that in all love there is and remains singularity, that
though self-acceptance has already taken place it has to take
place over and over, that self-acceptance is totally an act of love.
With respect to the love of neighbor self-love teaches me that
the other, just as I am myself, is involved in a process of growth
toward real self-acceptance; that the other is mortal, ambiguous,
inhibited, mysterious and open. Thus a process of learning gets
started in me who find myself in the tense triangle of the three
love-dimensions, a process of transformation the story of which
will never be finished because every person, in his or her uniqueness, discovers and walks his or her own life path in the midst of
these three love dimensions. In the meantime it has certainly
become clear that this threefold arrangement of love is the ultimate justice: it allows the riches of love to come to the truth of
its very being.

The shield of faith (trust)

The shield[262] offered the warrior protection from top to bottom:
it came down to his feet and concealed his entire body[263] in contrast to the small hand-shield (*clipeus*). Two forms existed: a square
shield so rounded that it furnished the warrior almost all-around
protection, and a longer oval-shaped shield.

> In all things is to be taken up
> the shield of faith,

[262] *Scutum* (Lat.) goes back to a root which originally means *protection*
(Dutch: *beschutting*).
[263] *Scutum* in *Paulus Realencylopädie der Classischen Altertumswissenschaft*, 2/
3:914-920.

Faith is trust in the faithfulness of another, the Other. From *my* perspective trusting is a leap into the dark: I cannot bring about the faithfulness of the other. To trust is to build on the faithfulness of another. It requires surrender but not to *nothing*. I give myself up to someone who vouches for me, even when I do not feel it; who sustains me, even when I do not experience it; who takes care of me, even though I do not know it. When speaking of trust in God, we are by implication dealing with the faithfulness of God.

Faithfulness and trust are preeminently divine virtues.[264] God is faithful (Ps. 31:6). The Psalms sing of his solidity in many different ways: faithfulness to his creation (Ps. 86:15; 89:15; 146:6; etc.); faithfulness to his word (Ps. 132:11; Ps. 119:43, 160); faithfulness in his deeds (Ps. 111:7); faithfulness in his gracious love (Ps. 25:10; 40:12; 57:4; etc.). "Although it is certain that the Old Testament in no way speculates about the nature of God as such, still we may venture to say that faithfulness belongs to God's essence".[265] He is "a God of faithfulness" (Deut. 32:4; Ps. 31:6). This fundamental fact constitutes the basis of the New Testament.[266] The core experience of the New Testament, after all, is that God's faithfulness survives the unfaithfulness of humans. "What if some were unfaithful? Will their faithlessness nullify the faithfulness of God? By no means!" (Rom. 3:3-4).

Trust is the characteristic way in which we affirm the faithfulness of another and give it a chance in our life. In my trust the faithfulness of another can be realized. The ability to trust is a creative faculty. By trust we realize that the world was called into being by the Word of God (Heb. 11:3). By trust we sense that in Jesus the Messiah God's preservation became flesh and blood among us (Rom. 10:9-14; 1 Cor. 1:21; Gal. 2:16; etc.). This faculty grows by trusting (2 Cor. 10:15; 1 Thess. 1:3; 2 Thess. 1:3).

Trust does not remain enclosed in its Source: the faithfulness of God. It becomes active and real in love (Gal. 5:6). Especially

---

[264] See *'aman* in *THAT* 1, 177-209; *TWAT* 1, 313-348.

[265] *'emuna* in *THAT* 1, 199.

[266] *pistis* ktl, in *Exegetisches Wörterbuch zum Neuen Testament* 3 (1983), 216-231.

the letters of James (Jam. 2:14-26) and John (1 John 3:18-24) stress the fruitfulness of a trust that becomes active and real in love (Jam. 5:17). This is "the breastplate of trust and love" (1 Thess. 5:8).

> with which you will be able to quench
> all the flaming arrows of the wicked one,
> for without faith
> it is impossible to please God.

Cracks and holes appear in my identity, however well I secure it with chastity and holiness, justice and hope. Only trust is able to mend the undermining and discouraging stitches I drop. Without trust the flaming arrow of the wicked one (Matt. 6:13; 13:19, 38; cf. 2 Thess. 3:3) penetrates my existence unobserved. For that reason Paul recommends: "Fight the good fight of trust; take hold of eternal life" (1 Tim. 6:12).

By trusting we not only build up resistance against destruction, but trust more especially makes us acceptable to God. Trust touches God in his essence: his faithfulness. We affirm him in his solidity. We give him a chance to be who he is: "I will be: I will be there [for you]" (Ex. 3:14). The fact that "I will be there" can *be* in my life is the outcome of my trust. I let myself be delivered from my fear and my "shut-down"-ness and open myself up to the Source of my trust: his faithfulness. I attach myself to his solidity. I learn to see the truth of the saying: "Without trust it is not possible to please God" (Heb. 11:6). It must be a moving thing to him to be understood above all in his faithfulness.

In the original Rule Albert adds the statement: "And this is the victory: your trust" (XIV). The victory applies in two directions: We quench the flaming arrows of the wicked one *and* we overcome the undermining force of our own distrust. Trust is the total victory over the destruction that comes from without and that which comes from within. It is the victory of Love.[267]

---

[267] It is not clear to me why this sentence was omitted from the Rule of Innocent IV. It is possible that as a result of a copyist's oversight it already dropped out in an early phase of the tradition.

The helmet of salvation

Soldiers originally covered their head with an animal skin; later they adopted a metal helmet.[268] The most important feature of a helmet is, of course, the cap which covers the skull, the temples, and the forehead. Often a plume was fastened to the cap as a symbol of rank or simply to impress people. Sometimes helmets were equipped with a visor in front to protect the face, as well as cheek-pieces to protect the sides of the head. In the back the cap extended downward as far as possible as a neck-guard. The ears and eyes remained uncovered. The idea of the helmet is to protect the head as much as possible without blocking observation. Just as the breastplate becomes dysfunctional when it is too heavy and rigid, so the helmet becomes dysfunctional when it is too closed-off.

> On your head is to be put
> the helmet of salvation,
> that you may hope for salvation
> from the only Savior
> who saves his people
> from their sins.

The helmet of salvation came into the letter to the Ephesians by way of Isaiah: "He put on justice like a breastplate, and a *helmet of salvation* on his head" (Is. 59:17). Salvation is part of the armor God wears. For that reason God is so often called "the God of our salvation" (Ps. 18:47; 25:5; 65:6; 79:9; 85:5; etc.). By salvation we mean the act, event, or process by which the integrity of a person or group is secured (see, e.g., Pss. 3, 4, 5, 7, 11; etc.). By God's personal address to a situation – "I will be there!" – an atmosphere of freedom is created in which my truth can totally *be* and therefore flourish (Pss. 26 and 27). As a people Israel experienced how it was set free by "I will be there" and later ever anew shielded from destruction (Ps. 80). Often God's salvation is

[268] Cf. Anthony M. Snodgrass, *Arms and Armour of the Greeks,* 1967, Cornell University Press, 19, 50ff.

connected with his justice (see Is. 45:8; 46:13; 51:5; 56:1; 61:10; etc.). That stands to reason: both are aimed at the preservation and protection of the wholeness of a person or group.

Because this wholeness is so often violated and can never be altogether safeguarded, salvation is especially linked with the End: "On that day it will be said, Lo, this is our God; we have waited for him, so that he might save us. This is God, for whom we waited. Let us be glad and rejoice over the salvation he will bring" (Is. 25:9; see 33:22; 35:4; 60:16; 63:1; etc.).

In the New Testament salvation is predominantly eschatological: it is ultimate deliverance from evil forces.[269] But this salvation is not totally restricted to the future. It has already been established in time by Jesus the Messiah (2 Cor. 6:2). Thus, salvation encompasses both salvation in time and the completion of it in the end. Christian communities are the first fruits of this end-time salvation (cf. 2 Thess. 2:13). Its definitive irruption occurs with the Lord's second coming (Heb. 9:15; 12:22-23). The tension between present salvation and the salvation to come is borne by trusting. This is precisely what is meant by "the salvation of your souls" (1 Pet. 1:9): the bridging of the distance between the salvation already realized and the salvation still awaiting us. The whole of Christian spirituality exists in this tension. In this connection Western spirituality stresses the salvation that is already present; in Jesus God's salvation has entered the world from above. By his suffering and death Jesus preceded us all toward resurrection. The salvation of souls consists in *following him* in all things. Eastern spirituality stresses the salvation that is to come: the salvation which ever again appears with increasing force in our world. The salvation of souls is *God's coming* among us. God's salvation, accordingly, has two poles: its incarnation in the history of salvation and its coming in the End-time.

Because the Rule connects salvation with the virtue of hope, it orients God's salvation to the End, a very biblical accent. We

---

[269] *sotèria,* in *Exegetisches Wörterbuch zum Neuen Testament,* Stuttgart-Berlin-Köln-Mainz 3 (1983), 784-788.

already saw what Isaiah says: "This is our God; in him we put our *hope* that he should *save* us" (Is. 25:9 *NJB*). Expectation and salvation belong together because salvation belongs to the end-time. It is precisely the New Testament,[270] the era which was privileged to experience salvation at close range, which knows that salvation can only be hoped for. Hope is the only appropriate way to appropriate salvation. Salvation is expectation – whatever else we may do about it (Rom. 8:23-25). The link between salvation and hope is intrinsic: "But since we belong to the day, let us be sober, and put on the breastplate of faith and love and for a helmet *the hope of salvation*" (1 Thess. 5:8). The hope of salvation protects all sides of our head down to our neck but must not make us deaf and blind to reality, nor muzzle our mouths at seeing so much in life that is dreadfully wrong. Therefore the helmet of salvation which safeguards us against violation is at the same time the helmet of hope because we have no illusions about the world.

As we look back on the last three parts of the soldier's armor (the breastplate, the shield, and the helmet), it is not hard to discover in them the core of the life of the virtues: faith, hope, and love. Though the Rule has changed the order – for a specific reason, as we will shall see – and has introduced certain accents of its own, the triad is recognizable. The triad, for that matter, is biblical through and through. Paul linked them inimitably in the context of love: Love *believes* all things, *hopes* all things, *endures* all things ... Now faith, hope, and love abide, these three; but the greatest of these is *love*" (1 Cor. 13:7-13). Elsewhere he had already linked them as well. He opens his first letter to the Thessalonians with them.

> We always give thanks to God for all of you and mention you in our prayers, constantly remembering before our God and Father your work of *faith* and labor of *love* and steadfastness of *hope* in our Lord Jesus Christ (1 Thess. 1:2-3).

[270] *elpis* ktl, in *ibid.*, 1 (1980) 1066-1075.

At the end of his letter he again brings them together but now – just as in the Rule – in the symbolic language of the armor of God.

> But since we belong to the day, let us be sober, and put on the breastplate of *faith* and *love,* and for a helmet the *hope* of salvation. For God has destined us not for wrath but for obtaining salvation through our Lord Jesus Christ, who died for us, so that whether we are awake or asleep we may live with him (1 Thess. 5:8-10)

In Pauline spirituality faith, hope, and love spontaneously elicit each other.

Not only Paul[271] but Peter as well is familiar with the triad faith, hope, and love. In his case hope comes first. In Jesus the Messiah we have been "given a new birth into a life of *hope*"; are "being protected by the power of God through *faith*", and we "await salvation in Jesus the Messiah whom we *love* "without having seen him" (1 Pet. 1:3-9). The links between the three are so vital they seem to work automatically: "through the Messiah you have come to *believe* in God ... therefore your *faith* in God is simultaneously *hope* in God ... you must *love* one another deeply from the heart" (1 Pet. 1:21-22). To Peter the divine virtues are intrinsically bound up with the salvation that is awaiting us. We saw it a moment ago: born again in hope, secured by faith, awaiting salvation, looking for the Messiah in love. "You will rejoice with an indescribable and glorious joy as you attain the goal of your faith, the salvation of your souls" (1 Pet. 1:8, 9).[272] The Rule takes over the classic triad of faith, hope, and love, but introduces accents of its own. *Love* is united with justice: justice-in-love. This justice plays an important role in the chapter on silence (XVI). Faith is made unconditional: by trusting, all that is from the devil is resisted and without trust we cannot possibly please God. Hope – linked with

---

[271] For the combination faith-love see also: 2 Thess. 1:3; Col. 1:4-5; Eph. 3:17-19; 6:23-24; etc.

[272] This casts a fascinating light in the section on chapter in its reference to the salvation of souls. Peter says outright the salvation of souls describes the goal of the spiritual life.

salvation and made the hope of salvation – constitutes the climax. It gives the Rule a prophetic-eschatological focus. The polar tension between *justice-in-love* and the *hope-of-salvation* is mediated by *faith-as-unconditional-trust* (Heb. 11:1-6).

The sword of the spirit

The ancient Roman sword was long, blunt, and one-edged for hewing into the enemy. Later it became pointed and was used like a spear.[273] From their wars with the Spaniards the Romans learned to value the short sword – almost a dagger – and took it over. After hitting the enemy with arrows and lances, they killed him with the short sword.

> And the sword of the Spirit,
> which is the word of God,
> should dwell abundantly
> in your mouth and in your hearts.
> And whatever you have to do,
> let it all be done in the Word of the Lord.

In various ways the last implement of the armor of God contrasts sharply with the preceding. It is the first offensive weapon. Also the Spirit and the Word of God do not fit in the series of virtues: love, faith, and hope. Neither are they goods of salvation like justice and salvation. On account of these differences from the preceding series Albert uses the moderately adversative word "now".[274] We will be able to measure the precise import of these differences only after patiently listening to the final passage on the armor of God.

In Scripture the Word and the Spirit completely belong on the side of God. Things came into being by the speech of God; and

---

[273] *Gladius,* in *Paulus Realencyclopädie der Classischen Altertumswissenshaft,* 7, 1, 1372-1376; for representations see: C. Daremberg-F. Saglio, *Dictionnaire des Antiquités Grecques et Romaines,* 2, 2, 1600-1608.

[274] One puts too much weight on *autem* if one renders it *however.* We are going to see that the last part of the armor, though it has several features of its own, fits perfectly in the preceding series.

by his Spirit he gave them soul, animation, zest for living (Gen. 1-2). Psalm 33 puts it in a nutshell: "By the *word* of the Lord the heavens were made, and all their hosts by the *breath* (spirit) of his mouth" (vs. 6). The idea that the enspiriting speech of God can work like a sword can be traced to prophetic circles.

> He made my mouth like a sharp sword,
> in the shadow of his hand he hid me;
> he made me a polished arrow,
> in his quiver he hid me away' (Is. 49:2).
>
> Therefore I have hewn them by the prophets,
> I have killed them by the words of my mouth (Hos. 6:5).

In the Jewish tradition the Torah is often represented as a sharp sword.[275] The militant side of God's word was cultivated in apocalyptic circles as well: "From his mouth came a sharp two-edged *sword*" (Rev. 1:16; see also 2:12; 19:15, 21).

In prophetic traditions the sharp edge of the sword is especially directed outward, but in the letter to the Hebrews it is directed inward.

> Indeed, the word of God is living and active, sharper than any two-edged sword, piercing until it divides soul from spirit, joints from marrow; it is able to judge the thoughts and intentions of the heart. And before him no creature is hidden, but all are naked and laid bare to the eyes of the one to whom we must render an account (Heb. 4:12, 13)

The word of the Lord is a surgical knife which pushes through to the most intimate intertwinings of our mind. It is the surgical knife of discernment.

But more important than the direction of the sword's thrust (outward or inward) is its structure: Spirit and Word at the same time. In early Christian spirituality the Spirit was the real bearer of the Word's meaning. The reading of Scripture was aimed – by way of various "senses" of Scripture – at arriving at "spiritual knowledge".[276]

---

[275] See H. Strack-Billerbeck, *Kommentar zum Neuen Testament*, München 1924, 3, 618.

[276] Cassian, *Conferences*, 14.8-19.

> For it is one thing to be a skilled talker and a shining speaker. It is something else to enter into the very heart and core of heavenly utterances, to contemplate with heart's purest gaze the deep and hidden mysteries. This is not something to be possessed by humanistic lore and worldly erudition. It will be gained only by purity of heart and through the illumination of the *Holy Spirit*.[277]

The Word of God, illumined by the Holy Spirit, refers to contemplation, the goal of the spiritual way. We shall return to this later. This contemplation is called a sword (among other things) because in contemplation discernment gains its definitive acuteness. In light of contemplation in Scripture – the Spirit! – motives and connections are discerned.

This, however, is a long journey, a journey which starts with reading *(lectio)*. Reading imprints Scripture upon our senses. By our looking, listening, speaking or singing Scripture enters our mind. By our repetitions, reflections, and soft hummings the Word gently descends into all our senses and finally into our heart. That is reflection on Scripture (*meditatio*). Once Scripture has been savored with the mouth of the heart it gets a chance to begin to speak. The love movement which animates Scripture takes possession of our heart and, from within the heart, causes it to bubble up to the Source of these love movements. That is prayer *(oratio)*. Finally the eye of our mind opens in the Spirit of God. That is contemplation *(contemplatio)*. The prayer of everyone who loves the Scriptures is fulfilled: "Open my eyes and I will see the wondrous world of your Scripture" (Ps. 119:18). Both the outer world and the inner world become transparent. In one sweeping movement the Word of God lays everything bare; like a sword it cuts through clichés and insularities, fixations and false defense mechanisms, screens and icons, and all that because the Word of God "dwells abundantly in your mouth and in your hearts". The overflow of the Word is the high point and source of all Scripture reading. The Word reaches such a depth in us that it rises up and moves outward in power and passion: the Spirit who digs up and carries along all that is within me.

[277] Ibid., 14.9; *CWS*, 163.

If, then, such matters are carefully received, if they are hidden and consigned within the quiet places of the mind, if they are marked in silence, they will later be like a wine of sweet aroma bringing gladness to the human heart. Matured by long reflection and by patience, they will be poured out as a great fragrance from the vessel of your heart. Like some everlasting spring they will flow out from the channels of experience and from the flowing waters of virtue. They will come bounding forth, running, unceasing, from, as it were, the abyss of your heart. There will happen to you what is said in Proverbs to the one for whom all such things have become utterly real: "Drink the waters from your own wells, fresh water from your own source. May the waters of your own spring pour out for you and may your waters pass over all your ways" (Prv 5:15-16). And, as the prophet Isaiah declares, "You will be like a well-watered garden, like a flowing spring whose waters will never fail. And places emptied for ages will be built up in you. You will lift up the foundations laid by generation after generation. You will be called the builder of fences, the one who turns the pathways toward peace (Is 58:11-12).[278]

The above is full of interesting paradoxes: a sword that dwells abundantly a sword which is like the sweet aroma of a mature wine; a sword which, like an everlasting spring, flows out from the channels of our experience. These paradoxes can only be understood in terms of the mystical love which constitutes the core of the Word. The *Book of the First Monks* knows of this love.

The sayings (promises) of the Lord are pure, silver refined by fire – i.e. love (Ps. 12:7). For, because you have, for the love of God, forsaken the world and the company of humans, in order from a pure heart to adhere to God, you will be rewarded with the abundant enjoyment of divine dialogue, so that mysteries, even future mysteries, are revealed to you by God in the meantime. Then you will overflow with inexpressible joy over the Almighty and the face of your spirit will be lifted up in order freely to behold God.[279]

---

[278] Ibid., 14.13; *CWS*, 168.
[279] *Decem libri*, 1.7.

It is self-evident that Scripture, once it has become the sword of the Spirit, will almost automatically dwell abundantly in mouth and heart and that everything that needs to be done will almost automatically take place in light of the lived and experienced Word of the Lord.

In later ages Carmelites saw this part of the divine armor as an incentive to preaching: let the Word dwell abundantly in your proclamation (John Baconthorpe, Philipe Ribot, John Soreth). But even then this preaching was viewed as flowing forth from contemplation *(contemplationem tradere)*. The nucleus of the last part of the armor of God is the contemplative transformation by the Word. Here again we witness the same dynamic we have consistently seen before: an attribute of God, become incarnate in the Messiah, is interiorized by song, speech, and action. There it touches the core of our existence, at the same time impacting our conduct from there. The power of the Word now flows from within. This dynamic is precisely the reason why Albert here cites the letter to the Colossians.

> Let the word of Christ dwell in you richly; teach and admonish one another in all wisdom; and with gratitude in your hearts sing psalms, hymns, and spiritual songs to God. And whatever you do, in word or deed, do everything in the name of the Lord Jesus, giving thanks to God the Father through him (Col. 3:16-17).

5.3.5 Connections

Depicted in the chapter on the armor of God (XIV) is the transformation of the life of virtue. In this transformation there are three discernible phases.

1. The first phase is marked by the chastity and sanctification of one's thoughts. This phase ties in with the practical objective of the preceding chapters: purity of heart. We saw, remember, that all elementary exercises have in common a single goal: ordering and purifying all that is present within us. This is the goal with which the chastity and sanctification of our thinking links up.

They not only continue the process of purification but also redirect it: toward the reception of God's attributes. The first phase (the chastity and sanctification of our thoughts) is aimed at inner purification, ordering, opening and reception.

2. The second phase is described by the three divine virtues: justice-in-love, unconditional-trust, hope-of-salvation. It is the intent of the Rule that the virtues be practiced at a deep level. Part of this process is

> To have our spirit shaped by their perfection, so that the soul is not, as it were, in thrall to them and violently subjected to their rule but, rather, is filled with a natural pleasure at their goodness, feeding upon them, delightedly climbing that high and narrow road.[280]

One lives by them just as one lives by eating and drinking. The second phase (justice-in-love, faith, and the hope of salvation) is aimed at actually living from the divine attributes.[281]

3. The third phase is aimed at contemplation. In this stage it continues to build on the practice of virtue.

> Hasten in all eagerness to acquire practical, that is, moral, knowledge. Without it, this contemplative purity, of which I spoke, cannot be acquired. This purity comes to those who are made perfect not by the words of those who teach them but rather through the virtuousness of their own acts. It comes as a kind of reward after so much work and labor. They will acquire knowledge not from meditation upon the Law but as the fruit of their work.[282]

Living the life of the virtues is the precondition for contemplation. The Word of God will only dwell abundantly in our mouth and heart when the divine virtues blossom. Just as the chastity and the sanctification of one's thoughts serve to prepare for the reception of the virtues, so the virtues serve to prepare for the

---

[280] Cassian, *Conferences*, 14.3; *CWS*, 156.
[281] Cf. *Conferences* 3.19; 10.7, 13.6, 13, 11.
[282] Cf. *Ibid.*, 14.9; *CWS*, 162.

reception of contemplation. But then the Word can indeed dwell in us richly, not only in our mouth, or in our heart, but in the whole of our conduct. Scripture, then, becomes in us a clear spring in which we view ourselves and the other as he or she is: as coming from God. Then we know the Scriptures from the inside. This is the contemplation of which the Rule speaks in the last part of the armor of God.

With the armor of God a new phase becomes visible in the spiritual way which is laid out for us in the Rule. This way begins with the systematic exercises of the basic provisions: remaining in the cell, reading in Scripture, saying the prayers, assembling in the oratory, etc. Their practical objective is purity of heart. This practical objective, however, is at the same time the starting point of mystical transformation: being clothed with the divine attributes. Purity of heart, after all, is simultaneously the reception of God: the first divine attribute granted us in the armor of God and the entrance to complete transformation in God, the final goal of the spiritual way.

Chapters I-VI	Basic Carmelite provisions
Chapters VII-XII	Elementary exercises
Practical objective: Purity of heart	
Receptivity to God: Final goal	
Chapter XIV	Being clothed with God's attributes – Final goal of mystical transformation

5.4 Preserving Contemplation (XV-XVI)

After contemplation (XIV), just what else can there be? Is not the overflowing fulness of God's Word the end? After being clothed with God's attributes, are not "some work" and "silence" (XVI) anticlimactic? Would not the chapter on work have been more fittingly located in the context of "remaining in the cell" (VII) or "the community of goods" (IX)? And what does work have to do with silence? Why devote so many words to the subject of work and silence? Are they not mere physical exercises, like fasting and abstinence? Why, of all things, does Albert devote so much space to work? Would it not have been better to enlarge upon prayer? Would it not have been enough to say: "And whatever you have to do, let it all be done in the word of the Lord' (XIV)? We can ask similar questions about silence. Within the tradition of the religious life there is no other Rule which reserves comparatively so much space for silence as this one (XVI).

To grasp the inner logic of the Rule we must know that on account of the weakness, instability, and superficiality of the humans receiving this abundance, contemplation is a fragile process, brief and limited in character. The spiritual authors refer to this fact constantly. The love of God is inexhaustible, eternal, and unfathomable. But our capacity for it is weak, our devotion is passing, and, as a result of our conceit, our appropriation is shallow. After contemplation the question is always, How can we preserve and validate this treasure?

A number of answers have come down to us. John Cassian refers to the fear of the Lord: "The riches of our salvation, namely true wisdom and the knowledge of God, cannot be preserved except by the *fear* of the Lord".[283] This is not the fear of punishment but the fear of the beginner. Contemplatives want to preserve love and "in all their deeds and words take the greatest care lest the warmth of that love should in any way diminish". The *Book of the First Monks* views submissive desire as the bedding of contemplation. After Elijah drank from the stream of the pleasures of God[285] comes the question: "How can you persevere in the perfection of the prophetic life of a hermit?"[286] There are two reasons why prophecy (= mysticism) breaks down: In his true and full reality God cannot be endured by human beings and we humans are fragile and limited in our receptivity. Only in the context of

[283] Ibid., 11.13; *CWS*, 152.
[284] Ibidem.
[285] *Decem libri* 1.7.
[286] Ibid., I.8.

perfect submissiveness and imploring desire [287] can we mortals endure the process of mystical transformation. To the question how mystical transformation can have ongoing impact in our life Albert furnishes an answer of his own. As the form (see XV) in which the ongoing interiorization of the abundant Indwelling of the Word can occur he offers: working in silence (XV-XVI).

5.4.1 Work (XV)

Stylistically and in content the chapter on work links up with that on the armor of God. This is instantly visible the moment we juxtapose the conclusion of chapter XIV and the beginning of chapter XV.

Conclusion of Ch. XIV	Beginning of Ch. XV
And whatever *you have to do* (*agere*) *let* it all *be done* (fieri) *in* the Word of the Lord.	Some *work* (opus*) *has to be done* (facere) by you.

1. The form of the gerundive ("... has to be done") which was so determinative for the chapter on the armor of God (six times) is continued: "Whatever you have to do" ... "it has to be done".
2. The two chapters are linked by words from the semantic field of "doing", must be *done (agere),* must *take place (fieri),* must be *done (facere),* some *work (opus).*
3. From the beginning the armor of God was aimed at warding off the assaults of the devil which threaten the *soul.* Now then the work to be done is designed "so that the devil may always find you occupied, lest on account of your idleness the devil manages to find some opportunity of entering into your *souls*" (XV).

Accordingly, the chapter on work is clearly an extension of the discussion on the armor of God. From a spiritual perspective, however, the contrasts between the two chapters are even greater than the similarities.

---

[287] Ibidem.

1. "Some work to be done" does not lie on the level of the attributes of God or of the theological virtues. The "language-game" here differs from that of chastity, justice, love, faith, and hope. One does not put on [the garment of] work the way one is clothed with chastity. "What has to be done", moreover, is not on the same level as "what has to be put on". For "what has to be done" is itself the object of being clothed: it must be done from within the word of the Lord!

2. The case is rather that the work to be done links up with staying in the cell, meditating on Scripture, etc. Remaining in the cell, like doing some work, is a way of being occupied. Doing some work, therefore, is more like a bodily exercise. The temporal references (always, day and night, night and day) belong to this level as well.

3. By comparison with the chapter on the armor of God, this one is expansive and paranetic in tone.

Some work to be done

All Rules have regulations concerning work. And in one way or another the influence of Augustine's *De opere monachorum*[288] consistently plays a role: physical work must be done with a view to the spirit and wellbeing of the community. Augustine, in turn, refers to Paul's Second Letter to the Thessalonians. That gives us two of the most important background texts.

The desert monks viewed work as something which accompanies, structures, and undergirds the life of prayer.[289] It is not clear just what attitude the new religious movements of the eleventh and twelfth centuries assumed toward working, but we do know that the hermits and early Franciscans gave priority to working for their livelihood and only reverted to begging when it was necessary. Not until later did they make *work* of their begging.

By "work" Nicholas the Frenchman, who at one time lived on Mount Carmel, understood spiritual work (reading, meditation,

[288] PL 40:547-582.
[289] Cf. Cassian, *Institutiones* 1.10.7-8.

prayer) as well as physical work (copying codices, agriculture).[290] After 1247 the accent shifted to the work of the apostolate. After that the Carmelites, like all other mendicants, lived from the gospel, which was viewed as work.[291] The question here is how the phrase "some work to do" must be understood in the context of the Rule.

Some work has to done by you,

Instinctively we read "some work" as meaning "not too much": we must always have something in hand to keep us occupied but must not get too busy. This interpretive track dead-ends, however, if put alongside Paul's example which is so emphatically recommended by the Rule: "*Labouring* and *weary* we worked *night and day*" (XV). That sounds a little different from having "some work". A second interpretive possibility is to understand "some work" as "work that does not matter much", work that is more or less routine in nature. This reading loses its attractiveness, however, when we note that the Rule views this work as something that "occupies", i.e. "engrosses" a person. There is good reason for this, for this being occupied – the opposite of being idle – has to keep the devil away from the door! Now then, those who do something routinely or mindlessly actually are not *working.* They are just doing something. Their minds wander. They are *not* occupied. The door stands wide-open to daydreams, illusions, self-reflections, woolgathering to no purpose. We will therefore have to seek the meaning of "some work" in another direction, taking both words – "work" and "some" – seriously.

First of all, the reference is to some *work.* To work is to be engaged in doing something with attention and concentration. Whether it is working the land, making implements, building and restructuring, the care of animals, copying codices, studying sacred texts or the apostolate, the work in question requires

---

[290] Nicolaus Gallus, *Ignea Sagitta* (1270), VIII; ed. A.Staring, in *Carmelus* 9 (1962) 237-307.
[291] Thomas Aquinas, *Summa Theologiae*, 11a-11ae, que. 187, a.3, m.n. ad 3um.

concentration. Hence it does not simply coincide with "whatever you have to do", the clause with which the chapter on the armor of God ended. For that encompasses everything: choosing a prior, obedience, receiving guests,[292] meditation, saying the prayers, coming together for the Eucharist, holding chapter, fasting, abstinence, being quiet. Within the context of "whatever you have to do", "some work" refers to specific activities (see also chapter VII!), which require concentration and render a person "occupied" (again see chapter VII). The question is whether the word "some" serves to limit the amount of work or qualifies its nature. We are inclined to read it as a limitation: "Be sure that this work does not fill all your time. Take care that you are not always working". We have already noted that Paul's example ("*night and day* we worked") and the Rule's own motivation ("to be *always* occupied") do not exactly support this "limiting" reading. Accordingly, I believe that "some" must be understood in a qualifying sense: it must deserve the name of *work*; it must qualify as labor; it must really be some sort of *work*.

Once we take this road we can go further. "Some work" can then get the associated meaning: *part* of the work that has to be done in the community. This harmonizes well with the chapter on the community of goods: Carmelites do not keep anything for themselves alone but all share and let others share in that which is common to all, work included. We must bear in mind that much work was assigned, as is evident from the life of the humble Abba Pinufius.

> All that his superior [a young brother in charge of a garden] ordered him to do and all the care of the *work* entrusted to him he carried out with a holy humility which was most admirable. At night he even performed in secret certain necessary duties which were shunned and avoided by others so that when morning dawned the whole community marvelled that this useful *work* had been done, though no one knew who had done it.[293]

---

[292] *agenda sunt* (VI)!
[293] Cassian, *Conferences*, 20.1.

The work I do, therefore, is not my work but some part of the community's work in which I take part. By doing some work I participate in the work-community. In so doing I adhere to the creation order as recorded in Genesis (3:17-19) and dissociate myself from the busybodies Paul had so little use for. Their conduct was dis-order-ly (*ataktos*).

Being always occupied

To have some work to do, then, is to be absorbed in doing something that deserves the name of work, something by which we fit ourselves into the creation order. While this helps to define the concept more sharply, it does not yet convey its spiritual significance, the thing the Rule is interested in.

> so that the devil may always find you occupied,
> lest on account of your idleness
> he manage to find some opportunity
> of entering into your souls.

Actually the Rule says the same thing twice. The first time the statement is positive: "so that the devil may always find you occupied". The second time it is negative: "lest on account of your idleness he manage to find some opportunity of entering into your souls". The contrasting parallelism is perfect: being occupied vs. being idle; the devil vs. the soul; "always occupied" vs. "entering into your souls"; both times the reference is to the devil stalking the soul. The positive and the negative statements literally reinforce each other. "Some work", in sum, has a single clear goal: to keep the devil absolutely outside the door.

In the history of Rule-making the subject of screening out and seeking protection from the devil[294] comes back in various ways. By working, Carmelites keep their senses busy. They distract them by engaging in exhausting labor. On the lee-side of this, consequently, the relationship to God can blossom. On this level, "some work" is comparable to the cell, for both are forms of remaining

---

[294] See Cicconetti, *Rule,* 279-281 (with examples).

occupied. The spiritual function of work is to concentrate the mind; to be brought into a single focus in solitude; to become familiar with the inner person; to be no longer a spiritual wanderer but to be turned inward and so to learn acutely to discern one's deeper motives.[295] The cell, by its insulation, its isolation, its inward focus, and its indwelling, supports this internal function of work. There is an intrinsic connection between the concentration of the work and the *simpli*-fication of the cell.

> Abba Serapion told a young monk not to be idle or footloose, friviously rushing in all directions, especially because he was young and strong. Instead, he ought to remain in his cell, as the teaching of the elders demanded, and he should choose to support himself by his own efforts rather than through the generosity of someone else.[296]

Restlessly lounging around outside one's cell and away from one's work makes a person extremely vulnerable, leaving him wide open to all sorts of influences. It leaves the door open to forces which are destructive of life. This is most detrimental to the soul: it coarsens, loses its coherence, and becomes vacuous. One's cell and one's work, on the other hand, point the way inward, or rather, they *are* the inward, the indwelling, the interiorization *itself.*

The example of Paul

The spiritual significance of work, far from being exhausted by its aversive effect vis-à-vis the devil, emerges in its full import when we carefully consider the teaching and example of the holy apostle Paul.

> In this matter you have both
> the teaching and example of the blessed apostle Paul,
> in whose mouth Christ spoke,
> who was appointed and given by God
> as preacher and teacher
> of the nations in faith and truth;
> *if you follow him you cannot go astray.*

[295] Cassian, *Conferences*, 24.4.
[296] Ibid., 18.11.

It is striking that Albert, who is succinct elsewhere, is so expansive here. What is the reason for this? Is he trying to overwhelm his readers? Why did he deem it necessary, precisely in this chapter, to posit such a powerful example? Reading this, one would think that the imitation of Paul is on a par with the imitation of Christ. Were the original Carmel-dwellers perhaps reluctant to go in this direction? Did they have another view of work? Or was it Albert's intent precisely to confirm their view?

Albert stresses first of all that both in his *teaching* and in his *lifestyle* Paul had a right to speak. In the quotation from 2 Thessalonians both aspects are expressly stated: "we wanted to present ourselves as a model for you so that you might imitate us. In fact, when we were with you we instructed you to this effect" (2 Thess. 3:9, 10). In a spiritual model we are, of course, dealing with the duality of instruction and practice.

Paul's teaching here is framed in the field of tension between Christ and the nations. On the one hand, Paul is he "through whose mouth *Christ* spoke" (cf. 2 Cor. 13:3); on the other, he was appointed and given by God "as teacher and preacher of the nations" (1 Tim. 2:7; cf. 2 Tim. 1:11). In light of this, Paul's instruction is marked as standing between the original source (Christ [Gal. 2:20]) and the goal. This source does not remain enclosed in Paul but flows out by way of Paul to all the nations. The river of his proclamation has its bedding in "faith and truth" (1 Tim. 2:7). Those who through Paul are gathered in the Messiah from among the Gentiles find the way to life that is life indeed: "if you follow him you cannot go astray". Thus the Rule recommends the teaching and life of Paul as a safe roadmap to salvation. This recommendation has a solemn adjuring quality, especially because of the dyadic rhythm the Rule employs: teaching and example; appointed and given; preacher and teacher; faith and truth.

Why is Paul so emphatically offered as our example? Answer: because of the weight he attributes to work. In Scripture work is viewed in various ways. In Genesis it is seen as a punishment imposed on humans by God (3:17-19). In Ecclesiastes it is considered vexation and vanity (2:18-23). To the psalmist of Psalm 104 work is a way of joining God in creating things based on his wisdom (vss. 23-24). Psalm 8 views human beings as God's deputies: humanity manages the creation on God's behalf and in the name of God. Thus human labor is seen from a variety of perspectives. Paul, for one, sees it from the perspective of the coming Son of man. In his writing everything, work included, is oriented to the End. From yonder side – past the horizon of time – God comes out to meet us in Christ. This precisely is the perspective in which Paul situates work. From the return of the Lord some draw their own conclusions: they quit working. No, says Paul, you must not stop working but work differently. This is the secret behind Albert's strong emphasis on Paul's teaching and life: he wants to instil this eschatological orientation in all our work. We will see what that means as we follow the further explication of this chapter.

> Laboring and weary we lived among you,
> he says,
> working night and day
> so as not to be a burden to any of you;
> not that we had no right to do otherwise,
> but so as to give you ourselves as an example,
> that you might imitate us.

This section of the quotation from Paul concerns especially the exemplary nature of Paul's *practice*. As preacher of the gospel Paul has the right to be supported by the churches, but he voluntarily refrains from asserting that right. He practices the tentmaker's trade and at the same time devotes himself to preaching the gospel among the nations. Doing both together means an overly full daily schedule. "So as not to be a burden to any of you" he invests all the time not given to preaching in the trade by which he earns his living. It is profitable for us to keep in mind the tension between Paul's occupation and his preaching. For working "night and day" does not mean that all the time available to him was invested in his trade as tentmaker. No: it is during the limited amount of time still left *after* he had done his apostolic work that he labored at his livelihood. That was what kept him busy day and night. In the Rule, too, the reference is to the *remaining* time, the time that is left *after* we have done all the necessary things.

It is Paul's intent to model a form of working which can be followed as an example by the members of the churches. In spirituality our goal is consistently to live a life form so intensely – labouring and weary – that by our example others may gain access to the experience which is fundamental to this form. This is a basic insight in every spirituality. A combination of preaching and working, as this was exhibited in Paul's life and as life form, is held up as an example to every Carmelite. Not that we have to give to our evangelical life and our work the same form and content as Paul did; but it does mean that in our life we must be willing to undergo a tension between the things we have to do on the basis of our calling (staying in the cell; reading Scripture; praying; the liturgy of the hours; etc.) and the work by means of which we earn a livelihood.

Having held up as exemplary Paul's *practice* Albert now brings his *teaching* to the fore.

> For when we were with you
> we used to tell you,
> If any are unwilling to work,
> let them not eat.
> For we have heard
> that there are certain people among you
> going about restlessly and doing no work.
> We urge people of this kind
> and beseech them in the Lord Jesus Christ
> to earn their bread
> working in silence.

This second part of the quotation from Paul concerns the *didactic* aspect: the instruction. Twice Paul mentions something he held up to them: "When we were with you, we used to tell you ... People of this kind we urge ...". He even goes so far as to implore the members of his church to earn their bread working in silence.

Accordingly, the imploring tone we detected earlier in Albert's recommendation derives its force in part from the adjuratory character of the quotation from Paul.

Just what was the focus of Paul's concern?[297] Some people in Thessalonica were of the opinion that the End-time (in the strict sense) was already in effect (2 Thess 2:2). Aside from the Lord's return this also meant the restoration of the paradisal state. An important part of this paradisal restoration was the lifting of the necessity to work. Before the end, i.e. as long as the present age lasts, the law of Genesis applies: humans must eat bread by the sweat of their brow (Gen. 3:17-19). The erring Thessalonians broke with this order. They believed the End had erupted in the present and so they were "dis-order-ly".[298] They have quit working, thus breaking with the tradition they received from Paul (2 Thess. 3:6). They are eating without having really exerted themselves (2 Thess. 3:7-8) and hang around idle spreading unrest everywhere (2 Thess 3:11-12). The order of this age, however, is that working and eating are integrally bound up with each other.

Paul's teaching can be pressed into a single saying: "Anyone unwilling to work should not eat" (2 Thess. 3:10). Expressed here is an intrinsic bond between labor and livelihood. This connection is part of the divine order for this age. This order may not be violated under the pretext that the End has come. It is not *working* that must be stopped; it is our *way* of working that must be changed – changed in view of the approaching End. How can we do our work in a way that corresponds to the order of this age and at the same time live totally in terms of the End?

What comes to mind is the statement of Leon Blum who, imprisoned in a Nazi camp, wrote: "We work *in* the present, not *for* the

---

[297] For background information see: M. Menken, *Paradise regained or still lost? Eschatology and disorderly behaviour in 2 Thessalonians*, in *New Testament Studies* 38 (1992) 271-289.

[298] Paul uses the word *atattos,* which means, "violating the divine order after the Fall"; cf. Menken, *ibid.,* 271-289.

present". Genuine dedication in working does not seek the applause
of one's own time. It devotes itself in dark trust to "a time which lies
past the horizon of my time". Surfacing here is the eschatological
meaning of "some work". Our work in this age is fragmentary, part
of a whole we cannot take in from where we sit. It is only a completely naked faith which knows that this "some" is bound up with
a body of the Messiah I can neither conceive or organize. By disin-
terestedly stepping outside of myself in work I exercise myself
in darkly trusting the End. As worker I abandon the prospect of
"personally experiencing the outcome" of my work. This work is
essentially prophetic: it works "without entering the Promised
Land". This prophetic eschatology is free: delivered from the snares
of calculation, delivered from the triumph of that which succeeded,
delivered from the nihilism of uncommitted game-playing and
waste. And stronger: in dark trust discerning a triumph "in a time
without me ...". The prophetism of this work is located precisely in
this "eschatology without hope for myself ...". Really working
exceeds the boundaries of one's own time. It is "action for a world
that is coming, action which surpasses this time, action in which I
surpass myself, and in which the yearning for an epiphany of the
Other is included".[299]

Now we understand why the Rule so emphatically features Paul
as teacher and example. Both in his teaching and example he
endures the tension between working in this age and working
in light of the End. By following Paul's example we share in his
prophetic-eschatological manner of working.

The way of work

Working is much more than completing an assignment or doing
one's share: it is a process-in-motion, a way. The Rule of Innocent
IV (1247) therefore concisely sums up the essence of the chapter
on work by adding this conclusion:

This way is holy and good:
follow it.

---

[299] Levinas, *Het menselijk gelaat,* 172-173.

With these concluding words the Carmelite Rule evokes the prophetic
traditions which give depth to Paul's eschatological-prophetic
lifestyle. Three passages from Scripture vie for priority.
1. First a text from Isaiah: "This is *the way; walk in it*" (Is. 30:21).[300]
   This text, taken from a chapter which the Rule again cites in
   the chapter on silence, accuses the Israelites of "carrying out a
   plan, but not mine" (30:1). They set out on their own to a
   goal they have set for themselves (30:2). But this way has no
   future (30:3-7). Self-determination has blinded Israel, closed
   its mind to the real instruction and to the genuine prophecy
   which comes from outside its own circular path (30:8-11).
   Because Israel seals itself off it destroys itself (30:12-14). The
   only thing that can really help is for Israel to seek its point of
   gravity in God and in silence to expect everything from him
   and no one else (30:15-17). But even past Israel's self-isolation
   and self-destruction, and grief, God's teaching will come
   through to it saying: "This is the way; walk in it" (30:20-21).
   Then everything will change between God and his people:
   prosperity *will* prevail (30:22-26). This text from Isaiah touches
   the core: in all work the pivotal question is whether or not we
   will isolate ourselves in our own plans. Work that isolates itself
   ruins itself. Work that permits itself to be directed from Beyond
   receives the right direction: "This is the way; walk in it".
2. The second quotation, one that is melted into the quotation
   we have just discussed, comes from Isaiah as well: "a highway
   shall be there, and it shall be called *The Holy Way*" (Is. 35:8).[301]
   The context speaks of the exiles" joyful return home through
   the desert. On this occasion the desert dresses itself in delight
   and blankets itself with flowers (35:1-2). The exiles who are
   returning need not be afraid; they will without trouble survive
   the wilderness journey (35:3-7). A paved road will be constructed through the desert, a road such as only the most holy
   cities know: splendid roads which lead into the sanctuary

---

[300] In the Vulgate: *Haec est via, ambulate in ea.*
[301] In the Vulgate: *Et erit ibi semita et via, et via sancta vocabitur.*

(35:8-10). Even more forcefully than the previous text this quotation stresses that the actual work comes from the other side. The exiles only set out on the journey – that is all. All the other things came over them: the blossoming steppe, the glory of the Lord. Essentially this way is God's own coming! "He will come and save you" (35:4). Everything is written from the perspective of God's coming: eyes and ears will be opened; strength enters people's legs; streams break forth (35:5-7). From within the sanctuary a holy way unwinds on which the exiles will walk "just like that" (30:8-10). They do not pave the way themselves! Applied to the work we do this means: in our fragmentary efforts there is one who works toward us. "Some work" is a holy way: a way that is paved from within the holy place by the Holy One of Israel himself.

3. The third Scriptural given, one that can hardly be restricted to a single text, stems from the spirituality of the wisdom litera-ture in which *the good way*, the *path of uprightness*[302] is a familiar motif. The good way leads to life,[303] the evil way to death.[304] As a result an interesting tension develops in the Rule. Wisdom, after all, viewed as such, remains within the order of this aeon. Intensely eager prophetic-eschatological hope for the End, past the horizon of the empirical present, is foreign – even fool-ishness – to this wisdom! To foster an expectation reaching beyond the boundaries of the present is the death of our entire working-world. How could there be life there? That is *not* a good way. However, because the Rule mixes the prophetic eschatology of Isaiah with the orderly mental processes of the wise, precisely that tension arises which is so characteristic for Pauline spirituality but now in the reverse order: quietly work-ing in expectation of the Approaching One who comes toward us from beyond the grave (the *holy* way) is the way to life (the *good* way).

[302] Cf. Prov. 2:8, 20; 16:5, 29; Sir. 37:11.
[303] Cf. Prov. 2:1-22; 16:2-9; 25-29.
[304] Cf. Prov. 2:12; 28:10; Jer, 18:11; 25:5; 26:3; etc.

Doing some work is a spiritual way, a way which essentially originates in God but is at the same time a way we walk. From our
perspective this way is meaningless because we are denied a view
of the End. Remaining to us is merely a quiet hope, patience, and
a going forth in darkness. This reaching out in darkness makes
clear the actual import of all our actions – *past* the meanings we
attach to them, however important and solid these meanings may
be. *Past* all meaning the Carmelite waits with eagerness for the
Coming One. To do some work is to go selflessly into the night
"with no other light or guide than the one that burned in my
heart".[305] Now all our knowing is a knowing in part – "some
work" – but then we shall be known as we are known. To do some
work is to go the way which leads into alterity. This way is holy:
it is presented to us from within alterity. This way is good, for it
leads us into life.

As we look back upon the chapter on work, we see that work fitting
into the Carmelite Rule as follows:

	The spiritual way of the Rule	The chapter on work
I-VI	Carmelite Basic provisions	Some work
VII-XIII	Basic provisions	have to be done by you
XIV	Being clothed with God's attributes	so that you may always be occupied
XV-XVI	Lasting interiorization of contemplation	Work now out of the End as Paul

1. Like the cell, Scripture, the oratory, etc., so *some work* is a basic
   provision. Several aspects run together in it: a communal aspect,
   insofar as in a cenobitic community "some work" gives us access

---

[305] John of the Cross, *The Dark Night* (Collected Works, 1979, 711).

to the work of the community; a personal aspect insofar as some work is set aside for each member of the community; a spatial aspect insofar as the work effects a material transformation of the place (in the cell or in the common space).

2. Like staying in the cell, reading in Scripture, saying the prayers, coming together in the oratory, etc., *doing* some work is an elementary exercise. The practical objective is to shape a fenced-off space, just as staying in the cell, muttering the words of Scripture, and saying the prayers do this. The work weaves a firm structure around the soul by which the soul is made receptive to the overflowing abundance of the Word.

3. This, in turn, *occupies* the soul. The devil, who in the chapter on the armor of God is the great antagonist of our transformation in God, is kept outside the door by work: "Some work has to be done, so that the devil may always find you occupied, lest on account of your idleness he manage to find some opportunity of entering into your souls" (XV). This aversive formulation in turn evokes the positive converse: work is an invitation to God to enter the soul and to take up residence in it.

4. Because the work naturally focuses on *the teaching and example of Paul,* it unfolds its disinterested character as orientation to the End. Because of this orientation it renders the reception of God's attributes permanent. "Some work" permanently interiorizes the influence of God's Word by extending it eschatologically. The overflowing Word of God by "some work", becomes a way.

5.4.2 Silence (XVI)

Albert, by a literary device, links the chapter on silence (XVI) to that on work (XV). First he expressly refers back to the apostle Paul: "The *apostle* recommends silence ...". Next, he expressly refers back to the motif of work: "The apostle tells us to *work* in silence". Albert thus places silence in the context of work: "the apostle recommends *silence* when he tells us to work *in it*". The spiritual relationship between work and silence is unclear. Just what is the meaning of silence in the Rule of Carmel?

Elijan silence

Before proceeding to the institution of silence Albert offers us biblical motivation for it: he repeats Paul's recommendation and twice quotes Isaiah.

> The apostle recommends silence,
> when he tells us to work in it.
> As the prophet also testifies,
> Silence is the cultivation of justice;
> and again,
> In silence and hope will be your strength.

The silence recommended by Paul and summed up in the Isaiah-quotations goes back to the traditions of Elijan prophecy. Characteristic for these prophetic traditions is that they confronted Israel with the deadly outcome of its own misconduct (cf. Am. 8:2; Hos. 1:9; Is. 6:11; Jer. 1:14). In exile – which was the death of Israel – the people were to remember the Elijan prophecies. They remembered that in Israel's misconduct Elijah heard the silence of death (1 Kgs. 19:12). He let himself be battered into silence by this vision of death. He grew silent and he *heard* (1 Kgs. 19:13).[306] This prophetic-mystical silence became a dominant feature in biblical silence, cultivated especially in the school of Isaiah. In the exile this silence was able to ripen into the tranquil hope of the quiet in the land. It became a spiritual way. The most significant phases of this way we wish to describe as follows.

1. *The silence of death.* Silence means death: the motionless darkness where the dead dwell (1 Sam. 2:9). They "go down into silence" (Ps. 115:17). To kill someone is to render him silent (Hos. 4:5-6; 10:15; Zeph. 1:11; Jer. 48:2; etc.). The silence of death has many faces. It can be the silence-in-death of a city or a people. A devastated city presents a scene of death and desolation (cf. Jer. 49:26). Elijah saw the silence of death in lifeless Israel: war, revolution, and divine judgment (1 Kgs. 19:12, 15-17). Also a person's own death,

---

[306] Cf. K. Waaijman, *Elia*, Nijmegen 1985, 17-19; 64-69.

in its lifeless silence, may suddenly appear before his mind's eye.
Thus a wise man grows silent at the thought of destroying himself
by living a sinful life (Ps. 39:2-4). It was a bold step in the Elijan
tradition to link the silence of the deadly ending with a theophany
(1 Kgs. 19:11-12). The traditional heralds (Breath, Earthquake,
and Fire) no longer announce God's appearance. The King passes
by only after a new herald, the Voice which batters into silence,
has announced him. In the exile this Voice, which announces the
death of Israel, will be heard by all.

2. *Cessation of speech.* Anyone touched by the silence of death
– war, sickness, decline, judgment, doom – is perplexed.[307] Nations
grow silent at sight of the destruction of Tyre (Ezk. 26:15-18).
Someone suddenly hit by a deadly disease is struck dumb (Ps. 31:18).
When mighty Egypt has to look on in dismay as Israel marches
away the nations become still (Ex. 15:16; cf. Lev. 10:3; Hos. 4:5;
Am. 5:13). Death renders one silent (Is. 6:5; 38:10). In the first
place this silence is a completely natural organic reaction. It happens automatically, as when a person gets gooseflesh. However,
one can also *maintain* this spontaneous reaction. That occurs when
people conduct a ritual of silence. When the friends of Job see
how his life is marked by death they stop speaking: They tear
their robes, throw dust in the air upon their heads, and sit down
by Job. No one speaks a word for seven days and seven nights
(Job 2:13). Tearing one's clothes and shaving one's head are rituals of self-abasement, as are lying still on the ground (Ps. 6:3-4),
stumbling forward in a bent posture (Ps. 38:18), clothing oneself
in sackcloth (Ps. 30:12; 35:13), fasting and keeping vigil (Ps. 35:13;
69:11).[308] Also the custom of remaining silent is such a self-abasement ritual: to live speechless and motionless through the crisis of
death. A great deal happens in this silence, as we can tell from
Psalm 39 which is cited by the Rule. The psalmist withdraws into

---

[307] *damah/dmm/dwm* in *TWAT* 2:277-283.

[308] We encounter these customs especially in psalms of illness. Cf. K. Waaijman, *Psalmen bij ziekte en genezing,* Kampen 1981.

a furnace of silence in which all his illusions and fixations are melted down (vss. 3-4b). This meltdown then brings him into contact with the insignificant mortal he is (vss. 4c-7).

3. *Quiet expectation.* The furnace of silence leads me to a place where I become imbued with the awareness of my own insignificance (Ps. 39:5-7). Neither externally nor internally am I able to give stability to myself. The only One who can give my life solidity is God. Apart from God "my world is nowhere" (Ps. 39:6). For that reason the transient creature I am, and in silence experience myself to be, turns from within to the Source of my life: "In You alone I hope" (Ps. 39:8-9). Thus the furnace of silence is inwardly transformed into the quiet glow of expectation. "In quietness I wait for the one who wills my deliverance" (Lam. 3:26).

The furnace of silence transforms us even more deeply when our expectation touches the self. For though my fixations were already melted away and my trust in God had already been born, it was still *my* quiet expectation that sustained me. I was still clinging to my lack which I projected outside of myself on *him*. Dare I admit that God could possibly be quite different from what I am quietly expecting him to be? Here my yearning is touched at the roots and hence uprooted (Ps. 39:10-12). This silence, while deadly, is also liberating: it frees me from the fear of death. The focus of *my* expectation shifts to expectation of *him*; it now becomes a matter of expecting and existing in light of who he is. This is the quiet trust which Isaiah recommends (Is. 30:15). Over against the short-term thinkers and short-winded planners of Jerusalem (Is. 30:1), who in their dread seek refuge in illusions (Is. 30:3-7; 12-14), he posits the long breath (Is 30:2; 8-11) of the non-manipulable future of God who makes his power felt in quiet expectation (Is. 30:15).

4. *Becoming silent.* Those who were led to the discovery of their insignificance and in that discovery caught fire in expectation, but then, delivered from that as well, became anchored in God, have nothing left to lose. Quiet hope has become their identity, their

strength. They enjoy themselves at the table of Life (Ps. 39:13). Everything is now a gift to them; they have nothing, but possess all things. The ravens feed Elijah, while he is hidden in the love-brook Carith. John of the Cross shelled peas in the morning. The disowned silence becomes quiet expectation (Ps. 22:3; 30:13; Is. 62:6-7). "The silence has become a celebration" (Ps. 65:2). It is the quiet triumph of a Presence which was not exacted, nor defined from within myself. This silence is incomprehensibly direct and distinguished. It is Life itself in its imageless Presence. This is Isaiah's quiet hope: "In silence and hope will be your strength" (Is. 30:15).

The institution of the silence of the night

Following Paul's recommendation and the double motivation from Isaiah in which biblical silence is made present comes the institution of silence in two stages. First, in just a few words, the silence of the night is instituted.

Albert's text	Text of Innocent IV
Therefore we direct that you keep silence	Therefore we direct that you keep silence
from after vespers until terce of the following day, unless some necessity or good reason, or the prior's permission, interrupts the silence.	*from after compline until after prime of the following day.*

All great Rules know the distinction between the silence of the day and the silence of the night (the latter is also known as the grand or supreme silence). The silence of the night was marked by a strict cessation of speech which was sometimes extended to certain places as well (oratory, refectory, walkway, dormitory). Some Rules were extremely rigorous in their enforcement of silence.

In the original rule the silence of the night lasted from nightfall around six in the evening (the hour of vespers) to the ninth hour on the next day (the time of terce). Innocent IV shortened the silence of the night: now it begins later (after compline) and ends sooner (after prime). The original length of the silence of the night was too hard for the community.

From the beginning of the day to terce and from the vespers to the end of the day numerous things – necessary to the brothers – often had to be done which could not reasonably be accomplished in silence, particularly things tied to instruction of the brothers.[309]

The papal advisors solved these difficulties by abbreviating the silence of the night.

More important than its length is the spiritual meaning of the silence of the night. "Night" and "silence" are closely connected in the history of spirituality. Night, with its terrifying sense of displacement from one's home, is a time of purification[310] – like the desert. The senses and the mind are stripped of their protective images. Night puts the immeasurability of God in the center. One who begins to sense this is drawn past all the images which up until then cast (an illusory) light on God – so far in fact that even the memory grows dim.[311] The night immerses us "in the nothingness, i.e., in the divine darkness, the supreme bliss of God and the saints".[312] A similar effect is attributed to silence. Silence pulls me away from the world of fixed patterns.

> Basil: "Silence makes it possible for us to forget old habits . . . and offers the opportunity to practice the good".

> Isaac of Nineveh: "By persistent silence and fasting a person decides to be continually occupied with service to God".

> Philoxenus of Mabbug: "Material silence leads us into spiritual silence and spiritual silence causes one to rise up to life in God".

> Isaac of Nineveh: "Love silence above all. It bears fruit such as no tongue can describe. At the beginning it is we ourselves who force ourselves to be silent. Afterward something is born out of our silence that lures us into silence. May God grant you the ability to grasp what is born out of the silence. Once you begin with this practice I would not know what light could not ignite in you through it".

---

[309] *Decem libri*, 8.4.
[310] See *Nuit*, in *DS* 11 (1982), 520-523.
[311] Herp, *Theologia mystica*, 2:61, Cologne 1545.
[312] Ibid., 3.30.

Dionysius the Areopagite: "The simple absolute, and unchanged mysteries of theology lie hidden in *the darkness* beyond light of the hidden mystical *silence*".[313]

Both silence and the night lead us to an imageless naked surrender to God who is imageless and inexpressible.[314] By keeping vigil at night we expose ourselves to this quiet Presence. Night is a symbol of the unknowable and unfathomable Presence. On this point the entire mystical tradition – from Gregory of Nyssa and Dionysius the Areopagite to Eckhart and John of the Cross – is unanimous.

> The tranquil night
> At the time of the rising dawn,
> Silent music,
> Sounding solitude.

> She [the soul] calls this music "silent" because it is tranquil and quiet knowledge, without the sound of voices. And thus there is in it the sweetness of music and the quietude of silence. Accordingly, she says that her Beloved is silent music because in Him she knows and enjoys this symphony of spiritual music ...[315]

The institution of the silence of the day

Following the silence of the night the silence of the day is instituted, a subject to which many more words are devoted! A rather large number of biblical reasons are advanced as well.

> At other times, however,
> although you need not observe silence so strictly,
> you should nevertheless be all the more careful
> to avoid much talking,
> for as it is written –
> and experience teaches no less –
> where there is much talk

---

313 Cited in *Silence* in: *DS* 14 (1990) 838-839.
314 For this "mystical silence" see: *ibid.*, 845-851.
315 John of the Cross, *The Spiritual Canticle,* Collected Works, 1979, 472-473.

sin will not be lacking;
and, He who is careless in speech
will come to harm;
and elsewhere, He who uses many words injures his soul.
And the Lord says in the gospel:
For every idle word that people speak
they will render account on judgment day.
Let each one, therefore,
measure his words
and keep a tight rein on his mouth,
lest he stumble
and fall by his talking
and his fall be irreparable
and prove fatal.
With the prophet let him watch his ways,
lest he sin with his tongue;
let him try attentively and carefully
to practice the silence
in which is the cultivation of justice.

The silence of the day breathes a different atmosphere from that of the night. At first blush it seems the Rule does not realize this. It expresses the difference between the two in quantitative terms: during the day you "need not observe silence as *(tanta)* strictly". It seems that during the day one must find the golden mean somewhere between *not*-talking (the silence of the night) and *much*-talking (the boundary of the silence of the day). This quantitative approach, however, fails to do justice to the quality of the silence of the day as it comes to expression in the Rule. We discover this qualitative silence by juxtaposing the beginning and the end of the silence of the day.

Beginning	End
At other times, however, although you need not observe silence so strictly, you should nevertheless be all the more careful to avoid much talking	let him try attentively and carefully to practice the silence in which is the cultivation of justice.

The silence of the day is not merely a diminished version of the silence of the night, or the avoidance of much talking; it is rather to be observed attentively and carefully. The reason for this caution is that this silence consists in the cultivation of justice.

This cultivation has both a negative and a positive component.

A. The *negative* component consists in guarding oneself against much talking. Five citations, supported by experience, serve to bring home the disastrous prospect of much talking.
1. The first citation is taken from the book of Proverbs (10:19). The spirituality of Proverbs circles around questions like the following: How can one build a "house" that is alive? How does one avoid a path that leads to death? In the face of these choices the tongue is of decisive importance: it gives direction to one's conduct. The tongue can speak both for good and ill, bless and curse. Especially in social settings it can be a wellspring of life as well as a fount of evil: (Prov. 10:11). "The mouth of the garrulous fool makes ruin imminent" (Prov. 10:19, 21). The prospect of death contains the incentive for restrained and truthful speech.
2. The second citation from Scripture also comes from Proverbs (13:3). Here, too, the prospect of death stands out, especially as a result of the antithetic parallelism: "Those who guard their mouths preserve their lives; those who open wide their lips come to ruin" (Prov. 13:3). This proverb gives expression to still another fundamental given: the law of reciprocity. "One who opens wide his mouth devours himself" (Prov. 13:2).
3. The third citation, taken from Jesus Sirach, further brings home the law of reciprocity: "Those who talk too much harm their own souls" (Ben Sira 20:8). This statement brings out into the open the core problem inherent in garrulity: those who talk too much and too fast estrange themselves from themselves by their many words (Ben Sira 20:8, 18). The result is that in our social relations also our conduct is not constructive. Reserved persons, by contrast, know how to restrain themselves. Such persons are themselves – do not "live" away from themselves. With their respect for others they build up community. They know what to say and when to say it (Ben Sira 20:1, 6, 7). They are viewed as wise and pleasant (Ben Sira 20:5, 8, 13).

4. The fourth citation, which comes from Matthew (12:36), brings the prospect of death to a (provisional) climax: "the day of the judgment". This puts garrulousness in a definitive context: final judgment. People will have to give an account of every careless word to the Son of Man when he appears as Judge. If our speech is empty, i.e. without relation to ourselves, our neighbor, the Messiah, the truth, we are lost. We have then in effect voided our own value.

5. The fifth citation is again from Jesus Sirach. After urging people to weigh their words carefully – "make balances and scales for your words and keep a tight rein on your mouth" (cf. Ben Sira 28:25), he adds as a deterrent prospect the words: "lest they stumble and fall by their talking and their fall proves fatal" (Ben Sira 28:26). The end suddenly comes upon us like a thief in the night, as the empty words suddenly turn against us, causing us to stumble on the brink of the abyss, and plunge us into the void of our own speech. This fall is irreversible.

B. The *positive* component consists in the obligation of all persons to weigh our words with care. And we must keep our mouth in check as though it were a horse. For this positive instruction the Rule again cites Jesus Sirach (28:25). If we are to escape the evil we do with our tongue, we will have to take great care not to harm our neighbor in his absence or insult him in his presence. To this end one must practice speaking well of people. The Teacher uses two images to make this point.

The first is that of a scale. Before one speaks one must carefully weigh the words one is about to use. That is: say exactly as much as there is in our heart to say and as is necessary for the matter under discussion – hence, in measured terms. But also: weigh your words against each other and choose the best.

The other image is that of the bridle and reins used to keep a beast of burden in check. By nature our speech is uncurbed or unbridled. Reins and bridle limit it. Also: the reins by which an animal is tamed make it useful.

Measured and controlled speech calls for "muzzling" (Ps. 39:2) the tongue and mouth, i.e. the inner direction of our conduct. If the psalmist remains true to this inner culture he will "guard his ways and not sin with his tongue" (Ps. 39:2). Silence has here become a kind of conduct: the core of just action and carefully measured speech. We must, says the Rule, attentively and carefully practice this silence, a silence which consists in the cultivation of justice.[316] As the *Book of the First Monks* states in a nutshell silence has community-building implications:

> The monks were so peacefully disposed to each other that there was no disunity among them. In their speech they were armed with silence, for there was no garrulousness among them. And because of this they were peaceful and self-assured: their heart did not accuse them before God.[317]

The structure of the passage on the silence of the day is clear. Following the course of the admonitions, while omitting the motivations, we note three elements.

Element A	Element B	Element C
At other times, however, although you need not observe silence so strictly, you should nevertheless be all the more careful to avoid much talking.	Let each one, therefore, measure his words and keep a tight rein on his mouth.	With the prophet let him watch his ways lest he sin with his tongue; let him try attentively and carefully to practice the silence in which is the cultivation of justice.

Element A presents the negative silence of the day: avoid much talking. This line is continued in element B: measure your speech.

---

[316] For this ascetic silence which takes shape in our dealing with ourselves and others, see *Silence, DS* 14 (1990) 837-839.

[317] *Decem libri*, 4.7.

Element C gives expression to the positive side of the silence of the day: speak with close attention and care. This line, too, is present in element B: speak well. Hence the silence of the day is situated in the field of tension between elements A and C as mediated by B: the little that is said during the day (A) must be interiorly cultivated into justice (C) by means of a scale and tight reins (B).

The silence of Carmel

The chapter on silence (XVI), in its very structure, portrays the silence of Carmel. The chapter is divided in two parts: part 1, consisting of the motivation for the Isaiah-citations and part 2, consisting of the religious institution of silence.

In part 1 the silence is motivated by the two Isaiah-texts which are cited in support of Paul's recommendation. These two citations together embrace the basic tension inherent in Elijan silence. The first citation: silence admits to one's consciousness the dark sides of life; does not run from them but lets their poison work like a fire which consumes our inner fixities and images until we are fluid. Now the silence is distilled into quiet respect: we allow ourselves and the other to come into their own. The second citation: our nothingness fervently hopes for life. The silence liberates this hope from its fearful egocentricity by fastening it onto the other (or Other) as the latter remains imageless in his impregnable silence. This is the quiet hope which seeks no other consolation than the silence in which the other in his alterity rises up before me, a silence in which I have nothing left to lose. That is the quiet hope Isaiah wants for us.

In part 2 of the chapter on silence, silence is instituted in two forms, the silence of the night and the silence of the day. First there is the silence of the night which, as mediatrix of the encounter with God, takes us out of the world of fixed mental imagery and patterns of conduct in order to lead us to naked trust in God, who is inexpressible and imageless. Then comes the institution of the silence of the day, a silence whose context is the field of tension between restrained speech (as little as possible) and careful speech (the culture of justice).[318]

The silence of the day is a form of quiet justice which opens itself during the silence of the night to the Inexpressible One as the actual form of our life. Conversely, the experience of being freed from one's images and forms makes us inwardly ready for an attitude of modest respect for ourselves and others. In that sense the repetition of the Isaian saying: "The cultivation of justice consists in silence' is significant. It can be read in two ways. The silence of the night constitutes the condition for just speech. And conversely: justice creates the condition for the silence of the night.

The structure of the chapter on silence, then, preserves the typical structure of Carmelite silence. Part 1 describes prophetic-mystical silence: the silence of death, the beginning and energizing principle of the practice of silence, leads to mystical silence. Part 2 describes the institutional silence: the institution of silence in the two forms of daytime silence and nighttime silence. Elijan silence and the institution of silence *together* form a spiritual path which invites us to walk it.

If now we compare the two silences with each other we are struck by a chiastic pattern (a-b b-a), which creates a balance. Elijan silence finds its dominance in the prophetic impulse to become silent. The sequence is (a) justice and (b) mysticism. Accordingly, that is how the Isaiah-citations are connected: "Cultivation of justice consists in silence" (a), is succeeded by "In quietness and hope will be your strength" (b). In the institution of silence that order is reversed: first (b) the mystical silence of the night, then (a) the just silence of the day. Not only as it concerns sequence but also as it concerns weight the silence of the night (with its few words!) seems to be the point of reference, for after it has been instituted

---

[318] In the tradition the dichotomy daytime/nightime silence is retained also in the word-pair being silent/being quiet where the first embodies the ascetic and the second the mystical aspect of silence (*Silence, DS* 14 (1990) 829).

the Rule continues with respect to the silence of the day as follows: "At *other* times, *however,* you need not ... as strictly ...". Thus the two, the value-sphere of Elijan silence and the architectonic structuring of daytime and nighttime silence, hold each other in balance.

The way of silence

Remaining in the cell, reading Scripture, saying the prayers and coming together in the Eucharist are elementary exercises. Maintaining silence as well is such an elementary practice of appropriation. Carmelites keep silence the way the Jews keep the Sabbath. All its activities are immersed in silence. But there is more going on. One who keeps silence offers shelter to it. Just as light gathers *and* spreads out in a crystal, so Carmel admits silence into its center in the hope that from that center it will radiate outward.

In all this a certain note of absoluteness is sounded. The reason for this is that *keeping* (tenére) silence is linked with *extending* (téndere) silence. One who keeps silence wants that silence to be absolute. To keep silence is to give to silence its full scope; it is to let it have its own full impact. One who keeps silence tries to let it be ever more unconditionally in control.

The practice of silence does not leave us untouched. We ourselves *become* silence. The keeper of silence has an intimate relationship with Silence. Just as a smoldering block of wood holds fire, so a Carmelites hold Silence. We carry it within ourselves. Just as iron-bearing soil is totally pervaded by iron and water-bearing matter by water, so silence-bearing humans are totally pervaded by silence. We, silence-bearers, bear silence within our whole selves.

That silence from then on leavens all our activities. The activities of the night – the evening prayer, the vigil, the nightly meditation in the instruction of the Lord and the simple handiwork done by the pale light of a lamp – all these activities, even including the sleep of the night,[319] become night silence. Similarly the silence of

---

[319] For the spirituality of sleep see: *Sommeil et vie spirituelle,* in *DS* 14 (1990), 1033-1041.

the day leavens all the activities of the day: the teaching, the work
on the land, the care of the house and animals, saying the hours,
muttering Scripture, the manual work of the day, the care of one's
body and social contacts. To keep silence is to expose all the activities of the day and the night to the transforming effect of Silence.
To keep silence is to break away from all the codes which keep us
captive and to open up to the Inexpressible One who wants us to
feel God's quiet Presence.

> Intelligent silence is the mother of prayer, freedom from bondage,
> custodian of zeal, a guard on our thoughts, a watch on our enemies,
> a prison of mourning, a friend of tears, a sure recollection of death, a
> painter of punishment, a concern with judgment, servant of anguish,
> foe of license, a companion of stillness, the opponent of dogmatism,
> a growth of knowledge, a hand to shape contemplation, hidden
> progress, the secret journey upward ...
>
> Lovers of silence draw close to God. They talk to Him in secret
> and God enlightens them.[320]

The way of silence fits in the spiritual architecture of the Rule
of Carmel as follows:

	The spiritual way	The way of the Silence
I-VI	Carmelite basic-provisions	Direction of night and day silence
VII-XIII	Elementary exercises	Keeping silence, cautious and careful
XIV	Being clothed with God's attributes	Cultivation of justice; interiorization of hope
XV-XVI	Lasting interiorization of contemplation	In quietness and hope will be your strength (Is.30:15)

[320] John Climacus, *The Ladder of Divine Ascent*, 11.3, 5; tr. Colm Luibheid
and Norman Russell, New York 1982, 158-159.

The way of silence fits in the spiritual way of Carmel as follows.

1. The *institution* of silence, including its division into the silence of the night and the silence of the day, applies to all spiritual communities. To the hermits the silence of solitude was self-evident. For the cenobites it had to be regulated. The institution of silence first of all touches the individual. It is a self-abasement ritual. But in the silence of the day it equally touches the community. The silence, especially at night because of the night's rest, also touches the place. Some places are quiet by definition: the chapel, the dormitory, the cloister, the refectory.

2. The silence is a provision which requires *practice*. Just as one stays in a cell, and reads Scripture, so one observes or keeps silence. Silence demands strict and careful appropriation. It seeks to penetrate all the layers of our personality, in order thus to leaven our speech and conduct from within.

3. Silence is an *attribute of God*. It unites within itself two parts of God's armor: justice and hope. Justice-in-quiet hope is a gift from God.

4. Like work, silence is *oriented to the End*. This orientation is brought about in several ways. First of all by the recommendation of Paul, a recommendation that is rooted in an eschatological context. Then by the two citations from Isaiah which direct us to practice quiet expectation – beyond the boundaries of our own plans. Finally, by the five quotations from Scripture which together guide us to the climax of the ultimate significance of our speech. All the signals point in a single direction: the silence of Carmel is prophetic-eschatological in character.

5.4.3 Connections

Running between the chapters on work and silence are several lines of connection.

1. Striking is the atmosphere of *modesty*: "Some work" has to be done; practicing silence is a ritual of self-abasement.

2. Though *time* plays a role, it is unrestricted time: the Carmelites must work night and day so that the devil will always find them occupied; silence, too, encompasses night and day.
3. There is a strikingly strong focus on a person's *inner life*: the devil may not gain access to the soul; much talking hurts the soul.
4. The *Messiah* plays an important role: through Paul's mouth Christ speaks; the Carmelites are solemnly told to work in the name of the Lord Jesus Christ; the Lord in the gospel has to avert the disaster of garrulousness.
5. Striking, too, is the *authority factor*: both work and silence are undergirded with an authoritative word from Paul. The apostle and the prophet are exemplary.
6. We again find elements of the *armor of God*. Paul is an example of faith and truth; he opened up a holy way; silence is viewed in the perspective of justice and hope.
7. Remarkable is the *eschatological* note: very clearly in the citation from the Letter to the Thessalonians, no less clearly in the quiet expectation passage and the final judgment on excessive talk.
8. Striking, again, is the focus on *activity*. This is natural in the chapter on work but also the silence is linked up with working.
9. Finally there is some concentration around the features of the *mouth* and the *ear*: Christ speaks by the mouth of Paul, who is the preacher and teacher of the Gentiles; having heard that some are disorderly, Paul charges and implores them; and, of course, the chapter on silence circles around the mouth.

The question now is: how do these connecting lines make up a meaningful whole? For an answer we will hook up with the end of the chapter on the armor of God. There we saw how the virtuous life blossoms in the abundant way in which the Word dwells in heart, mouth, and hands, and how, conversely, all our conduct returns in the Word of God. This lived contemplation of Scripture, however, is fragile, brief, and limited in its profundity. If contemplation is to have lasting impact a specific receptivity is needed. Within the Rule of Carmel, that receptivity comes through working in silence. Inherent in contemplation is the wish that it be preserved in our life at ever deeper levels. That is the reason why the cure (care) of the soul is central here (see 3 above). The Word seeks to prepare a holy way (XV) in us as it did in the life of Saint Paul, who precisely on this account became a paradigm for an ever deeper and more pervasive impact. Silence aims at an ongoing process of interiorization. Continually and full of expectation it holds itself in readiness to receive the Word. Its purpose is that the Lord will become increasingly more vocal in our life. That is the reason why in chapters XV-XVI there is such frequent reference to the Lord speaking (see 4 above). Paul models confidence and truth for us (XV); Isaiah extends the silence for the sake of justice and hope (XVI). The whole point of silence is the permanently ongoing, invasive and pervasive effectiveness of the armor of God (see 6 above). The process of interiorization constitutes the time dimension: time in chapters XV-XVI is not external (as in the case of the canonical hours, the celebration of the Eucharist, the chapter, and fasting) but the enduring interiorization of the Word. That is the import of the unrestricted duration of which the Rule speaks (see 2 above).

And where must this enduring impact occur? Answer: in our heart, our speech, our conduct. That is how the description of the armor of God ended: "Let the Word of God dwell abundantly in your *mouth* and *heart,* and whatever you have to *do,* let it all be done in the Word of the Lord" (XIV). Well then: chapters XV-XVI symbolically represent the entire layeredness of our existence. We already talked about the "soul" which represents the activated interior. But also speaking and listening are dealt with at length and in various ways (see 9 above). Heart and mouth, however, are not sufficient. Working, a key word in these two chapters (see 8 above), falls within the horizon of this continuing impact as well.

The all-around impact of the Word can only have its way if the obstacles we have raised up are destroyed. To that end the Rule shatters three "power lines".

1. There is, first of all, the power line of conceit: our tendency to determine the meaning of the work ourselves, to seek to be the focus of the noisy applause of the community. The humility which Ribot deems necessary for the durability of contemplation is reached by my taking part in the work assigned to me, the scope of which I cannot measure ("some work"); and by abasing myself in silence and letting myself be stripped of my false self-image, not clinging to anything external (see 1 above).

2. The second power line is I-centeredness. The Rule shatters this I-centeredness from within the relation to others. It does this by working with the authoritative examples of apostles and prophets (see 5 above). This I-centeredness is shattered by the authority of the apostle Paul who asserts that people must work, and by the word of the prophet Isaiah within which the two silences are instituted.

3. The third power line is the illusion of the day, called "the glitter of the present world" by the *Book of the First Monks*.[321] The Rule shatters this illusion by placing our time within the perspective of the End-time (see 8 above). The perspective of the End-time turns Carmelite mysticism into an eschatological form of contemplation as Cassian characterizes it: some contemplatives are drawn away into the mystery of creation; others are fascinated by the mystery of the Incarnation; still others, in eschatological contemplation, marvel at his unfathomable being that is hidden in hope.[322] It is this last form of contemplation we see emerging in the Rule of Carmel. Working in silence trains us in eschatological mysticism. That is the reason why after the armor of God there most certainly is a further dimension. This explains as well why work and silence are so expansively dealt with and so Scripturally orchestrated.

> Eschatological contemplation is fundamentally prophetic. It allows the absolute working-in of the Infinite, which transcends the totality of all that happens, to enter that totality. The End, which exceeds

[321] *Decem libri* 1.8.
[322] Cassian, *Conferences* 1.15.

our comprehension, within history impacts the persons who are thereby removed from the jurisdiction of history. History does not have the last word – which is true even now. The Infinite directly addresses persons in history and calls them to give an account. This is the prophetic content of eschatology. Not the person is subject to the judgment of history but history is subject to the judgment of persons who expose themselves to the Infinite. Prophetic escha-tology breaks through every totalitarian regime, not because it is directed to the end (of history) but because it exposes itself to the Infinite who transcends all that happens. Meaning is no longer derived from the context (of all that is) but from the eternally Com-ing One who is already on his way in simple thought – past-the-End. Eschatological contemplation is the "breakthrough of totality, the possibility of *meaning without context*". Working in silence pre-serves it.[323]

What is the role of working in silence within the Rule as a whole? We note that chapters XV and XVI function on four levels.

1. Work and silence are *basic provisions*. These provisions are not specifically Carmelite. They are integral elements in the orga-nization of the cenobitic life.
2. Work and silence are *elementary exercises*. The work must be done, the silence maintained. On this level they share in the practical objective of all the elementary exercises: the purity of heart which is inwardly directed toward the reception of God.
3. Work and silence receive the *divine attributes*. "Some work" can be clothed with confidence and truth, as Paul shows us. Silence shares in the divine gifts of justice and hope.
4. As a result of being placed in the Rule after the armor of God, work and silence gain an additional meaning: *keeping contem-plation sound*. Carmelite work, in imitation of Paul, rids itself of all appreciation arising from the present, imbued as it is with the End, the coming Messiah. Carmelite silence, in imitation of Isaiah, rids itself of all self-willed planning, in order to find its only strength in quiet expectation. This eschatological

---

[323] E. Levinas, *De totaliteit van het Oneindige*, Baarn 1987, 15-21.

orientation empties work and silence of all self-conceit and thus makes it especially well-suited not only to receive the abundance of the Word of God but to permanently interiorize it as well.

Eschatologically working in silence is a form of humility which keeps contemplation healthy. It insures that contemplation does not deteriorate in conceit and self-sufficiency. Working in quiet expectation turns Carmelites into "young black ravens". According to Ribot, "old black ravens" (mystics) can only feed their young when the latter are dressed in black feathers; otherwise the old ravens do not recognize their young. "Black feathers" symbolize humility. God's overflowing Word can only continue to feed us when we are completely unpretentious. That is precisely what silence and work aim at: they give us black feathers. They unsettle our self-conceit by lifting us out of our center and directing us toward the Messiah who is coming from the End.

I-VI	Carmelite Basic Provisions
VII-XIII	Elementary Exercises Practical objective: Purity of heart, for the sake of the rceptivity to God: Final goal
XIV	Being clothed with God's attributes Final goal of mystical transformation
XV-XVI	Working in silence out of the End as a lasting interiorization of contemplation

The specific function of working in silence has now become clear. On the one hand, working in silence forms an inclusion with the other basic provisions, insofar as work and silence must be observed. At this level they constitute the reception of transformation in God. However, because working in silence has been placed in the Rule *after* the armor of God it now gains the added function of preserving the abundance of God's Word. By their profound humility work and silence serve the lasting interiorization of contemplation. As a result of their prophetic-eschatological reach they are extremely well-suited to that end. Contemplation calls for preservation-in-truth, without a limit in time, without being screened through the *Zeitgeist*. It is devoid of context, directed toward God alone. Hope and confidence are recipient of God's coming. In silent work the growth of justice is removed from the illusion of the day. Justice is definitely removed from the circle of self-involvement. It consists in doing good without calculation. It is blind trust, quiet expectation.

With the chapters on work and silence (XV-XVI) Albert has come to the end of his exposition, an exposition in which he unfolds the Carmelite life formula. In retrospect we can observe that his exposition is marked by a clear structure. First he described the most important provisions (I-VI). Next he indicated how these provisions can be observed (VII-XIII). The goal of the exercises is purity of heart which aims at receptivity to being clothed with God's attributes (XIV). This being clothed with God's attributes, which is a mystical transformation, requires ongoing interiorization (XV-XVI). Conclusion: Albert achieved balance in building up his exposition.

Ascetic transformation: 402 words		Mystical transformation 455 words	
Basic provisions	Elementary exercises	Being clothed with God's attributes	Ongoing interiorization
129 words	273 words	156 words	299 words

6. Request (petitio)

A standard letter, says Guido Faba, grand master of the letter-writing art and Albert's contemporary, must stand like a house.[1] The foundation of the house is laid along with the *starting point*. On this foundation rest the four walls of the *exposition*. The roof is the *request*.[2] It completes the house. The metaphor of the house makes clear that a letter had to be solidly constructed. Earlier already we saw the masters in the art of writing letters viewed a letter as a syllogism: the starting point was the major premise, the exposition the minor, and the request the conclusion.[3] Applied to the Rule of Carmel: All religious should live in allegiance to Jesus Christ (*starting point* as major premise); the Carmelite form of life is a religious life form (*exposition* as minor premise); therefore, Carmelites should live in allegiance to Jesus Christ (*request* as conclusion).

6.1 The prior makes the Messiah present

Albert directly addresses the Carmelites: "And you, brother B., … You other brothers, too". He looks first from the viewpoint of brother B. and the "priors" after him.

> And you, brother B., and whoever may be
> appointed prior after you,
> should always have in mind
> and observe in practice
> what the Lord says in the gospel:

[1] Faulhaber, *Summa dictaminis,* 94.

[2] The *petitio:* the request made; the statement of what the writer desired of the reader; the recommendation submitted.

[3] Ibid., 97; Constable, *Letter-Collections,* 17.

> Whoever wishes to be the greatest among you
> will be your servant,
> and whoever wishes to be the first
> will be your slave.

From the viewpoint of content Albert here refers back to chapter I, where he instituted the priorate. This institution makes possible successive appointments of new priors.[4] Albert foresees a long future for this institution: for "brother B. and *whoever may be appointed prior after you*". It is a succession without end.

The "priors" are exhorted to bear in mind and really to put into practice the word of the gospel in which is described the messianic ministry of the leader.

> You know that the rulers of the Gentiles lord it over them, and the great ones make their authority over them felt. But it shall not be so among you. Rather, *whoever wishes to be great among you shall be your servant; whoever wishes to be first among you shall be your slave.* Just so, the Son of Man did not come to be served but to serve and to give his life as a ransom for many (Matt. 20:25-28).

This passage occurs in the context of a request made by the mother of John and James. She hoped that her two sons might sit "one at your right hand and one at your left, in your kingdom" (Matt. 20:21). Jesus then asks her sons whether they can share in his death. When they say "yes" to this, Jesus nevertheless replies: "to sit at my right hand and at my left is not mine to grant but it is for those for whom it has been prepared by my Father" (Matt. 20:23). Then follows Jesus' statement, cited above, about the way earthly rulers exercise their power. Messianic leadership, he says, is not exercised in that fashion: the leader is the servant and the first is the least.

As a result of the context in which Jesus' statement is framed, leadership, messianically exercised, acquires eschatological import: the conversion of power into service reaches to the End. Applied

---

[4] This appointment is foundational *(institutus)*: it institutes the office of prior in the midst of the community which, by that token, officially receives its basic structure.

SEELING CHRIST IN THE PRIOR

to the priorate it means: the "prior", in the exercise of his authority as "prior", makes present the coming of the Messiah to the degree we distance ourselves from the usual practices of people with power and approximates the servanthood of the Son of man.

The "prior" is invited to realize on the *cognitive* level what this word of Christ means: "Always bear in mind". The prior was taken, by an election process, from amidst the other members of the community and clothed with authority in the midst of the community. We might perhaps forget the ultimate goal for which the institution of the priorate is designed. We might perhaps get entangled in the practical objective, viz. that the community structures itself on the level of authority and power. We might overlook the final goal of all religious systems: making the Messiah present in the midst of the community.

This representation, however, is not only a matter of cognitive relation; it is above all *praxis*. Albert now repeats the words he used at the beginning of his Rule. There he stated: ... Each of you "is to promise him obedience and strive to fulfil his promise by the *reality* [truth] of his *deeds*". Here he says: you should always "*observe* in *practice*". What matters here is the realization in practice of the messianic saying just mentioned. The person who as "prior" and superior has been placed in the midst *by* all makes his way out of the midst *to* all so as to be of service for the benefit of each. In that way this person *really* makes the Son of man present to all. Accordingly, the focus of the Rule is Christological but in such a way that the institutional layer of the community is fully involved and consonant with this focus.

6.2 Seeing Christ in the prior

The other Carmelites as well have a possibility of realizing the Messiah in the leader they have elected.

> You other brothers, too,
> hold your prior humbly in honor,
> thinking not so much of him

> as of Christ who placed him over you,
> and who said to the leaders of the churches,
> Who hears you hears me;
> who rejects you rejects me.

Again there are two levels: the cognitive and the practical.

On the *cognitive* level the "brothers", like the "prior", may get entangled in the institutional: one of them was removed from their ranks and placed in their midst. They may get fixated on this one and regard the "prior" solely as *this* person whom *they* have chosen. At best, they then reach their practical objective (*skopos*): they are indeed being moved outward but they have not arrived at receptivity, at thinking of the one who placed this person at the head, the final goal (*telos*), the Messiah. When someone has been "set up as head"[5] this means juridically that a community accepts religious authority over itself and thus becomes a religious community.[6] But past the juridical dimension what matters is the religious reality. For the one who is the head of the community makes present the One who is the head of the church, indeed the head of the whole creation (Eph. 1:10; Col. 1:18). The "prior" is not simply the one who unites the many on the basis of their unanimous assent; as one he symbolizes the One who is the Messiah (Eph. 2:14-18; cf. 4:3-5). The Messiah is the center of the community, a space of reconciliation, forgiveness, unity: seeing each other, giving each other space, bringing each other into being from face to face. Of this reality the "prior" is the symbol. In their person they remind everyone of the unity which the community invested in them but, through this, of the unity which the Messiah establishes among people.

In the case of the members of the community as well the cognitive level is supplemented with the level of *practice*. They are invited to hold their "prior" humbly in honor, that is, generously accord this person the place which is due. This they do by hearing the "prior". Hearing the "prior" here means to effectively accept

---

[5] This phrase was derived from Psalm 65:12.

[6] *Decretum Gratiani* II, XVI, qu. 1, cap. 12.

the Messiah. When the disciples – the later leaders of the church – are later sent out by Jesus through all the cities and villages of Palestine, there are people who reject his message about the coming rule of God (Lk. 10:1-16). This rejection has larger implications, however, than they can surmise at the time. The truth is that along with the disciple they are rejecting their Lord and along with their Lord they are rejecting the God who sent him: "Whoever hears you hears me; whoever scorns you scorns me".

In the "prior" we Carmelites can hear a voice greater than we opted for: the voice of the Messiah who speaks to us in the "prior". This is the final goal (*telos*) of the election of a prior.

For Albert this orientation to the Messiah is not without strings. He relates it to the final judgment.

> In this way you will not come into judgment for contempt,
> but through obedience will merit
> the reward of eternal life.

Allegiance to the Messiah, who makes himself present in the "prior", is decisive for the final judgment. Those who despise the Messiah by maligning the "prior" condemn themselves. "*At the judgment* it will be more tolerable for Tyre and Sidon than for you. And you, Capernaum, will you be exalted to heaven? No, you will be brought down to Hades" (Lk. 10:14-15). And again Albert infuses his instructions with eschatological implications. Those who, both on the cognitive level and on the level of action, convert the power of the community into service and allegiance will go their messianic way to the End. Messianic leadership and messianic obedience go past the End and from there they penetrate this world, where they establish the Kingdom of God.

Entrusting oneself to this leadership bears within itself "the reward of eternal life". It leads *past* the power structures. It breaks through the patterns of power in which we keep each other imprisoned. Where messianic power-relations prevail people are born again in the liberty of the children of God. Eternal life becomes visible on *this* side of the End. The End paves a way for itself in the here-and-now.

6.3 Connections

In an ill-constructed letter the request dangles at the end. It shows
no intrinsic connection with the introduction and the exposition.
The same is true for a badly constructed syllogism. In such a
syllogism the conclusion is drawn from the premises mechanically.
In a well-constructed syllogism, on the other hand, the major
premise and the minor premise are read confrontatively in each
other's light, and the conclusion flows as a vital truth from the
confrontation. Example: there is the profound human experience
that we, humans, are mortal (major). This truth is confronted by
the awareness that I, Thomas, am human through and through
(minor). From this flows the vital awareness that I, Thomas, am
mortal through and through (conclusion). This is not an external
logical inference but a creative realization which grows out of a
living confrontation. The same applies to a well-constructed letter.
The request flows naturally from the introduction and the exposition. In the field of tension produced by the introduction and the
exposition there arises a growing awareness of the real point of it
all: the request.

Albert wrote a good letter. His request flows naturally from his
introduction (all religious life subjects itself in servanthood to the
Messiah) and his exposition (this is the religious mode of life of
the Carmelites). One who creatively relates the two begins to see
both the Carmelite way of life as a way of subjecting oneself in
servanthood to the Messiah and the Messianic servanthood present in the Carmelite way of life.

As an example in which this creative process comes to expression
Albert chooses obedience, the obedience with which he started his
exposition (I). To gain a clear view of what Albert is doing we
need to bring to the fore the different levels which come together
and resonate in his request. Then, in light of the concrete paradigm (priorate and obedience), the dynamic structure of Albert's
request may become visible.

1. The priorate is set up by Albert before all else. It is a *provision*
   by which the hermits can start to form a community. Once

instituted it can be regularly reactualized by the election proce-
dures (I) by which every "prior" succeeding brother B. is
appointed (*petitio*). This is the level of having a prior (I).

2. The priorate must be *observed* by the members of the community, on the level of principle by promising him or her obedience, and on the level of practice by actually keeping this
promise (I).

3. The priorate along with obedience gives access to the armor
of God. The "priors" realize and actively uphold the Word of
the Lord in the gospel: the messianic leader humbles himself
(*petitio*). The members of the community in their respect for
the "prior" are mindful of the Word of Christ: in servant leadership the Messiah himself speaks (*petitio*). Thus both the "prior"
and the other Carmelites are clothed with an essential aspect of
the armor of God: "Whatever you have to do, let it all be done
in the *Word* of the Lord" (XIV).

4. The prophetic eschatological orientation – as *permanently
ongoing interiorization* of contemplation – is already heralded in
the opening words of the request: "Whoever may be appointed
prior after you ...", words in which the perspective of an
unlimited future looms before us. A chain of successors continuing right into the End is suggested. The gospel passages
cited, moreover, stem from an eschatological context. Most
important, however, is the prophetic-eschatological thrust:
messianic reversals (greater-servant, first-servant), perishing in
the final judgment, and the reward of eternal life. By listening
to the Word coming from the (messianic) "prior" brothers and
sisters encounter the Lord who is coming to them from the
End. This form of leadership and listening takes us past the
boundary of this age, an age characterized by the thirst for
domination.

5. The *essence* of the request consists in creatively relating the
exposition to the introduction. Allegiance to the Messiah particularizes itself in servanthood to the "prior". In the process of
obeying the "prior" the Carmelites attempt to *hear* the coming
of Christ. By this servanthood vis-à-vis the others the "prior"

seeks to make the Messiah present in the service to the community. By creatively and confrontatively reading the introduction and the exposition in each other's light on the point of
obedience, Albert brings to expression the entire thrust and
intent of the Rule – that which it calls for (the *petitio!*).

From a literary point of view the request seems to form an inclusion with the institution of the priorate (I). The verbal repetitions
speak for themselves: brother, set up or appoint, you, have, prior,
obedience, in reality, observe. Opposed to this, however, is another
literary fact, viz., that the request brings together two "power lines":
the general principle of the introduction and the concrete argu-
mentation of the exposition. Only in light of this latter literary
fact does the meaning of the verbal repetitions become really clear.
In the exposition the promise of obedience to the newly chosen
"prior" is kept in actual deeds, while in the request the "prior"
must keep the Word of the Lord in actual deeds. It is precisely in
these verbal correspondences that the shift intended becomes visible! In his request Albert again picks up the subject of the priorate
(hence the verbal repetitions) but he does it in light of the introduction (hence the shift in meaning).

Accordingly, the request is not an inclusion in the literal sense
of enclosure but rather an invitation. Just as work and silence (XV-
XVI) indeed materially form an inclusion with the other provisions
to be observed (I-XIII), but from a spiritual viewpoint aim at constantly ongoing interiorization by a prophetic-eschatological manner
of life, so the request is indeed materially an inclusion with chapter
I but from a spiritual viewpoint an invitation to reinterpret Christo-
logically the entire life model (I-XVI) in light of the introduction.

Albert only works out his *petitio* in terms of the example of obedience. This is logical, for the structuration of the cenobitic life is
precisely what is new in the life model he is presenting to the hermits. He does not work out the other provisions, leaving that
to the Carmelites themselves. It is, after all, a letter (*brevis*) and a
letter must be brief (*brevis*). From the one example he does work

	Introduction *Service in obedience to the Messiah*
I-VI	Carmelite Basic Provisions
VII-XIII	Elementary Exercises Practical objective: Purity of heart, for the sake of the rceptivity to God: Final goal
XIV	Being clothed with God's attributes Final goal of mystical transformation
XV-XVI	Working in silence out of the End as a lasting interiorization of contemplation Request *Awareness of the coming of the Messiah*

out we can tell how this can be done. The request is an invitation to the Carmelites, as it were, to reinterpret the entire Carmelite life model as a Christ-icon. The request calls for meditation on Christ: searching for the Messiah in light of the life form and looking at our way of life with the eyes of the Messiah. It is the intent of the request to set in motion a search process: a process of learning to see the Carmelite way of life as salvation in the Lord (*salutatio*), so that we begin to experience ever more deeply what it means to be "beloved sons and daughters in Christ".

> To remain in the cell is to remain in the vine (John 15:1-11). Praying is a fresh internal recollection of him: "In the days when he was in the flesh, he offered prayers and supplications with loud cries and tears to the one who was able to save him from death" (Heb. 5:7). The disappropriation of all private possessions recalls what it means that "foxes have dens and birds of the sky have nests, but the Son of Man has nowhere to rest his head" (Matt. 8:20). In coming together "we, like living stones, are built into a spiritual house" of which the Messiah is "the cornerstone" (1 Pet. 2:4-9). Where the Carmelites build one another up, there "he stands in their midst" (Jn. 20:19-23). One who fasts is tested along with the Messiah in the desert (Matt. 4:1-11). One who puts on the armor of God is "clothed

with the Messiah" (Gal. 3:27; Rom. 13:14; Col. 3:10; Eph. 4:24; 2 Cor. 4:16). One who works in silence "will himself do the works that I do" (Jn. 14:12).

The request sets in motion a search process, one which the Rule itself does not work out in detail. It only asks that each Carmelite will personally seek to go on the messianic journey.

7. Conclusion (conclusio)

The conclusion of a letter can be very brief: Farewell! (*Vale!*), with the name of the sender added. The final greeting can also be longer, however, and with a word or two refer back to the content of the letter.[1] The main function of the conclusion – as counterpart to the greeting – is to say good-bye to the person addressed and to wish him or her the best. A variety of secondary functions may be served as well: a further elaboration of the wish; a final reference to the content; a stylistic rounding-off plus authorization by means of an embossed stamp or signature.

The conclusion of Albert's letter consists of two parts: the first part looks back at the literary form and the content of the letter; the second looks ahead.

7.1 A formula for your way of life

In the first part of his conclusion Albert looks back at what he has done: "We have written these things briefly for you". His writing is now referred to in the perfect tense: "We *have* written these things". The author withdraws from the scene, no longer able to direct his readers in their interpretation of the letter. Where the author takes his leave, an open space, a possibility for spirituality, comes into being.[2] With the act of lifting up his pen the author withdraws from his writing, leaving the text behind as orphan. While this leave-taking would seem to be a pure loss, in fact this act of disappearing creates a spiritual space for the reader, *every* reader, including ourselves.

---

[1] For the closing formulas see: Lanham, *Salutatio Formulas*, 69-88.

[2] P. Ricoeur, *Tekst en betekenis. Opstellen voor de interpretatie van literatuur*, Baarn 1991, 150-151.

> We have written
> these things briefly for you,
> thus establishing a formula
> for your way of life,
> according to which you are to live.

The words "these things", both literarily and materially, refers back to the preceding.

1. *The literary level.* When Albert says: "we have written these things briefly to you", he is really saying: this is my letter. The idea of brevity was such an integral component of the style of a letter (*modus* or *stylus epistolaris*) that the idea of writing a letter was synonymous with writing briefly.[3] A letter was generally characterized by brevity. Albert of Monte Cassino, grand master in the art of writing letters, regularly and cleverly reminds his students that in writing a letter (*brevis*) one must always remember its etymology: short (*brevis*). It is not so strange, therefore, that both quantitatively and qualitatively Albert's letter is short. Quantitatively, the Rule of Carmel is significantly shorter than the other Rules. Qualitatively, Albert's writing is modest, does not try to settle everything, respects the unforeseen, does not lose itself in secondary matters, is not roundabout but goes straight for the core of an issue.[4] By keeping his letter brief Albert enlarges the spiritual space which he opened already by his departure from the text.

2. *The content.* Materially, in speaking of "these things", Albert is referring to the form of conduct he described in his letter. He succinctly defines this backward reference to the material content in the words: "thus establishing a formula for your way of life, according to which you are to live". Although from a literary viewpoint the Rule of Carmel is a letter, in terms of content he is laying down a Rule: "a formula ... according to which you are to live".

---

[3] Constable, *Letter-Collections,* 18-20.

[4] For these meanings see *Oxford Latin Dictionary*, Oxford 1968, 241-242.

Again, materially "these things" refer to the "formula of life" Albert is presenting. This can be clearly seen when we place the beginning of his exposition alongside the conclusion.

Exposition	Conclusion
A. that in keeping with your proposal we give you a *formula* of *life*	A. thus establishing out a *formula* for your way of *life*,
B. to which you may hold fast in the future.	B. according to which you are to *live.*

In the first place, in both cases (A) we are dealing with a *formula* which shapes the conduct and life of the Carmelites. The reference is to a formula for life in its full scope: not only the provisions (I-VI) but also the full armor of God (XIV), including the form of God we know as the Messiah (*petitio*). Then in both cases (B) he refers to processes of appropriation: the elementary exercises (VII-XIII), being clothed with the attributes of God and their ongoing interiorization (XIV-XVI). This is what Albert sought briefly to communicate to the hermits on Mount Carmel: he wanted to give them a form of conduct which, inwardly as well as outwardly, so transforms their life that it can permanently receive the form of God who is Love. This form of conduct, far from being an inflexible model, proceeds from the experience of the hermits themselves: "You desire us to give you a formula of life in keeping with your purpose" (*narratio*). This formula grew out of an intensively lived-through experience of commitment to the Unconditional.[5] Precisely as such, as a formula which arose from their own conduct, the Rule is a way which in turn sets in motion

[5] Clifford Geertz calls this aspect "a model of reality": the embodiment and symbolization of an experience of Reality; see Geertz, *Religion as a Cultural System,* in *Reader in Comparative Religions. An Anthropological Approach,* New York 1979, 81.

a new experience: people discover in it their own commitment to the Unconditional.[6]

7.2 If anyone will have spent more

Having looked back, Albert now looks ahead.

> If anyone will have spent more,
> the Lord himself, will reward him,
> when he returns.

After everything that has been said what more could anyone do? Just what does it mean to do *more*? Does it mean more than the formula for life asks? This approach does not satisfy: anyone taking a careful look at the model for life embodied in the Rule can easily tell that at virtually all points it exceeds all boundaries. From the institution of the priorate up to and including the institution of silence something *more* is continually being suggested in the formula of conduct itself. For example: the stipulations relative to meditating on Scripture, day and night, working night and day, practicing silence day and night give to the formula of conduct a scope which far exceeds any precise definition of boundaries. The same is true for the armor of God. At almost all points it crosses boundaries: chastity, the sanctification of one's thoughts, faith, hope, and love – they all open up ways which are designed to exceed boundaries. And "let the Word of the Lord dwell abundantly in your mouth and in your hearts". We can safely say that the Rule itself everywhere already ignores all stop signs.

We could also try another approach. "More" could mean "to experience and follow the model more intensively". We might look in the direction of greater zeal: the zeal with which one meditates on Scripture, the zeal with which one prays and works, the zeal with which one fasts and keeps silent. But this approach also comes

---

[6] Clifford Geertz would call this "a model for reality": symbolic structures by which the experience of reality can be channelled. *Ibid.*, 81.

to a dead-end. At several places it is already incorporated in the Rule. For example, they must do their best to fulfill the promise of obedience in actual fact. They must take the utmost care to put on the whole armor of God. As to silence, they must "try attentively and carefully to practice it". Accordingly, at essential points zeal already belongs to the formula of conduct as the Rule laid it down. And the intent can certainly not be that this prescribed zeal should itself be surpassed in a kind of extreme form. Such an overzealous application is expressly rejected by the Rule (chapter XI). In fact, a formula of conduct is even established to correct this kind of excess: the weekly discussion on Sunday with "in the midst of love". To do *more* in the sense of doing the same things more intensely does not seem to me to be the key to an understanding of Albert's comment.

We must consult the parable of the Good Samaritan to which the Rule refers.

Luke 10:35	The Rule
If you will have spent more, *I* shall reward you, when *I* return.	*If anyone* will have spent more, *the Lord himself,* will reward him, when *he* returns.

The Good Samaritan was moved with pity over a traveller who had been robbed and mistreated (Lk. 10:33). So he went to him, bandaged his wounds and, putting him on his donkey, brought him to a nearby inn. The next day he gave two denarii to the innkeeper and continued his journey. His last words were: "Take care of him. If you spend more (than what I have given you), I shall *reward you when I return*" (Lk. 10:35).[7]

It is worth noting the two changes Albert makes in the story. First of all he introduces a change which, though logical from the viewpoint of the Rule, does not carry much weight: he changes the *second* person (2 x you) and the *first* person (2 x I) into the *third* person (anyone, the Lord himself, him, he). The other change is more significant: he alters the *practical* points in Luke into

---

[7] *Et quodcumque supererogaveris, ego cum rediero reddam tibi* (Vulgate).

a *personal* one: "Should *anyone* spend more, the *Lord himself* will reward him, when he returns". Luke highlights the business expenditure in excess of the two denarii paid. In the Rule the accent lies on the personal gift of self: "If anyone will have spent more ...". That is: give more of ourselves; rather: give ourselves more; still better: *give* ourselves. The Rule leaves the domain of business transactions behind and speaks the language of personal commitment.

Still this reading is not altogether satisfactory either. Though it moves in the right direction, it does not yet hit the bull's eye. The reason for its not being satisfactory lies in the fact that the Rule itself repeatedly and explicitly discusses the motif of personal commitment. In the context of the armor of God, for example, the Rule explicitly mentions loving God and neighbor with all one's heart, mind, and strength. The same area is broached when the Rule speaks of quiet hope. For that matter the entire Rule was written in part from the perspective of the soul whose salvation it has in view. The perspective of the soul consists precisely in the fact that it is gradually being led to "live in allegiance to Jesus Christ with a pure heart and a good conscience". And that is precisely the perspective of never-ending self-commitment.

I believe we must look for the "boundary-crossing" element the Rule intends in an area which as such lies *beyond all that is regulable*. In line with the ongoing transformation which is inherent in every spirituality, pursuant to an ever more intensive commitment and ever-growing self-offering, and in the perspective of a prophetic eschatology the Rule takes us *past every formula of conduct* into an area that cannot be described or regulated.

We can best get at this area from within Ruusbroec's *The Sparkling Stone*. In his book this fourteenth-century Brabant mystic depicts ongoing transformation in God by contrasting four relational forms (hired servants, faithful servants, secret friends, hidden sons): hired servants and faithful servants; faithful servants and secret friends; secret friends and hidden sons. The contrasts have been selected in such a way that together they depict a spiritual way.[8] In the case of the hired servant the relationship is governed by profit and reward. Personal advantage is uppermost. Faithful servants, on the other hand, turn away from the self-centeredness which characterizes hired servants and focus on the other. Their vision ends in the works they do and the satisfaction these give them. Secret friends break out of this self-sufficiency: beyond the deeds of love they perform they fasten themselves onto the other person. But that, precisely, is their limitation. Secret friends are always still consciously present in the outgoing movement of their love. This final attachment to self is overcome by the hidden sons. "Overcome" as an act of self is not the right idea: we are dealing with something that lies outside our own possibilities. We cannot step outside of ourselves to the point where we forget ourselves. That is something which comes over us. Of ourselves, that is from within our own pathos, we are imprisoned within our own selves. The hidden 'son' takes us into an area which lies beyond every form and all self-centeredness. In self-forgetfulness we live in terms of the other, lost in the love of God. As hidden sons or daughters we are no longer aware of self or of our motives. We live the pathos of God's love. This is the *beyond* to which the Rule refers when it suggests the contrast between the established formula of conduct and the "more" of the parable of the Good Samaritan. This "more" symbolically represents everything that is no longer specifiable, devoid of form, non-regulable. Symbolically, "spending more" stands for that which is beyond every order: the trackless desert of love, the night of faith which leads me outside of myself. This is the hiddenness of giving as such which has no awareness of self.

Beautiful – the way the future perfect tense now works: "If anyone will have spent more". It seems as if in the end the giver is surprised at his or her own giving! In the parable the difference is still measurable: the amount advanced is two denarii. Whatever is more can be calculated. In the Rule this basic amount is

---

[8] See H. Blommestijn, *Initiation into love: The mystical process according to Ruusbroec*, in *Studies in Spirituality* 2 (1992), 99-126.

CONCLUSION

unknown. The Rule gives us a formula of conduct which – in scope, intensity, and degree of personal commitment – is itself unmeasurable. How then can we know when we have given more? We cannot; indeed, the more given by the hidden son or daughter is measureless because it surpasses all measure. This "more" loses itself in the measurelessness of God's love, a love which never adds things up, which without any calculation invests itself in his creatures, which is essentially hidden, because it is totally absorbed in giving. In that sense God's love is itself the paradigm of this "more".

Via this contrast between the established formula of conduct and that which is "more", the Rule takes us into the area where God's love prevails in a way which causes us to live out of that love spontaneously without thinking. This is the real End: God's coming into our conduct. This coming cannot in any way be registered, regulated, or recorded. It occurs for the *Lord's own reasons.* For that reason the slight nuance the Rule introduces into the parable of the Good Samaritan is so meaningful: in the parable the reference is to a traveller who on his or her way back – "when I return" – will pay up the additional costs; in the Rule an eschatological perspective opens up because it is said: *the Lord himself,* when he returns, will reward us. The combination of "the Lord himself" with the clause "when he returns" evokes the association of the return of the Lord in the End (1 Thess. 4:15-17; cf. 1 Thess. 3:11-13; 5:23; 2 Thess. 2:16; 3:16). The Rule leads us into complete transformation in God – *past* all our own perspectives, *past* our own horizon, *past* the regulations of this time: "God himself will be with them; he will wipe every tear from their eyes. Death will be no more; mourning and crying and pain will be no more, for the first things have passed away" (Rev. 21:3-4).

The innkeeper is our guide. On a given day, without any advance notice, a traveller enters the inn, bringing with him a man who has been beaten up and is half-dead. The traveller leaves this penniless person behind in the inn. The innkeeper finds himself obligated to take care of someone whom he does not know and who has been dropped off at his place by a stranger. Such innkeepers are not, like the Good Samaritan, in the grip of deep pity. As owners of the inn they are in all respects "dis-ordered"; they receive instructions from a guest; they have to choose in an emotional void; they are left to themselves; they can only wait for their guest's return. These innkeepers are held hostage by a guest! Now the Rule puts us in the role of the innkeeper: innkeepers who were lifted out of their own role, hosts who were totally "dis-ordered" by a traveller who for only a short while was a guest: the Messiah. Unasked, the Messiah has entrusted our neighbor to us: a legacy we never asked for, left us by someone who stayed with us overnight and then continued his journey. In his absence we must have compassion on his own, without having his emotions. We are responsible for a poor and suffering world solely because we are living in allegiance to Messiah. We are the innkeeper who carries out the orders of a divine guest. Giving here loses all support and control: it is no longer rooted in our feeling or in our choice; it is no longer rooted in our status or in our knowledge. Here the only guideline is the darkness of selfless giving. The left hand no longer knows what the right hand is doing. Abba sees in secret, in the secrecy of giving. Real giving is essentially giving in darkness. This is the "more" of the expropriated innkeeper. For this "more", this desert of love, this night of trust, Albert recommends to us discernment as our guide.

> Use discernment, however,
> the guide of the virtues.

In this expropriation by God's Love – is there any role left for discernment? In this solitude – is this still a guide? Does not the darkness of being offered up lead to death?

These questions betray a limited view of discernment. At the beginning of the spiritual way discernment appears as a prudent builder who sees to a good structuration of the basic provisions. Then it shows itself as the golden mean which neither exercises us too little or too much. It senses what can be done conveniently. Via the elementary exercises it teaches us to sense where the exercise of virtue can be let go so that God himself can do his work in

us. After that it directs our minds past the horizon and teaches us to
see through the relativity and responsibility of our life. Anthony
was right: "Discernment is the mother, the guardian, and the guide
of all the virtues".[9] Discernment goes down the road with us every
step of the way. It is like Scripture: "As our mind is increasingly
renewed by this study, Scripture begins to take on a new face. A
mysteriously deeper sense of it comes to us and somehow the
beauty of it stands out more and more as we get farther into it.
Scripture shapes itself to human capacity".[10]

Discernment grows as we grow. It is neither a provision, nor an
exercise, nor a virtue. It consistently accompanies us in its own way.

What can discernment do for us in the desert of love, in the
night of trust, in the "more" of the Rule? Over and over discernment brings home to us the painful realization that our love is
always and only *our* love, however noble and generous. The pain
of this realization causes us to desire a passion and pathos which
originates solely in You. It leads us into quiet expectation. It makes
us hope for a gesture from You. By the pain of discernment's
understanding it brings us to the boundary of the desert. There it
is no longer our guide but our conception. It has become the
night which leads us, the desert which has become a highway. It
is no longer a capacity separate from us, from the virtues, from
the institution. It is itself that which in great clarity receives the
Beloved. Discernment, which always guided all the institutions
and exercises, the virtues and self-knowledge, has not itself been
brought *past* its function as guide. In it the light shines out. It is
the living flame of love (John of the Cross); it is the night which
accompanies me, the night that unites the Lover with his beloved.

> On that glad night,
> In secret, for no one saw me,
> Nor did I look at anything,
> With no other light or guide
> Than the one that burned in my heart;

[9] Cassian, *Conferences,* 2.4; *CWS,* 64.
[10] Ibid., 14.11; *CWS,* 165.

This guided me
More surely than the light of noon
To where He waited for me
– Him I knew so well –
In a place where no one else appeared.

O guiding night!
O night more lovely than the dawn!
O night that has united
The Lover with His beloved,
Transforming the beloved in her Lover.[11]

---

[11] John of the Cross, *Collected Works,* 711.

8. The Spiritual Way of the Carmel Rule

From a literary point of view the Rule is a letter. From a historical point of view it documents the period in which the Carmelite Order originated. From a juridical point of view it reflects the dialogue between the church leadership and a group of hermits seeking recognition. From an intertextual point of view it constitutes a link between the religious traditions from which it draws and the Carmelite tradition which it spawned. From a spiritual point of view the Rule of Carmel delineates a spiritual way. It is this spiritual way which, in and through all the different readings, fascinates us.

The desert monk Abraham compares the spiritual way with the construction of the vault of a dome: with every stone the mason puts down, with every circle he makes, he is guided by an extremely precise central point. Around this center, layer upon layer, the dome is erected. Both horizontally and vertically the circles come into being around this center. The more the construction advances, the more the invisible center which shapes the dome from within becomes visible.

> If someone wishes to complete the dome of an apse to its summit, he must continually follow the line around the exact center in keeping with that infallible norm and assemble with precision the entire symmetrical circle. One who attempts to build it up without close observation of this center, however skillful or gifted he may presume himself to be, cannot possibly maintain without error the symmetry of the circle or be able to tell by appearance alone how far he has strayed from the true beauty of the circle. He must return again and again to that standard of truth. By its authority he corrects the inner and outer circumference of his work. He completes the structure of so lofty a magnitude by the rule of a single point.[1]

[1] Cassian, *Conferences* 24.6.

This is, for several reasons, a splendid picture of the spiritual way.

1. In the construction of a dome, as in spirituality, there are two constantly interactive movements. On the one hand, there is the working of the Center which, like an invisible hand, directs every movement. On the other hand, there is the action of the mason who, stone by stone and layer upon layer, brings the dome into being. In the Rule of Carmel a double perspective is similarly at work: on the one hand, there is the Messiah who, from the greeting to the conclusion, forms the essence of the spiritual way; and, on the other, the way every soul advances from the most elementary exercise up to and including its highest wellbeing.

2. Both in the construction of a dome and in spirituality there is a practical objective and a final goal. The practical objective is the horizontal circle which comes into being stone by stone and on which the next layer is built. The final goal is the whole structure which the Center unfolds. I am being deliberately ambiguous here: the whole and the Center can both be subject as well as object. The Center, as it were, bears the dome on its hands from within and the dome, as it were, unfolds the Center in all directions. The unfolding of the Center and the formation of the whole interlock indivisibly. In the same way the chapters of the Rule seem initially to be linked together without purpose. But on closer scrutiny it is clear that first the circle of the basic provisions is laid (I-VI). The circle of the elementary appropriations which follows refers back to and builds upon it (VII-XIII). The appropriations make people receptive to the virtues in which God communicates himself (XIV). The self-communication of God demands constant interiorization which is shaped in quiet labor done in light of the end (XV-XVIII). Gradually there awakens a practical sense that this Messianic Life is the eternal Center in which we may live (*petitio*).

3. The construction of a dome gives pictorial expression to the fact that spirituality is a spiral-like process. Constantly new layers of

ourselves and of reality about us are drawn into the process of transformation. Over and over we pass through the entire process; still,
each time, new areas present themselves to be brought into touch
with the Center. It seems we are not making any progress. Over and
over we come back to the same point. This, however, is merely
appearance. In reality the process becomes ever deeper and more
dense; as a result the dome is constantly in process of being formed
more firmly from within the Center. Thus, for example, remaining
in one's cell is initially merely a physical fact. But gradually, after
we have repeatedly run through the entire course of the Rule, this
remaining in our cells begins to shape our durability, our being
established in Scripture and in prayer, our attachment to the Messiah as a branch in a vine. Thus an elementary exercise – remaining in one's cell – affects and transforms deep layers in our being.

4. Constructing a dome and spirituality are both fragile occur-
rences. As long as the dome is incomplete it is extremely flimsy.
Given a little push, the whole structure collapses. But when the
dome has been completed all points on the dome are centers of a
powerful field of forces. A completed dome is almost impossible
to tear down. The same is true for spirituality: only from within
the whole do the parts possess a firm place and inner strength of
their own. Apart from the whole they fall apart like a suddenly
released handful of marbles. The Rule of Carmel is above all a
complex whole held together by the Center. Only from within
this complex as a whole do all the constitutive elements get their
firm place and inner strength. No matter where we start, we are at
the Center of the dome, for all the lines of power come together
at that point. So we can say that remaining in our cell is the center of the Carmel dome. For there everything comes together:
Scripture reading, prayer, vigils, work, silence, hope, trust. But the
Eucharist, too, forms the center: all the cells come together in it,
as do all the hours of the day, the remaining in the Messiah, provisions for the journey, brotherhood or sisterhood, hoping for
the end. No matter at what point on the Carmel dome we start,
always the lines of power of the whole converge there.

Now, on the basis of the interpretation we offered we wish to describe the spiritual way of the Rule of Carmel. In this we will follow the Rule itself, which from chapter to chapter becomes more complex and profound. This is in accord with the progression of the spiritual way itself, a progression which, according to the desert fathers, in this respect resembles learning an art or a trade.

> This is what we think. In any art or discipline, perfection can be reached only from beginnings which are necessarily very simple. One starts off from what is easier and gentler. The soul is nourished by the milk of reason, grows bit by bit, rises up gradually step by step from lowly things to the very highest. When one has taken hold of the simpler principles, when one has passed through the gates of one's profession, then as a consequence and without constraint one reaches the inner recesses, the high points of perfection.[2]

8.1 The basic provisions as spiritual symbol

A foundational given in spiritual transformation is the way (*modus vivendi*) in which a spirituality is structured, the form (*formula vitae*) which is handed down to be learned, the plan (*propositum*) that is presented, the religious manner of life (*religio*) which is chosen; in short: the how (*qualiter*) of the order (*ordo*) of things. We call this foundational given a *structure*. This structure is instituted (*instituere*), even decreed (*statuere*).

Structure must not be interpreted superficially. We are dealing, after all, with a religious way of life. An entire world opens up in it. It is something created. This kind of creation is attributed to "founding fathers or mothers": "In many and various ways the holy *fathers have laid down ...*" (*exordium*); "according to the *institution* of the holy *fathers ...*" (VIII). It is the *Patriarch* of Jerusalem who instituted the Carmelite formula: "We *establish* first of all ..." (*narratio*); "Therefore we *direct* ... " (XVI); "We have written these

---

[2] Ibid., 10.8; *CWS*, 130.

things briefly for you, thus *establishing* a formula for your way of life…" (*conclusio*). This architecture is specifically realized in such structuring acts as: the choice of a prior (I), the choice of a site (II), the assignment of the cells (III and V), the reception of the guests (VI), the division of the goods (IX), etc. Everything that concretely structures the Carmelite formula of life shares in the originating charism of the founding "fathers". While the institution of the basic Carmelite form is the primary focus in section 1 (chapters I-VI), it injects itself into the entire Rule as an undertone. When from this foundational angle we look at the architectural design as it emerges in the Rule of Carmel as a whole we get the following picture.

1. The focus is a *community*. On the level of authority-relations this community is structured in accordance with the prior-and-brothers pattern (I, XVII-XVIII). Important decisions are channeled through this pattern (II-III and IX). But the community also manifests itself in the act of assembling: eating together, listening to Scripture together, celebrating the Eucharist together, discussing essential matters together (IV, VIII, X, XI). Also, the community orders itself economically: all members contribute their bit to the community of goods, which, along with the gifts, is large enough to give to each person his own (X, XII, XIII, XV) via the hand of the Prior (XV). Finally, the community manifests itself in a silence which respects the other and creates space for God's presence (XVI).

2. This community inhabits a *place*; originally this was the Carmel range, later a location in the desert or the city. This place offers space to each person in virtue of the fact that each has a cell (III). It gives shape to the community, especially in the oratory and the refectory (IV, X), and is accessible to people from the outside (VI).

3. Living within the community and the place are the *brothers* or sisters individually. All of them have the active and passive right of suffrage (I). All have their own cell (III) but not as a private

possession. Consideration is given to the age, primary needs, and state of health of each (IX, XII, XIII). The Carmelites perform their work in silence (XV-XVI). The wellbeing of the individual souls has the attention of the community (XI).

4. The unique space of every Carmelite in the place and within the community gets its grounding in the *cell*. There we enter into confrontation with the silence. From there we come to the center of the community.

5. The local community exists in dialogue with its *context* on four distinct levels. First: the origin of the Rule shows that there was a lively dialogue between the church leadership (Albert and the popes) and the Carmelite community – originally in the field of tension between structure and antistructure. Second: as the Rule shows, there was lively interaction with sympathizers. The latter offered living space and/or buildings (II), gave alms and gifts for the brothers' maintenance (IX), visited them for various reasons (VI), and joined them in prayer (VIII, X). Third: there was a link with other communities. Carmelites view themselves as *a* form of religious life (*exordium*). Most vital is their connection with the religious renewal movement. For that reason, we daresay, the contact with Albert was as cordial as it was (*salutatio*). The brothers must have warmly welcomed the modifications introduced by the two Dominicans. When the Carmelites were forced to return to Europe they effortlessly resonated with the mendicant movement: the element of community (brotherhood) was reinforced; the meaning of certain elements (meditation, choral prayer, the Eucharist, the word of God as sword of the Spirit) shifted in the direction of the apostolic life; new elements were integrated (the refectory, itinerancy and begging, international connections). Fourth: they situated themselves in the changing culture. The point of gravity in society shifted from the countryside to the cities. Within this urban culture (domestic industry, city schools, burghers, freedom of trade, the right to own property, political independence, democratization) the Carmelites chose a place of their own. Within

the poverty movement (renunciation of property) they opted for the "lesser" (*minores*) and the "least".

6. This local community has a *time order*. There are activities which form a kind of continuum, described by the words "day" and "night": meditation on Scripture and prayer in the cell (VII), working in silence (XV-XVI). Other activities are limited to certain times: the canonical hours (VIII), the daily celebration of the Eucharist, the weekly chapter meeting (XI), the periods of fasting and abstinence (XII-XIII).

This architectural design is not merely a practical arrangement. It is a spiritual symbol in the sense ascribed to it by Victor Turner and others. In speaking of a spiritual symbol we are referring to a plastic structure which works in two directions *at once*. On the one hand, such a symbol elicits fundamental *values*: it points to a complex of values and truths and makes it present; it opens a window on a spiritual reality. At the same time the symbol touches deep layers in the *person* who interacts with it: it awakens longings, memories and experiences in him or her, and provides an unobstructed view of a person's core. This is also true for the Carmelite architecture described above. The *place* must become a Carmel, as we saw in the interpretation of Chapter II. It does not matter whether a monastery is located on Mount Carmel or away from it, in a solitary place or in the city, if only the place becomes a Carmel. And that can be the case only if the Carmelite realizes self-awareness there as the solitary one who – like the great example Elijah – is up to the challenge of solitude as the way to the Wilderness which is God.

This is how the *community* becomes the body of the "Messiah". The Rule expressly states this where it speaks of the "prior-and-the-brothers" structure: they present the Messiah to each other (*petitio*). Where the brothers or sisters eat together they listen to the Word of the Lord (IV). Daily they assemble around the Word and the Body and Blood of the Messiah (X). During their discussions they know him to be in their midst (XI). What the Lord provides is distributed by the "prior" to each (IX). Generally speaking, the messianic community of Acts 2 and 4 is in the background. Even the isolated *person* in his or her own *cell* has a symbolizing effect: the cell in its solitude isolates the person's uniqueness conceived by the Shekinah. The same applies to the context. Praying together with ordinary people, going around begging in their midst and participating in their life is a way of life which unites itself with the Church's act of praying, at least where the institution is *fluid*: not determined by hierarchy, class differences, pretensions to status, and discrimination. Finally, the purpose of the structuring of time is not to ward off boredom and long duration but to mediate a focus on the End which lies beyond the circle of our horizon. Accordingly, all the components of the structure are ways of mediating a perspective of values. They open up a view of the messianic world. *At the same time* they awaken the messianic human being deep within us. They are aimed at the divine birth in us, at the brothers or sisters who know their own solitude and therefore do not put on airs and elevate themselves above the others, the brothers or sisters who know themselves born in the human community, indeed, who know themselves to be simple creatures, children of God who "wait with eager longing for the revealing of the children of God" (Rom. 8:19-22).

8.2 Spiritual exercise

The Carmelite architecture can work only if there are inhabitants who appropriate it. It can only become an inhabitable interior if it is interiorized. The desert fathers and mothers already said that one can only come to a knowledge of everything by the experience of doing.[3]

Hence the importance of exercise, which is the main focus in section 2 of the Rule (chapters VII-XIII), but consistently plays a role outside of that section as well. The Rule expressly touches on this subject several times. Every religious chooses a specific religious

---

[3] Ibid., 18.3.

way of life (*exordium*). To this we must adhere (*narratio*) or rather, this we must keep the way we keep silence (XVI). Keeping silence we become silence-keeping persons: we become filled with silence and live in it as in our cell. We observe (II) and keep (XI) a certain regulation; we live in accordance with it (*conclusio*) just as we live in a melody or a language or a dwelling.

So the core of exercise is not accommodation but the practice of really appropriating the language presented to us, which *thereupon and through* this process constitutes a possibility of perception and action. Thus actual obedience (I and *petitio*) is a kind of exercise which makes possible the hearing of a voice other than one's own. Such a form can be replaced by another: for example, by group dialogue. But even then I will have to so appropriate this form that I begin to hear the voice of the other and not abuse the group as a platform for my own monologues. The place must be inhabited, and one must stay in one's cell in order through this experience to realize how generous the reality is which receives me (II-III and VII). The outcome can, of course, also be different. But even then the concrete act of learning to accept oneself, the gratuitous conception into life, will require exercise. Experience teaches us that self-hatred is not easily overcome. Scripture, particularly the Psalms, represents a culture which is permeated with the experience of God. If I wish to live in and on the basis of this experience, then the deepest possible interiorization is needed: Scripture must be heard (IV) and recited (VII), the Psalms must be spoken (VIII). Of course, within Scripture one can underscore different things and within the tradition one can choose different texts (patristic texts, mystical texts, modern texts), but even then the truth is that if they are really to open our eyes and to orient our conduct we must of necessity ingest and assimilate the material. If a text has not entered into me, I cannot enter into it. And if I have not entered into it, it cannot (yet) be my faculty of perception and orientation. The same is true for the communal person I may become.

The Rule offers a few sure-fire practice models (IX-XI): communalize that which is one's own (things, talents, skills, intuitions, etc.); come together, from within one's own space, in communal prayer (the hours, the Eucharist); jointly discuss that which pertains to each and to all (the wellbeing of each and the ordering of the whole). These models only become parts of my actual identity as fellow member if I frequently repeat the exercise, over and over step out of myself toward the center and in the process take along with me all that I have and am. Of course, other forms are conceivable which interiorize the act of really stepping outside of myself. But even then I will repeatedly have to bring on myself the pain of giving up the positions I have adopted, of opening up the territories I have marked off, and of marshalling my potential. Fasting and abstinence (XII-XIII) are forms which affect our bodies in two ways. They will empty out the (over) fullness of our bodiliness and undo our estrangement from our own physical selfhood: unavoidable exercises to create space for the Other and live authentically, however one shapes these practices. Working in silence is a way of instilling respect and restraint (XV-XVI). It weaves into being a space in which false hope is banished and spiritual realism is inwardly rehearsed. False imaging with regard to oneself and the other is transformed into quiet expectation.

Accordingly, we note that all the forms handed down to us are designed to become parts of our exercise. Such exercise is not accomplished all at once. To really learn to live from within the Rule demands incessant reflection: daily Scripture reading, a continual saying of the Psalms. I do not become a brother or sister at one stroke. If the brother or sister in me is to awaken, I will each day anew have to find concrete ways in which to step outside of myself. This, in fact, is the meaning of the time order presented by the Rule. Some things are so difficult or so much a part of the Carmelite identity that they demand constant appropriation. In any case, this is true for reflection on Scripture and prayer: they demand observance which continues day and night (VII). But also the practice of working in silence is part of such a form (XV-XVI). In connection with work we find the words "always" and "night and day". Silence even knows two forms which encompass the entire 24-hour period: the silence of the day and the silence of the night. The liturgy, too, knows such steady appropriation: all the hours of the day have their prayer-component while the Eucharist occurs at the pivoting movement when night turns to day. Looking at the ordering of time in that way we note that it marks out for us the time-path of continuous exercise.

The working goal of this appropriation is a pure heart. The Rule itself says this: we should live a life of allegiance to the Lord from a pure heart and a good conscience (*exordium*). This purity of heart has three aspects:

1. *Interior.* Just as a body cannot function without adequate defenses, so also the spirit cannot function when it has no interior, no heart. For that reason several form-elements are designed to create an interior. The "place", the cell, Scripture and the prayers create an open form which is receptive to the attributes of God. This is why meditation on Scripture and prayer can be mentioned in the same breath with other activities which ensure that we will be occupied (VII). Also the phrase "something to do" is designed so that we will always be occupied (XV). The symbol which best depicts this interior is the cell. The cell, as form, makes visible the purpose of Scripture reading, the Psalms, the work, silence: the formation of an inner world.

2. *Purification.* One's inner world must be purged of inauthenticity. This cleansing is most vividly represented in abstinence. Abstinence from certain foods and drinks, after all, is aimed at safeguarding the body, our interior, from enslaving and alienating influences: narcotics and artificial "needs" we have been talked into. But that which is clearly visible in abstinence is latent in all form-elements. Silence safeguards us from alienating gossip. "Some work to be done" ensures that I will not become a workaholic. Scripture furnishes us with experiential language that has been tested through the centuries. And so forth.

3. *Receptivity.* The cleansed interior is not intended to be a closed interior. It aspires to become receptive to the Other, the Living One. Consequently there are form-elements which relieve us of being overstuffed. A clear example is fasting. By emptying

out our interior – by eliminating our "overstuffedness" – room is created for that which is not-I. This becomes physically perceptible in the lack. But the real receptivity is active: the inner observance of an outgoing movement. This is the core of all purification. Virtually all form-elements are immediately adapted to this end. Naturally the community exercises are first: the communalization of all that comes into my territory, the going out to the Center in communal prayer, the act of stepping out of myself in genuine dialogue. But obedience has the same aim: deliberately going out to listen to "non-I". Prayer is aimed at vigilance. Working in silence is inwardly designed for quiet expectation. Simply put: the formation and purification of one's interior only attain their practical objective in the receptivity which reaches out to the Other.

8.3. Transformation in God

Now that the physical structures have been formed, purified, and made receptive down to the heart, they can be clothed with the attributes of God: the divine virtues, the messianic Body. This is the salvation of the soul (XI), salvation in the Lord, the blessing of the Holy Spirit (*salutatio*). This is the final goal the Rule envisions for all religious ways of life: "to live in allegiance to Jesus Christ and to serve him faithfully" (*exordium*). This transformation in the power of God is the main focus in section 3: the chapter on the armor of God (XIV). Three thematic components are important here.
1. In the first place, the heart which is pure and receptive is confirmed by being clothed with God's purity and God's sanctification of one's thoughts. It is essential, of course, that the interior self be structured by elementary exercises, that it rid itself of excess and inauthenticity, that it reaches out in receptivity. But it is only the reverent Presence of the Other which consecrates the interior, loves that which is my own, and fulfils the outward-looking posture. I may prepare myself as I please, but only the Other can confirm this preparation. And that is more

than merely ascertaining that it is there. Only now the purity is activated: in pure reverence. Only now the interior is activated: in reception. Only now the receptivity is activated: in the encounter. Only now the self-consecration is activated: in the sanctification.

2. Sanctification and purity are, as it were, the points of entry for the Self-communication of the Other, God's self-giving in love. That is not to say that the soul is purely passive here. Just as purification down to the level of the heart is preparatory to the purity and sanctification of our thoughts – a purity and sanctification which in *essence,* however, are *given* – so we receive God's preservation by works of the love of God, the love of neighbor, and the love of self. We receive God's trust by taking steps into the dark without any support other than that which comes from taking them. And we receive God's expectation by looking forward to the Salvation he has reserved in the only Salvation that heals everything: Messiah Jesus.

3. In purity and holy reflection God prepares us to receive him in the big three: faith, hope, and love. It is his will to fill us with his Presence and that in such a way that we will overflow with it. This is clear in the case of the Word: in the solitariness of the cell it is appropriated by meditation (VII) that ultimately it may dwell abundantly in our mouths and our hearts (XIV), and everything we do is prompted by the Word of the Lord (XIV). This is the realization of the final goal of Scripture-meditation. Thus all the basic provisions envisage their final goal: that the Messiah be heard in obedience (XVII-XVIII); that the Messiah is actually received in the Eucharist (X); that following the time of fasting we bodily experience Easter (XII); that the Lord is present with his favors in the midst of our conversation (XI).

8.4 Continual interiorization

Contemplation remains incidental if it does not find a bedding in our life. It can easily be corrupted by conceit. It can decline as a result of superficiality. For contemplation to be deepened and to become ongoing it needs specific provisions and observances. Section 4 of the Rule offers "some work to be done" and silence as a bedding for contemplation (XV-XVI). This also explains why in such a short letter so much is said about working in silence. Nowhere else does Albert speak as motivatingly as he does here. Except in connection with the armor of God, he nowhere else works at such length with Bible citations as he does here. Also interesting is the fact that here the Rule seems to wish to rehearse the entire transformational process all over again. In fact, work like silence also belongs in the class of the basic provisions. In the case of silence this is explicit: "Therefore we direct ..." (XVI). Work and silence are institutions. To do work and to keep silence are exercises. Still it is patently clear that the Rule wants to say more than that. Otherwise these chapters would not have had to be so long, so full of exhortation and citation. Just look at the important chapter on remaining in one's cell where in two lines four basic exercises are presented: remaining, meditating, praying, and watching. Hence the Rule does more than introduce a new institution and present exercises. It also seeks to do more than offering a new part of the armor. Faith, hope, and love – the big three! – together have only 72 words devoted them, as compared to 299 in the case of work and silence.

For the rest, we are not dealing with work and silence as such. I mean: we are not dealing with work and silence in the way we were dealing with the cell, the prior, the oratory, etc. Work and silence, aside from being ordinary provisions, are above all provisions which must, as it were, take care of contemplation and keep it healthy. Precisely with this in mind – silence and work as the continual interiorization of contemplation – they are set in a prophetic-eschatological key. Precisely *that* makes them into interiorization of contemplation.

Life in terms of the End deprives us of all pretension. The End dispossesses us of the illusions of the day. This fact cuts deeply into our consciousness of self. It draws us out of ourselves. It makes us wait with eager longing. It deepens in us the reality of quiet expectation – until nothing is left but seeing and being silent. The prophetic-eschatological import of "some work to be done" and quiet expectation makes these exercises into a durable bedding for the overflow of the Word. Their eschatological import makes them into a means of continual reception of God's attributes. But that in turn means that other provisions and exercises as well can receive this prophetic-eschatological import and thus become a means of interiorizing contemplation. In fact they already bear this eschatological import within themselves! This is suggested by six signals:

1. Actually the eschatological import already comes across to us in the opening words: "Salvation in the Lord" (prologue 1). Salvation, as we saw, is a word which on the one hand refers to the salvation already realized in Jesus the Messiah but which on the other reaches out to the salvation awaiting us from the End. The salvation of our souls (XI) lies beyond the circle of our horizon and still it draws nearer to us every moment that we draw nearer to it. Salvation is not only the pith of Albert's greeting (*salutatio*) and the pivotal point of chapter conversation (XI) but also the apex of the divine virtues: following preservation by God in love and the faith that pleases God, comes, as last and highest, the "*salvation* you hope for from the only *Savior*, who *saves* his people from their sins" (XIV).

2. A second signal of eschatological import is audible in the insistence on being watchful in the prayers (VII). The reference here, as we saw earlier, is to the first letter of Peter: "The end of all things is near, be therefore soberminded and watchful in your prayers" (1 Peter 4:7). The reference is to a watchful looking out for the Coming of Jesus and the Kingdom of God beyond the horizon of our conceptions and organizations.

3. A third signal of orientation to the End is implicit in the introduction to the section on the armor of God. In this introduction we are given the motives for putting on the armor of God. There is mention of trial and persecution, both of them words which signal the End. But also the roaring lion which goes about seeking whom it may devour evokes the end of time.

The battle in which the armor of God aids us is an Endtime battle. The lion which from within its ambush seeks to devour the soul is out to destroy our salvation.

4. The fourth signal can hardly still be called a signal: the chapters on work and silence (XV-XVI). In the interpretation we showed that the work in question, because it is situated in the context of 2 Thessalonians, is completely permeated by End-time expectation. This is then reinforced by the fact that this work must be done in silence, a silence which the Isaiah-citations then qualify as a quiet expectation which fosters strength and righteousness. All the other citations also confront us with the End: the ultimate consequences of our speech.

5. The obedience (XVII-XVIII), which is designed to mediate the Messiah to us – as a result of the citations which have this time been taken from the New Testament – is totally dominated by the theme of the End-time.

6. This perspective finds its culmination in the epilogue. There we read: "If anyone will have spent more, the Lord himself will reward us, when he returns". Here we read explicitly that which, with mounting intensity, is woven through the Rule as a whole. Carmelite contemplation is focused, past the horizon of our working, our speaking, and our power relations, on his coming.

8.5 Transformation in Christ

As the starting point of all the forms of religious life the Rule posits the following: "To live in allegiance to Jesus Christ and to serve him faithfully from a pure heart" (*exordium*). This is the fundamental pattern the Carmelite life-form must be woven into and bring to light. For that is the import of Albert's request, a request in which starting point (introduction) and exposition merge: the Christocentric orientation of the Carmelite way of life. The central reference in the Rule is to *transformation* in the Messiah. In this connection our thoughts turn to Paul who exclaims:

"I live, yet not I, but Christ lives in me" (Gal. 2:20). Everything in Paul's life is focused on being in Christ. To that end he gives up everything; for this he deploys all his energies. Everything within him is oriented to Christ toward whom in his preaching and quiet labors he reaches out, fervently hoping for his coming (XV).

From a spiritual point of view it is no accident that allegiance and faithful servanthood come before all else in the Rule. One could view religious ways of life, remember, as forms which mark the transition from hireling to faithful servant. Faithful servants turn away from self-involvement and focus on purity of heart in order thus to be able to receive their Lord. In everything they try to accommodate their Lord in order with ever-increasing faithfulness to be bondservants to him. This is the perspective in which the provisions and observances are situated.

One of the central exercises which is designed to lead us into such servanthood is the daily reading of Scripture: "to meditate day and night on the Word of the Lord" (VII). The Word of the Lord occupies a central place. It leavens, as it were, both day and night. Scripture can be heard in the Hours and in the Eucharist, in the refectory as well as in the cell. Always the Word is in our mouth so that it may be tasted with the mouth of our heart and realized by our hands. The Word is the cell's cell. It weaves Carmelites into being on all levels: physically insofar as we memorize the words of Scripture, cognitively insofar as we reflect on them, affectively insofar as we taste them, agogically insofar as we act on them. Thus the Word gradually becomes the element in which Carmelites live.

We are at home in it.

Thus, from being faithful servants we have now become family friends. All of life is lit up from within the Word of the Lord. Family friends live from within the Word of the Lord. By its light we learn to look at things creatively. We recall that all authority is controlled by messianic self-evacuation (*petitio*). We are reminded that in listening to the leadership we must not get caught up in psychologisms but look past the bearer of authority and seek the Word of the Lord and listen to him (*petitio*). We remember the

Lord – how he stands in the midst of the community, pronounces his peace, and grants forgiveness. We remember the Lord: drawn so deeply into Abba that he saw everyone as brother and sister and was no longer able to discriminate.

The core of transformation is transformation in Love: learning to live on the basis and from the perspective of Love – something to which everyone is invited by the Word of the Messiah: "Love the Lord your God with all your heart and all your soul and all your strength, and your neighbor as yourself" (XIV). This Love permeates the life of prayer (VII-VIII), our mutual associations (XVI), and the manner in which we relate to ourselves (III-VII). Our praying and our working, our silence, and our speech, our fasting and feasting all eagerly long for the salvation of the all-around Love which is God.

The Rule's fervent hope is that "the Word of God may dwell abundantly in our mouth and in our hearts, so that whatever we have to do may be done in the Word of the Lord" (XIV). Without so much as a moment's thought – as of itself – the Word abounds in us. This is the Resurrection of the Lord, not the Resurrection that is celebrated on Sundays and feastdays or during the daily Eucharist, but the Resurrection of the Lord which we live bodily. "I live, yet not I, but Christ lives in me" (Gal. 2:20). It is this on which the Rule focuses: life in Christ (XIV), being clothed with Christ as God's armor so that he lives. "I must decrease that he may increase" (XII-XIII; cf. John 1:19-34). This is the salvation in the Lord with which Albert greets the hermits (*salutatio*), the salvation which overflows and abounds, for in the same breath he adds: "and the blessing of the Holy Spirit". This is the salvation which all the parts of the armor of God long for: "… On your head is to be put the helmet of salvation, that you may hope for salvation from the *only* Savior who *saves* his people from their sins" (XIV). This is the salvation of souls which is central in the weekly discussion (XI). Those who without a moment's thought overflow with it are no longer secret friends but beloved sons or daughters in Christ (*salutatio*). Our life is marked by Love. Sometimes we are momentarily given the privilege of tasting this life.

This again is followed by working in silence (XV-XVI), awaiting his coming. That, finally, is the only thing left for us to do: to linger, in quiet expectation, over his coming. We do all the other things because it has been entrusted to us. What we produce over and above that is something we at every moment receive from himself! It is the Lord himself who comes to us even now, from the End, in the midst of our days. It is a matter of discerning it.

8.6 The mystical dynamic

In the Rule of Carmel there is at work a dynamic which we can characterize with the word "forward". I am thinking in this connection of the opening poem of *Markings*: [4]

> I am being driven *forward,*
> into an unknown land.

This *forwardness* is something I cannot bring about in my own strength. I am being touched by someone on the other side of my horizon:

> A wind from my unknown goal
> stirs the strings
> of expectation.

I am being drawn, past the boundary of my horizon, into an unknown land, the domain of the Other who recedes from me but precisely in that way lures me out of myself. This attraction does not fail to have its effect. It touches the whole construction of the dome. It both unsettles and unties this process. It completes the whole and tears it open. Take, for example, purity of heart: initially it is merely a practical objective on which all the elementary exercises are focused and in which they find their restingplace; but it turns out not to be a final point and not at all a restingplace, but a matter of ever further reaching out in questioning receptivity:

[4] Dag Hammarskjöld, *Markings*, New York 1964.

> Still the question:
> shall I ever get there?
> There where life resounds,
> a clear pure note
> in the silence.

And being clothed with God's attributes proves to be much more than the reception of God's attributes. It is to be drawn outside myself into God's keeping. Though, to be sure, we already saw it during the interpretation, now at the end we are acutely conscious of it: God's attributes draw us out of ourselves and into God's love. And there our senses are overwhelmed. Our work and our silence are no more now than relics which continue to vibrate, stirred by a wind from my unknown goal. Waiting marks the silence in which my work happens. The core of this waiting is obedience (*ob-oedire*: to listen [*audire*] obediently) to what resounds from *beyond* my horizon, "there where life resounds – a clear pure note in the silence".[5] Faithful servanthood and silence belong together. The silence is the intensity of waiting which hears the Voice from beyond my horizon.

This is prophetic eschatology. The innkeeper of the parable of the Good Samaritan embodies this *further* dimension, this *more-than-is-possible*. In the innkeeper this being drawn past the horizon is present in concentrated form. It is his life-form to be on the lookout for the Guest who, each time upon his arrival, again forms the center of our living space. Even when this Guest brings along another guest for us to care for we will obey.

> On the edge of the wilderness there was a small inn. A space to eat in, a few beds, and a stable for the animals – that was all. The inn was the innkeeper's life. He kept everything in good order. The rooms were spick-and-span and there was enough to eat and drink.
>
> When a traveller entered the inn, the innkeeper made himself totally available. He tried to guess his guest's wishes. "My guest is my boss", he mused.

[5] Ibidem.

Often his eyes strayed into the wilderness. In a sense he expected unexpected guests. He was known as an innkeeper you could always count on, one who would always somehow meet your needs.

One evening – it was late; the guests sat outside, still chatting – a traveller approached from the wilderness. On his donkey he brought in a badly wounded man who had been manhandled by robbers. The traveller was visibly touched. Turning to the innkeeper he said: "*Please* take care of this man. Here is an advance on the account. I will make good the rest when I come back". He ate some bread, drank a little wine, kissed the wounded man, and disappeared into the night.

"A fine bit of generosity!" complained the guests. "He sticks us with the noise of this man's howling and then leaves". The innkeeper said nothing, bound up the wounds of the sick man, gave him food and drink, and put him to bed. The advance was bound to fall short but he did not care. Would the traveller ever come back? It did not matter to him. He did what was asked of him.

When the wounded man finally fell asleep, the innkeeper stepped outside for a moment. Quietly brooding, he peered into the wilderness – till the sun came up.

PRINTED ON PERMANENT PAPER • IMPRIME SUR PAPIER PERMANENT • GEDRUKT OP DUURZAAM PAPIER - ISO 9706

ORIENTALISTE, KLEIN DALENSTRAAT 42, B-3020 HERENT